THE CONSTITUTIONAL
STRUCTURE OF THE
COMMONWEALTH

THE CONSTITUTIONAL STRUCTURE OF THE COMMONWEALTH

BY

K. C. WHEARE

F.B.A.

RECTOR OF EXETER COLLEGE
OXFORD

OXFORD
AT THE CLARENDON PRESS

Oxford University Press, Amen House, London E.C.4

GLASGOW NEW YORK TORONTO MELBOURNE WELLINGTON
BOMBAY CALCUTTA MADRAS KARACHI LAHORE DACCA
CAPE TOWN SALISBURY NAIROBI IBADAN ACCRA
KUALA LUMPUR HONG KONG

© *Oxford University Press 1960*

FIRST PUBLISHED 1960
REPRINTED 1961, 1963

PRINTED IN GREAT BRITAIN

PREFACE

THE text of this book describes the constitutional structure of the Commonwealth, so far as I can understand it, at 31 March 1960. Although there have been changes since that date, and although other changes are already foreseen or foreseeable, nothing has occurred which, in my opinion, conflicts with the exposition I have given in this book of the fundamental principles of that structure. None the less it is necessary to set down briefly the principal changes that have occurred or are expected to occur in the near future, as the position appears at this moment of writing.

To the list of Members of the Commonwealth given in the first footnote on page 1, Nigeria should be added on 1 October 1960. The Nigeria Independence Act was passed in July 1960, and appears as Appendix VII to this book. The meeting of Commonwealth Prime Ministers in May 1960 agreed in advance to accept Nigeria as a Member of the Commonwealth when it became independent.

It was announced on 4 May 1960, at the conclusion of a constitutional conference, that Sierra Leone would become independent on 27 April 1961. If Sierra Leone expresses a wish to remain in the Commonwealth, the question of its becoming a Member will be considered and decided by the Members.

Cyprus is to become an independent, sovereign republic on 15 August 1960, by the terms of the Cyprus Act which was passed by the parliament of the United Kingdom in July 1960. Thereafter it is for the Republic to decide whether or not it wishes to be a Commonwealth country; if it decides that it does so wish, the Members of the Commonwealth will consider and decide whether or not it is to be a Member. In the meantime the Republic is to be treated, in the words of the Secretary of State for the Colonies, in moving the second reading of the Cyprus Bill in the House of Commons, 'as if it was with, but not of, the Commonwealth'. This expression is, no doubt, politically valuable, but it is legally less than clear. Apparently the Republic will not be a Commonwealth country but will be treated, in the eyes of the law of the United Kingdom, as if it is. Whatever the final choice of the Republic and of the Members of the Commonwealth, the appeal to the Judicial Committee of the Privy Council is no longer to lie from Cyprus; it was abolished by section 5 of the Cyprus Act.

Of the three Members which had discussed the possibility of becoming republics at some future time—Ceylon, Ghana, and South Africa—Ghana became a republic on 1 July 1960, and continued as a Member of the Commonwealth by the agreement of its fellow Members expressed at the meeting of Commonwealth Prime Ministers in May 1960. What is said about its relationship with the Crown in Chapter VII must therefore be modified. On p. 164, for example, it should be grouped with India and Pakistan.

Whether South Africa would become a republic and, if so, continue as a Member of the Commonwealth remained for decision in the future. So far as Ceylon is concerned, it has not yet become a republic, but if it does so, its continued Membership of the Commonwealth as a republic was agreed to in 1956 (p. 123).

On 1 July 1960 Ghana not only became a republic; it brought into force an entirely new Constitution which supersedes that described and discussed in the text of this book. It has not been possible for me to study in detail the legislative history of this new Constitution and I am not able, therefore, to express an opinion whether or not it provides an example of an 'autochthonous' constitution, as that term is used in the discussion in Chapter IV of this book. One further important change was announced. With the coming into force of Ghana's new Constitution appeals to the Judicial Committee of the Privy Council were to cease.

I would like to record my thanks to my friend Mr. Geoffrey Marshall, Fellow of The Queen's College, Oxford, for reading my manuscript. I have learnt a great deal from his criticisms and suggestions, as well as from all that he has written on this subject. I owe a great deal to my wife's encouragement.

K. C. W.

Exeter College, Oxford
1 August 1960

CONTENTS

TABLE OF CASES

TABLE OF STATUTES

UNITED KINGDOM

TABLE OF STATUTES

PAKISTAN

SOUTH AFRICA

I · VOCABULARY

I

THE word 'Commonwealth' has come to be accepted as the new name for the British Empire. The parts of the Commonwealth are called 'Commonwealth countries' and the self-governing Commonwealth countries are called 'Members of the Commonwealth'.[1] Whether the Commonwealth is spoken of as the 'British' Commonwealth or not will depend essentially upon who is speaking and to whom they are speaking. The Members of British stock—including Australia, New Zealand, and the United Kingdom—in speaking to or of each other may well talk of the British Commonwealth. Australians will have an additional reason of convenience for so doing, because in ordinary speech 'the Commonwealth' is to them the Commonwealth of Australia or its government, so that to avoid misunderstanding they will say 'British Commonwealth'. But when countries in the Commonwealth of non-British stock speak of it or are spoken of in relation to it, it is more likely that the adjective 'British' will be avoided. Its use is evidently going out of fashion.

There is no official, rigid rule about the words. 'All constitutional developments in the Commonwealth, the British Commonwealth, or the British Empire—I use the three terms deliberately—have been the subject of consultation between His Majesty's Governments', said Mr. Attlee, then Prime Minister of the United Kingdom, in the House of Commons on 2 May 1949, 'and there has been no agreement to adopt or to exclude the use of any of these terms, nor any decision on the part of His Majesty's Government in the United Kingdom to do so.'[2] Sometimes a compromise is sought by using them interchange-

[1] But it is possible to be a self-governing Commonwealth country and yet not to be a Member of the Commonwealth. It has not happened yet, but it could. The distinction is discussed below, pp. 120 ff. The Members are the United Kingdom, Canada, Australia, New Zealand, South Africa, India, Pakistan, Ceylon, Ghana, and Malaya. Among Commonwealth countries that approach near to the status of Members are Nigeria, the West Indies, and Rhodesia and Nyasaland.

[2] 464 H.C. *Deb.* 5 s., cols. 643-4.

ably. When the Commonwealth Prime Ministers met in April 1949, in London, to discuss India's relation with the Commonwealth when it should become a republic, they issued a communiqué which began by describing the United Kingdom, Canada, Australia, New Zealand, South Africa, India, Pakistan, and Ceylon as countries 'united as members of the British Commonwealth of Nations', and went on to refer to 'the Commonwealth' thereafter six times, and made no further use of the adjective 'British'.[3] As Mr. Attlee remarked: 'Opinions differ in different parts of the British Empire and Commonwealth on this matter, and I think it better to allow people to use the expression they like best.'[4]

Yet while the use of the terms is officially optional, official and unofficial usage have tended strongly towards the supersession of 'British Empire' by 'British Commonwealth' and of 'British Commonwealth' by plain 'Commonwealth'.

2

There have been some odd and unexpected happenings in the history of these terms. The use of 'Commonwealth' as a new name for the British Empire began to come into fashion after Lionel Curtis published his two books, *The Problem of the Commonwealth* and *The Commonwealth of Nations*, in 1916. It is true that Lord Rosebery, in a speech in Adelaide in 1884, had described the Empire as a 'Commonwealth of Nations',[5] but there can be little doubt that if Curtis had not popularized the word, Lord Rosebery's remark would not have been exhumed by research students. Hard upon the publication of Curtis's books came the passing by the Imperial War Conference of 1917 of a resolution which spoke of the 'autonomous nations of an Imperial Commonwealth'.[6] General Smuts, in speaking upon the resolution, referred to the 'equal governments of the King in the British Commonwealth'.[7] Although the opening words of the Articles of Agreement for a treaty between Great Britain and Ireland, dated 6 December 1921, referred to Ireland's constitutional status 'in the Community of Nations known as the

---

[3] Text printed in Mansergh, *Documents and Speeches on British Commonwealth Affairs*, vol. ii, pp. 846–7.   [4] 464 *H.C. Deb.* 5 s., cols. 643–4.
[5] Crewe, *Lord Rosebery*, vol. i, p. 186.   [6] Cd. 8566, p. 5.
[7] Ibid., p. 47.

British Empire',[8] in a later passage there was a reference to Ireland's 'adherence to and membership of the group of nations forming the British Commonwealth of Nations'.[9] Yet, by a curious contradiction of history, as Curtis's word came into fashion, it came to mean something quite different from what he had intended it to mean. Indeed, 'Commonwealth' today stands for a situation which Curtis in his writings had deplored and which he had devoted his energies to avoid and remove.

Put quite shortly, what Curtis meant by a Commonwealth of Nations was a federal union. He had a perfectly logical case. A commonwealth, he said, was 'a state in which government rests on the shoulders of all its citizens who are fit for government. It exists to enlarge that class, and can afford to spare from its difficult task none who are equal to sharing it.'[10] The characteristic of a commonwealth was the government of men by themselves. But the British Empire in 1916 was not founded on this principle. The control of defence and foreign policy rested upon the shoulders of the people of the United Kingdom alone; the peoples of other parts of the Empire had no say in it. 'A commonwealth in which the final responsibilities of government have come to be regarded as the peculiar attribute of citizens inhabiting one locality is ceasing to realise the principle of its being.' 'Until that final responsibility is shared between all the peoples of the self-governing Dominions with those of the United Kingdom, this Empire will remain what it has been since its first colonies were planted in Ireland, not a commonwealth, but the project of a commonwealth, which must be completed if it is not to be brought to an end.'[11] The solution, as Curtis saw it, was to establish a parliament and government for the whole Empire to deal with defence, foreign affairs, and other important common matters, while national parliaments dealt with national matters. Through such machinery and the progressive extension of the franchise, the principle of the Commonwealth, already realized in the United Kingdom, and beginning to become established in the self-governing colonies overseas, would attain its fulfilment. If, on the other hand, each part of the

[8] Article 1. The text is found in the Irish Free State Constitution Act, 1922 (13 Geo. V, c. 1).   [9] Article 4.
[10] *The Commonwealth of Nations*, p. 702.
[11] Ibid.

Empire attained full self-government and control over foreign affairs and defence for itself, then you would not have a commonwealth of nations but a collection of independent, and, at the best, merely co-operative national commonwealths. 'In plain words, the issue, as seen by the writer, is whether the Dominions are to become independent republics, or whether this world-wide Commonwealth is destined to stand more closely united as the noblest of all political achievements.'[12]

The choice was made soon after by the Imperial War Conference in 1917, which, by its reference to 'the Dominions as autonomous nations of an Imperial Commonwealth' at one and the same time accepted Curtis's word and rejected his idea. General Smuts, in his speech on the resolution at the conference, made the position explicit.

If this Resolution is passed [he said] then one possible solution is negatived and that is the Federal solution. The idea of a future Imperial Parliament and a future Imperial Executive is negatived by implication by the terms of this Resolution. The idea on which this Resolution is based is rather that the Empire would develop on the lines upon which it has developed hitherto, that there would be more freedom and more equality in all its constituent parts; that they will continue to legislate for themselves and continue to govern themselves; that whatever executive action has to be taken, even in common concerns, would have to be determined, as the last paragraph says, by 'the several governments' of the Empire, and the idea of a Federal solution is therefore negatived, and, I think, very wisely, because it seems to me that the circumstances of the Empire entirely preclude the Federal solution.[13]

3

The word 'Commonwealth' as it is used today, then, does not mean what Curtis meant by it. Nor does it mean what it meant in the years between the two world wars. In the usage which came to be adopted after 1919, the Commonwealth was thought of as the self-governing countries of the British Empire. In the Balfour Report, adopted by the Imperial Conference of 1926,[14] this idea finds expression. Great Britain and the Dominions were described as 'autonomous communities within the British Em-

[12] *The Problem of the Commonwealth*, p. vii.
[13] Cd. 8566, p. 47.   [14] Cmd. 2768, pp. 13–30.

pire' and 'freely associated as members of the British Commonwealth of Nations'.[15] It was common to interpret this statement as meaning that the Commonwealth consisted of the autonomous parts of the Empire; each of these parts was a 'Member' of the Commonwealth, and indeed the Commonwealth consisted only of 'Members'. They were 'within the British Empire', which meant that the Empire was the larger unit. It included the Commonwealth, but it included also various non-self-governing countries—colonies, protectorates, mandated territories, and the like. This use of 'Commonwealth' as a word to describe a part only of the British Empire and not as synonymous or interchangeable with it was not universally adopted but it was fairly strongly established in the inter-war period.

It raised certain problems. What, for example, was one to call that part of the British Empire which was not included in the Commonwealth? This was referred to sometimes as 'the Colonies', 'the Colonial Empire', or 'the Dependent Empire'. Thus it was possible to say that the British Commonwealth plus the Colonial or Dependent Empire made up the British Empire.

Another expression which came into use in this period and has persisted is 'British Commonwealth and Empire' or 'Commonwealth and Empire'. This is an ambiguous expression and is all the more useful on this account. It found favour, for example, with those who preferred the old-fashioned term 'British Empire', but felt obliged to recognize the new fashion of 'Commonwealth' while at the same time not entirely giving way to it. In the mouths of many such it amounted to saying 'British Commonwealth or Empire'. Mr. Winston Churchill's use of the expression during the Second World War and afterwards very well reflected this attitude. There were others who used the expression because they meant by 'Commonwealth' the self-governing communities and by 'Empire' the non-self-governing communities, and they therefore called the whole collection of countries 'the Commonwealth and Empire'. For them the Commonwealth was not part of the Empire; it was distinct from it and made up with it a larger collection. This usage cannot be easily reconciled with the words of the Imperial Conference of 1926, but it was not less respectable on that account. The changing Commonwealth needed a changing vocabulary.

[15] Ibid., p. 14.

When the stage was reached at which, as now seems established, 'Commonwealth' stands for the whole collection of communities, self-governing and non-self-governing, the need for the expression 'Commonwealth and Empire' disappears. All are countries of the Commonwealth and the self-governing countries are Members of the Commonwealth. And it is not perhaps surprising that 'Commonwealth' should be extended so widely in scope in the years since 1945. For with the granting of independence to India and Pakistan in 1947 and to Ceylon in 1948, the overwhelming majority of the peoples of the 'Empire' were now citizens of Members of the Commonwealth. With the prospect of still further additions to the list of Members it seemed reasonable to anticipate the course of history by calling the Empire 'the Commonwealth' a little ahead of time.

4

In the course of these developments one term came into fashion, had a useful and honourable career, and was finally declared obsolete. This was the term 'Dominion'. Its history was interesting. A good starting-point is the Colonial Conference of 1907. At that time two uses of the word were common. First of all it occurred in the King's title where Edward VII was described as 'of the United Kingdom of Great Britain and Ireland and of the British Dominions beyond the Seas, King'. Secondly, it had become the practice to speak of 'the Dominion of Canada' and 'the Dominion of New Zealand', though Australia had chosen to be called 'the Commonwealth'. These two uses of 'Dominion' were not identical. 'Dominions' in the King's title comprised all the territories overseas, self-governing and non-self-governing. The Dominions of Canada and New Zealand had the common characteristic that they possessed a considerable measure of self-government.

In the light of these two usages we may consider a discussion that occurred at the Colonial Conference in 1907. It lasted for two days, 18 and 20 April, and is reported word for word in an official publication,[16] and deserves to be read. It was initiated by a resolution concerning the future constitution of the confer-

---

[16] *Minutes of Proceedings of the Colonial Conference*, 1907, Cd. 3523.

ence which was submitted by Lord Elgin, the Secretary of State for the Colonies, and which was in the following terms:

That it will be to the advantage of the Empire if Conferences, to be called Imperial Conferences are held every four or five years, at which questions of common interest affecting the relations of the Mother Country and His Majesty's Dominions over the seas may be discussed and considered as between His Majesty's Government and the Governments of the self-governing Colonies. The Prime Minister of the United Kingdom will be *ex-officio* President, and the Prime Ministers of the self-governing Colonies *ex-officio* members of the Conference. The Secretary of State for the Colonies will be an *ex-officio* member of the Conference, and will take the chair in the absence of the President and will arrange for such Imperial Conferences after communication with the Prime Ministers of the respective Colonies.[17]

This resolution underwent a good deal of amendment before it was finally passed. It is not necessary for us to follow its fortunes in detail. Our principal concern is with the word 'Dominion'.

It will be noticed that in this first version of the resolution 'Dominion' finds a place and it is used obviously in the sense in which it was found in the King's title—'His Majesty's dominions over the seas'; it was not used in the sense of a self-governing territory. Indeed it is the word 'colony' which is used to describe Canada, New Zealand, Australia, Newfoundland, and the South African territories. They are spoken of as 'the self-governing colonies', and are thus distinguished from the non-self-governing colonies which were not represented at the Colonial Conference of 1907, and were not intended to be represented at the future proposed Imperial Conferences.

Some extracts from the discussion on 18 April will show how the statesmen were groping, somewhat incoherently, towards a new vocabulary.[18] Sir Wilfrid Laurier, the Prime Minister of Canada, said:

'. . . I am not satisfied as to the words "Dominions beyond the Seas." It is a good expression, but I do not know that it is correct as it is used here, and I should like to see it in a corrected draft. I do not know that it may not include Trinidad as well as Australia and

Canada. It is not limited, so far as I can see, to the self-governing Colonies.'

Chairman [Lord Elgin, the Secretary of State for the Colonies]: 'That is what is meant in the first place.'

Sir Wilfrid Laurier: 'Yes.'

Sir Joseph Ward [Prime Minister of New Zealand]: 'Why not use the words "self-governing Colonies"?'

Sir Wilfrid Laurier: 'Or "self-governing Dominions beyond the Seas." As drafted, it seems to me it could as well apply to Trinidad or Barbados as to Canada.'

Chairman: 'I think we will have to introduce the words "self-governing."'

Sir Wilfrid Laurier: 'I would like to use some expression which would make a differentiation between the self-governing Colonies and the other Colonies. So far as the Colonies represented here are concerned, I wish we could drop the word "Colonies," and try to invent something which would strike the imagination more.'

Mr. Deakin [Prime Minister of Australia]: 'Certainly; if anybody can do that it is you, Sir Wilfrid' . . . .

Chairman: 'Would the words "self-governing communities of the Empire" do?'

Sir Wilfrid Laurier: 'Perhaps they would, but I would like to consider the suggestion. It is worth taking twenty-four hours over it. I talked it over yesterday with a friend, and we agreed that we have passed the state when the term "Colony" could be applied to Canada, New Zealand, and Australia. I would like to have suggested the word "state" but for the fact that in Australia they call states what we call provinces, and it might lead to confusion. Perhaps one of us can make a better suggestion. I would rather sleep upon it, unless somebody else has any other suggestion to make today.'

Mr. Deakin: 'Would this term do: "British Dominions possessing responsible government"?'

Sir Wilfrid Laurier: 'I would prefer "self-governing dominions beyond the seas."'

Sir Joseph Ward: 'I am agreeable to that.'

Mr. Deakin: 'We need not add "beyond the seas." "Self-governing Dominions" will do.

Sir Wilfrid Laurier: 'If you designate all those countries that have been known up to the present time as self-governing Colonies "self-governing Dominions" we can then give out to the public that henceforth these are "self-governing Dominions," but I would like to have a single apt word which may be taken to mean "self-governing Colonies."'

Mr. Deakin: 'We recognise that the "Dominion" is the senior of the "Commonwealth", and therefore, the name "Dominion" has a claim. Again, we recognise that in his Majesty's official title the word "Dominion" is used where the word "Commonwealth" is not.'[19]

Sir Wilfrid Laurier: '"Dominion" is a general term which covers many words which it is not possible to define otherwise. . . .'

Sir Joseph Ward: 'As long as it is understood that New Zealand is a Dominion, I do not object to the word "Dominion." We ourselves understand New Zealand is a Dominion, but I would like it understood that our country is covered by that term here.'

After a little further talk, the discussion was adjourned until 20 April when it was quickly concluded.[20] Lord Elgin raised an interesting point:

We agreed [he said] and I am not going back upon the agreement, that instead of the word 'Colonies' we should use the word 'Dominions'; but is it sufficiently defined if we use the word 'Dominions' alone throughout? After all, we, in this country, are part of His Majesty's self-governing Dominions strictly speaking, and I would suggest that we might take what is really the official term 'the Dominions beyond the seas' in the first place where it occurs—'the Governments of the self-governing Dominions beyond the seas,' and any other reference to it in the course of the Resolution might very well be 'Dominions'. That would make it absolutely clear what we mean by the expression in the first place.

It was agreed, and the words 'beyond the seas' which Mr. Deakin had had removed were thereupon reinserted.

The relevant part of the resolution as finally passed is as follows:

That it will be to the advantage of the Empire if a Conference, to be called the Imperial Conference, is held every four years, at which questions of common interest may be discussed and considered as between His Majesty's Government and His Governments of the self-governing Dominions beyond the seas. The Prime Minister of

---

[19] When Mr. Deakin says that the 'Dominion' is the senior of the 'Commonwealth', he means that Canada is senior to Australia. He is not using 'Commonwealth' in its modern sense. It is interesting to note a hint, however, that he might have proposed 'self-governing Commonwealths' in place of 'self-governing Dominions' had it not been for the two reasons he mentions, which favoured the term 'Dominion'.

[20] Cd. 3523, p. 89.

the United Kingdom will be *ex-officio* President, and the Prime Ministers of the self-governing Dominions *ex-officio* members of the Conference. The Secretary of State for the Colonies will be an *ex-officio* member of the Conference, and will take the chair in the absence of the President. He will arrange for such Imperial Conferences after communication with the Prime Ministers of the respective Dominions.

5

If the adoption of 'Dominion' as a name for the self-governing parts of the Empire beyond the seas, and the reasons for its adoption, are to be identified with any particular time and place, then there is little doubt that they are to be found in this discussion and the subsequent resolution of the Colonial Conference of 1907. 'Dominion' really was short for 'the self-governing Dominions beyond the seas'. It was a natural abbreviation. No one could be expected to repeat the longer phrase time after time. Indeed, the framers of the resolution soon flagged. They began, as will be seen, with 'the self-governing Dominions beyond the seas'; in the next sentence they say 'self-governing Dominions'; and in the final sentence they say merely 'Dominions'. Yet it is an odd abbreviation, for it leaves out the significant words 'self-governing' and 'beyond the seas' and is really open to the objections which Sir Wilfrid Laurier and Lord Elgin had advanced. None the less it became established, fortified no doubt by its use in such expressions as 'the Dominion of Canada' and 'the Dominion of New Zealand'. The ambiguity remained, however, for the royal title continued to include the words 'the British Dominions beyond the seas', until the Coronation of Elizabeth II in 1953 so that the two uses of 'Dominion' continued side by side.

The use of 'Dominion', with 'self-governing' and 'beyond the seas' understood, flourished between 1919 and 1939. Along with it there went the expression 'Dominion Status'. No very precise meaning was given to this phrase at first. When Mr. Lloyd George asked in the House of Commons on 14 December 1921, 'What does "Dominion Status" mean?' he answered his rhetorical question by saying that it was 'difficult and dangerous to give a definition'. He had been obliged to ask the question because he was speaking on the motion that the House approve the Articles of Agreement for a treaty between Great Britain and Ireland, signed on 6 December 1921, in the opening words of which it was stated that 'Ireland shall have the same constitutional status in the Community of Nations known as the British Empire as the Dominion of Canada, the Commonwealth of Australia, the Dominion of New Zealand and the Union of South Africa. . . .' But what was that status? In the end all that Mr. Lloyd George could say was: '. . . Whatever measure of freedom Dominion Status gives to Canada, Australia, New Zealand or South Africa, that will be extended to Ireland. . . .'[21] So the position rested in 1921.

But it could not stay like that indefinitely. The Dominions were not in law, at any rate, fully self-governing, although they were called 'the self-governing Dominions'. Their position in foreign affairs was still obscure; they were subject to certain legal restrictions on the part of the parliament or government of the United Kingdom. Some did not mind this. At the Imperial Conference of 1921 Mr. W. M. Hughes, the Prime Minister of Australia, said that there was no need 'to set down in black and white the relations between Britain and the Dominions'. 'In effect,' he said, 'we have all the rights of self-government enjoyed by independent nations. . . . What other worlds have we to conquer? . . . I know of no power that the Prime Minister of Britain has, that General Smuts has not.'[22]

General Smuts could not afford to be so contented. He had said, indeed, at the Imperial War Conference of 1917, that 'although in practice there is great freedom, yet in actual theory the status of the Dominions is of a subject character. Whatever we may say, and whatever we may think, we are subject Provinces of Great Britain. That is the actual theory of the Constitution, and in many ways which I need not specify today that theory still permeates practice to some extent.'[23] The position had not changed in 1921, and General Smuts had not changed his view that 'too much . . . of the old ideas still clings to the new organism'.[24]

It was not until 1926, however, that an attempt was made to clarify the relations between Great Britain and the Dominions.

[21] 149 *H.C. Deb.* 5 s., cols. 27–28.
[22] Cmd. 1474, pp. 22–23.
[23] Cd. 8566, p. 47.
[24] Ibid.

By that time General Smuts had been replaced by General Hertzog; the Irish Free State was a full member of the Imperial Conference; and Mr. Mackenzie King, the Prime Minister of Canada, had just fought a general election in which he had professed to see issues involving Canada's status as a self-governing country. With the declaration of the Imperial Conference of 1926 that Great Britain and the Dominions were 'autonomous communities within the British Empire, equal in status, in no way subordinate one to another in any aspect of their domestic or external affairs, though united by a common allegiance to the Crown and freely associated as members of the British Commonwealth of Nations' it was possible to say something rather more definite about 'Dominion Status'. But it should be noted that the conference did not define Dominion Status. If it defined anything, it defined the status of a Member of the British Commonwealth of Nations. But it was possible to discover from it what the status of a Dominion was. There were three criteria. It was completely self-governing; it owed allegiance to the Crown; and it was freely associated with other self-governing countries, which also owed such allegiance, as a member of the British Commonwealth.

What these three criteria meant in detail and in practice was a matter for argument in the years after 1926. Each Dominion had its own views upon the subject. They will be explained and discussed in the succeeding chapters. There was indeed a good deal of ambiguity and compromise in the declaration of 1926. Moreover, the declaration was not a legal enactment, and some parts of it could not be made effective without legal action. For practical purposes, however, the declaration of 1926 had made it clear that no Dominion need tolerate a position of subordination to Great Britain. The Dominions were in fact independent nations within the Commonwealth.

To ensure that the old word 'colony' should no longer be used even in legal documents to describe the 'Dominions', it was enacted in 1931[25] that thereafter 'Colony' should not be used to describe Canada, Australia, New Zealand, South Africa, the Irish Free State, and Newfoundland or any province or state of those countries. So at last the new terminology seemed established.

[25] By s. 11 of the Statute of Westminster, 1931 (22 Geo. V, c. 4).

6

Yet quite soon after the Second World War the term began to go out of favour. It is not easy to explain, yet some of the considerations may be mentioned. By a curious turn of events, it was Canada, the country which had done so much to make the term acceptable, which had a considerable influence in removing it. From the passing of the British North America Act, 1867,[26] when certain of the British North American colonies federated, Canada was known as 'the Dominion of Canada', a title chosen by the Canadians. We have seen how Sir Wilfrid Laurier used it at the Colonial Conference in 1907. Yet when in later years Canadians looked rather more carefully at the British North America Act they noticed that although the name 'Dominion of Canada' had become generally accepted, that was not the name given to Canada in the act itself. Section 3 of that act provided that the provinces 'shall form and be one Dominion under the name of Canada'. 'Canada' was the name given to the new political community in its birth certificate. Canadians were therefore able to object that they were calling themselves and were being called by an incorrect name.

A second difficulty peculiar to Canada was that the word 'Dominion' did not appeal to French-Canadians as a name to describe Canada or the government of Canada. They seldom used it; they usually spoke of 'La Confédération'. Where English-speaking Canadians described the meetings between the government of Canada and the provincial governments as 'Dominion–Provincial Conferences', French-Canadians preferred to call them 'Les Conférences Fédérale–Provinciales'. Their objection to the word 'Dominion' arose not so much from the fact that the word was not easily translatable into French or from the fact that it was not Canada's proper name, as from their desire to assert the independence of the province of Quebec inside the union of Canada. They wished to assert that Canada was not a unitary state and that the government at Ottawa had limited powers and must not transgress those limits; it must respect provincial powers. This they could assert more effectively by speaking of 'La Confédération' and of 'the federal

[26] 30 & 31 Vict., c. 3.

government' at Ottawa than by speaking of 'the Dominion' and 'the Dominion government'.

Both these points led to action in Canada. In 1947 new letters patent were issued constituting the office of Governor-General and in them the word 'Canada' replaces 'Dominion of Canada' or 'Dominion' where they had occurred in the former letters patent. At a meeting of the Dominion–Provincial Conference in January 1950, it was decided that in future it should be called the 'Federal–Provincial Conference', and its report and later reports appeared under that title. Thus was the French-Canadian attitude recognized. As opportunity offers in the Canadian parliament the words 'Dominion of Canada' and 'Dominion' are removed from previous acts of Parliament and are replaced by 'Canada'. It is now the official usage in Canada. And although it may be thought of as no more than a Canadian matter, it is legitimate to conclude that Canada in changing its name was registering also its objection to the use of the word 'Dominion' to describe it as a part of the Commonwealth.

But the matter may be considered on wider grounds than these. There were at least five objections to the use of Dominion as a name for the overseas self-governing countries of the Commonwealth. There was, first, the view that the word suggested domination, that the Dominions were territories over which Britain had 'dominion'. This implication seemed to be contained particularly in such phrases as 'the British Dominions' or 'Britain and her Dominions'. Historically there was something to be said for this view, though the dominion was the King's dominion, not Britain's, and usage, since 1907 at least, had, as we have seen, established the position gradually that the Dominions were precisely those territories not subject to Britain's dominion. However, a flavour of inequality could attach to the word.

This possible implication was strengthened, it was felt, by the fact that the word 'Dominion' did not apply to the United Kingdom. We have seen how Lord Elgin tried to deal with the ambiguity of the word by inserting 'beyond the seas' after it and although these words had dropped out, their sense remained invisibly attached. So that although the United Kingdom was one of the King's self-governing Dominions, usage had confined the word to those beyond the seas. Although the United Kingdom had equal status with the Dominions, it was not a Dominion.

It was convenient, of course, to have a collective word by which to describe, in the United Kingdom, the overseas members of the Commonwealth. But it was possible to misconstrue the position and think that the difference in name implied a difference in status between the United Kingdom and the overseas members.[27]

A third objection was that 'Dominion' had been used to describe so many different degrees of self-government that it was too ambiguous a term. What it meant in 1947 was not what it meant in 1907 or in 1917 or in 1927 or in 1937. To call countries which in 1907 were not self-governing in foreign affairs, for example, by the same name as countries which in 1947 were officially described as independent was misleading. To describe the Members of the Commonwealth as enjoying Dominion Status was to use an obsolete term. It was like calling an adult an adolescent.

When the time came to invite Ireland to accept the membership of the Commonwealth a further difficulty about 'Dominion' revealed itself. The Dominions, historically speaking, were all grown-up or growing-up daughter nations of the United Kingdom. They had been subordinate colonies; their peoples had come from the British Isles, though in Canada and South Africa they had united themselves with people of non-British stock; they were daughter nations, or at least daughter-in-law nations. The word 'Dominions' had about it this history of growing up as daughters of a mother country. Ireland could not accept these historical implications. She was not a daughter nation but a mother country. She had not begun as a colony but as an ancient kingdom; she was not a daughter but a sister kingdom with Great Britain.[28] For the Irish Free State the term 'Dominion Status' was not appropriate. If this was true of Eire, it was also

---

[27] This point was made by Professor F. R. Scott of McGill University in an article entitled 'The End of Dominion Status', published 38 *American Journal of International Law* (Jan. 1944), pp. 34 ff. at p. 47. Considerably rewritten, it was re-published in 23 *Canadian Bar Review* (Nov. 1945, pp. 725 ff.).

[28] It is interesting to recall that the Irish House of Commons had resolved on 16 Apr. 1782 that, 'the Kingdom of Ireland is a distinct kingdom, with a parliament of her own, the sole legislature thereof'. The Irish House of Lords had concurred in a resolution passed the next day, and the parliament of Great Britain had conceded the claim in the Renunciation Act of the next year (23 Geo. III, c. 28). The documents are printed in C. Grant Robertson, *Select Statutes, Cases and Documents*, pp. 250-60.

true of India, Pakistan, and Ceylon, who, though for long sub-ordinate to Britain, were not peopled by British stock and had had a history of independence in the past.

But, and this was the fifth objection, there was something un-satisfactory about the word 'Dominion' even for those who were, in truth, grown up daughter or daughter-in-law nations. When people have grown up they do not like to be referred to always as 'the daughter of So-and-so'. They have an adult exis-tence in their own right. The time comes when the fact that they have grown up must be taken for granted. So the word 'Dominion' must be superseded by 'Member of the Common-wealth' which applied alike to mother and daughter and stresses neither the family relationship nor the days of childhood.

These objections to the use of 'Dominion' and 'Dominion Status' were not all held by all oversea Members of the Com-monwealth, and those that held them did not hold them all with equal intensity. Nor were they ever set out in a schedule of objections. From time to time, however, actions were taken which showed that some Member at any rate felt the force of these objections, and it would be true to say that the use of the terms declined from 1945. An important step was the announce-ment in London on 2 July 1947, that the name of the Secretary-ship of State for Dominion Affairs in the government of the United Kingdom was to be changed to that of Secretary of State for Commonwealth Relations, and that of the Dominions Office to Commonwealth Relations Office. Oddly enough, however, when, two days later, the Indian Independence Bill, by which India and Pakistan were to be given full self-govern-ment, was presented to the House of Commons, it provided for the establishment of two 'Dominions'. India and Pakistan con-tinued to be Dominions until their new constitutions came into force on 26 January 1950 and 23 March 1956 respectively, whereby the Indian Independence Act of 1947 was repealed. But the word has now almost gone. The new Members of the Commonwealth since 1947—Ceylon in 1948,[29] Ghana and Malaya in 1957—did not call themselves 'Dominions'. New Zealand is the last Dominion.

What is the significance of the change? In so far as there was

[29] For the discussion in Ceylon see Sir Ivor Jennings, *The Constitution of Ceylon* (3rd ed.), especially pp. 15–16.

attached to 'Dominion' some remaining notion of inferiority to
the United Kingdom, some historical memory of subordinate
status, of adolescence, of the Mother Country's apron strings,
it is true that 'Member' has no such associations; it contains no
embarrassing reminders of past subjection. It applies and can
only apply to fully self-governing nations. Yet it would be an
exaggeration to suggest that it means much more than 'Dominion
Status' did in practice and in potential in 1926. 'Dominion
Status' was a growing and developing concept. Independence
and equality were its essential characteristics. It is true that it
implied independence within the Commonwealth, but that
surely is precisely what 'Member Status' must mean. The new
terminology is very little, if anything, more than new labels on
the old bottles, new names for old things. It should not be under-
estimated on that account. Names are of great importance, as
the history of the Commonwealth has shown. If it was wise to
replace 'Colony' by 'Dominion' why should it not be wise to
replace 'Dominion' by 'Member of the Commonwealth'?

7

By 'the constitutional structure of the Commonwealth' I
mean that collection of rules, understandings, and practices by
which the position and mutual relations of the countries, and,
more particularly, of the Members of the Commonwealth, are
regulated and described. It would be shorter to speak of the
'constitution' of the Commonwealth and would accord with
British usage to do so. For the British constitution itself is a collection of rules, understandings, and practices. But in almost all
other countries of the world, and certainly in all other Commonwealth countries, 'constitution' means a specific legal document which contains a selection of the most important legal
rules that govern the government and usually has some priority
over other legal rules. The Commonwealth (like the United
Kingdom itself) has no constitution in this sense and it seems
better therefore not to use a word which could so easily produce
ambiguity and misunderstanding.

It has been thought wise also to avoid the term 'constitutional
law'. To begin with it is too narrow in its connotation. The rules
and practices which concern the relations of the countries of

the Commonwealth with each other are not only and not mainly rules of law; they comprehend much that is non-legal in character. There are conventions and customs and understandings and usages which would not normally be recognized, by courts in Commonwealth countries at least, as legal in nature.

But 'constitutional law', too, is commonly regarded as a branch of national or municipal law, whereas most of the rules and practices we are considering concern the relations of independent nations. It could be claimed that they are part of international law, not of national or municipal law. It may be doubted whether this objection to the use of 'constitutional law' can claim today the force it used to have. With the development of international institutions, established and regulated by documents such as the Charter of the United Nations, it is possible to see the development of an international constitutional law. These documents are constitutional in their subject-matter and nature, and they have as much claim to be called law as any other part of international law. I would be prepared to claim, indeed, that the constitutional structure of the Commonwealth is composed of international constitutional law and of national or municipal constitutional law—in so far, that is, as it contains rules of law at all. But as 'constitutional law' still connotes principally municipal constitutional law, it has been thought best not to use it in the title of this book on the ground that as commonly used it is too narrow.

When we come to consider the constitutional structure of the Commonwealth in detail we shall find that it is composed of several distinct elements, some legal, some non-legal. Among the legal elements are statutes passed by the legislatures of Commonwealth countries, and subordinate legislation passed under the authority of these statutes. There are also judicial decisions handed down by the courts of Commonwealth countries. Associated with the strictly legal rules there are non-legal rules which are described variously as constitutional conventions, usages, practices, or customs. These non-legal elements in the constitutional structure do not operate in isolation from the strictly legal elements. Though distinct, they are not disconnected. They supplement, modify, and even nullify the operation of the strictly legal rules. Their constant interaction will be illustrated in the following chapters.

It is convenient to make one or two distinctions within the non-legal category. 'Convention' connotes a binding rule, while 'usage' or 'practice' connotes what is usually done but is not or is not yet obligatory.[30] 'Conventions' may come to be established in a variety of ways. A usage or practice may, through long observance, come to be regarded as binding. 'Custom' is commonly used to describe a rule which by long observance has in this way come to be accepted as binding. In this sense 'custom' may be said to be one kind of convention. But conventions may be established quite quickly, perhaps by an agreement between parties to behave in future in a particular way. No previous history as usage or practice, no slow building up of precedent, no hardening into custom may have occurred. Much of the element of convention in the constitutional structure of the Commonwealth has been constructed in this way. Rules have been written down by agreement among the Members of the Commonwealth. It will be apparent that conventions of this kind have a good deal in common with those agreements in international relations which are called conventions also. The fact that the same word is used to describe both need not lead to misunderstanding; though it is possibly wise to remember that the conventions spoken of in describing the constitutional structure of the Commonwealth are constitutional conventions, whereas conventions in international relations may deal with almost any subject-matter, including constitutional matters. It is proposed in this book to speak of binding non-legal constitutional rules as conventions, and to employ the word 'usage' to describe what is usually done but is not yet required to be done. It may be valuable also to have available such words as 'habits' and 'practices', to describe the relations of the countries of the Commonwealth, for the structure is far from rigid, and what is done is often more revealing and more important than what is written down.

[30] There is a valuable critical discussion of conventions in G. Marshall and G. C. Moodie, *Some Problems of the Constitution*, chap. 2.

II · EQUALITY

I

'EQUALITY of status,' said the Imperial Conference of 1926, 'so far as Britain and the Dominions are concerned, is then the root principle governing our Inter-Imperial Relations.'[1] Though 'Dominions' and 'Inter-Imperial' may now be dated words, the principle of equality of status remains as an essential characteristic of Members of the Commonwealth. It is indeed what marks off Members from other Commonwealth countries. Equality means equality of status, not equality of stature. Members differ in power and potential. Equality means also no subordination. Members are 'in no way subordinate one to another in any aspect of their domestic or external affairs'. It means no dependence; it means independence. And yet it is interesting to see how reluctant, at first, Members were to use the word 'independence'. It was not until twenty years after the declaration of equality of status in 1926 that 'independence' was officially used. When, in 1947, India was granted full self-government, the parliament of the United Kingdom passed the Indian Independence Act,[2] which was described as 'an act to make provision for the setting up in India of two independent Dominions'. The same language was used later in 1947 when the Ceylon Independence Act[3] was passed. And the notion of independence was stressed and illuminated also by the language used when Burma decided to leave the Commonwealth and form a self-governing country outside. The parliament of the United Kingdom passed in 1947 the Burma Independence Act.[4] By using the same title for an act granting full self-government outside the Commonwealth, it was demonstrated that Members of the Commonwealth were considered to be no less independent or free as nations in the world than were those which retained no link with the United Kingdom and other Members of the Commonwealth. And the same language was used when in 1957 parliament passed the

[1] Cmd. 2768, p. 15.
[3] 11 Geo. VI, c. 7.
[2] 10 & 11 Geo. VI, c. 30.
[4] 11 Geo. VI, c. 3.

Ghana Independence Act[5] and the Federation of Malaya Independence Act.[6]

When equality of status is granted to a Commonwealth country what constitutional changes occur? What are the inequalities which must be removed? It is worth while to set out briefly the principal elements in that inequality of status which marks Commonwealth countries which are not yet full Members of the Commonwealth.[7] Though there is great variety in detail in the working of the instruments by which the United Kingdom controls dependent Commonwealth countries and in the intensity of that control, the instruments themselves are much the same.[8]

2

There is, first of all, the inequality which arises from what is usually called 'the sovereignty of the imperial parliament'. The parliament of the United Kingdom is both imperial and sovereign. It is imperial in the sense that it has the power to make laws for the overseas dependent territories of the Commonwealth; it is sovereign in the sense that such laws when made prevail over laws made by the overseas territory in so far as they conflict. The situation was defined in 1865 by the Colonial Laws Validity Act,[9] section 2 of which is as follows:

Any Colonial Law which is or shall be in any respect repugnant to the provisions of any Act of Parliament extending to the Colony

[5] 5 & 6 Eliz. II, c. 6.   [6] 5 & 6 Eliz. II, c. 60.

[7] This subject was fully expounded in the *Report of the Conference on the Operation of Dominion Legislation and Merchant Shipping Legislation* of 1929 (Cmd. 3479) in relation to the old Dominions—Canada, Australia, New Zealand, South Africa, the Irish Free State, and Newfoundland. The conference was set up as a result of the declaration of equality of status at the Imperial Conference of 1926. Its report was considered by the Imperial Conference of 1930 and adopted with certain modifications (see Cmd. 3717). Although the report does not deal with the position of India and the new Members of the Commonwealth, the principles which it enunciated and which the Imperial Conference of 1930 endorsed were continuously applied in Commonwealth relations after 1945. They are part of the constitutional heritage which new Members of the Commonwealth acquire.

[8] I confine my discussion to the position of Commonwealth countries dependent upon the United Kingdom. It should be remembered that there are Commonwealth countries dependent upon other Members of the Commonwealth; Australia and New Zealand both have dependent territories.

[9] 28 & 29 Vict., c. 63.

to which such law may relate, or repugnant to any order or regulation made under authority of such Act of Parliament, or having in
the Colony the force and effect of such Act, shall be read subject
to such Act, order or regulation, and shall, to the extent of such
repugnancy, but not otherwise, be and remain absolutely void and
inoperative.[10]

This act, it should be emphasized, did not create the power of
the parliament of the United Kingdom to make supreme laws
for the overseas territories. That power was assumed already to
exist. What the Colonial Laws Validity Act did was first to
declare and describe the nature, extent, and effect of the power.
In particular it was made clear in the Colonial Laws Validity
Act that mere repugnancy to the law of England did not invalidate a colonial act. It could not be claimed, for example, that
repugnancy to the common law of England necessarily involved
invalidity. 'No colonial Law', says section 3 of the act, 'shall be
or be deemed to have been void or inoperative on the ground of
repugnancy to the law of England, unless the same shall be repugnant to the provision of some such Act of Parliament, order
or regulation as aforesaid.'

Secondly, and not less important, the act contained a rule of
construction to determine when this power should be deemed
to have been exercised. 'An Act of Parliament, or any provision
thereof, shall, in construing this Act, be said to extend to any
Colony when it is made applicable to such Colony by the express
words or necessary intendment of any act of Parliament.'[11]
Before it could be claimed, therefore, that a colonial law was
void on the ground of repugnancy to a British act, it must be
shown that the British act did really extend to the colony, and
in order to show this it must be possible to demonstrate that the
'express words' or the 'necessary intendment' of the act required
this interpretation. A British act which merely dealt with the
same subject as a colonial act did not thereby prevail over a
colonial act. It was necessary to show that the British act extended to the colony, and, if so, that the colonial act was repugnant to it.

[10] The act did not apply to the Channel Islands, the Isle of Man, or India,
but in fact the position was substantially the same there as in the colonies. For
the Isle of Man and the Channel Islands see G. W. Keeton, *The British Commonwealth*, vol. i, *The United Kingdom*, pp. 486, 1144-6.
[11] S. 1.

The most important example of legislation by the parliament of the United Kingdom extending to a colony has usually been the constitution of the colony itself which almost invariably is embodied either in an act of parliament itself, or in an order-in-council passed under the authority of such an act. For the rest there have been certain general acts dealing with such subjects as merchant shipping, copyright, naturalization and citizenship, and the like, which have extended to colonies to a greater or less extent, and colonial laws, repugnant to them, have been void to the extent of their repugnancy.

The greater part of the law of a Commonwealth country, however, even when it is in a subordinate or dependent status, is enacted by the country's own legislature. Such control as the United Kingdom may wish to exercise over the legislation is provided by a variety of methods embedded within the constitution of the colony itself, rather than applied from outside by the parliament of the United Kingdom through the cumbersome method of legislation by act of parliament. There is, for example, the power granted to the Governor in some Commonwealth constitutions to enact laws himself if the legislature refuses to do so; or the legislature may be so composed that it contains a majority of official members who may be required to vote in accordance with instructions from the Secretary of State for the Colonies. Then there is the power of reservation by which a Governor, when presented with a bill duly passed by the legislature, may, instead of giving his assent to it, reserve it for the signification of Her Majesty's pleasure. Reservation is of two kinds, discretionary and obligatory. Where reservation is obligatory the Governor is required, either by his Instrument of Instructions, or by a specific instruction from the Secretary of State, or by the terms of the constitution of the colony, or by some act of parliament to reserve a bill if it falls within some specific class or category.

Even when an act has been passed by a colonial legislature and assented to by the Governor and is in full operation, it is still possible, by the terms of some Commonwealth constitutions, for the government of the United Kingdom to render the law of no effect. This is done by the exercise of the power of disallowance. An act of a legislature may, within a specified period, be disallowed by the Sovereign on the advice of the

Secretary of State. It is most rarely exercised, but its existence is a potential instrument of control over a Commonwealth legislature.

It will be noticed that, in a dependent territory, the Governor is not only the representative of the Queen, but the representative of Her Majesty's Government also. To this extent an institution of the colonial constitution is subordinate to another government in the Commonwealth. To the extent that the Governor acts not upon the advice of ministers or of an executive council responsible to the colonial legislature, but is responsible to the Secretary of State and subject to his instructions, to that extent the colonial government is dependent upon the government of the United Kingdom. It is not surprising, therefore, that one of the significant changes which occur when Commonwealth countries attain independence is the change in the status of the Governor both within the colony and in relation to the government of the United Kingdom.

Dependent Commonwealth countries exhibit their subordinate position also in the field of external affairs. They are unable, as a rule, to make laws with extra-territorial operation and must rely upon legislation by the parliament of the United Kingdom in such a matter. They are restricted in their intercourse with foreign states and are normally unable, formally at any rate, to accredit or receive diplomatic representatives, to negotiate, sign, or ratify treaties, or to belong to international organizations in their own right. The use of their defence forces, particularly outside their own territories, is usually subject to control by the government of the United Kingdom.

In the judicial sphere, it is usual for an appeal to lie from the courts of a colony to the Judicial Committee of the Privy Council sitting in London. The extent of the appeal and the manner of its exercise varies from country to country. There may be a right of a litigant to appeal from a decision of a colonial court without asking the leave of that court; or appeal may be by leave of the colonial court; or finally, appeal may be by special leave of the Judicial Committee itself. If the Judicial Committee is regarded as a British court, it is clear that if an appeal lies to it from courts in Commonwealth countries, these courts are subordinate to it and to that extent the Commonwealth country is dependent upon the United Kingdom. Moreover, as the appeal is regulated by acts of the British parliament, in particular the Judicial Committee Acts of 1833 and 1844,[12] it is not possible, under the provisions of the Colonial Laws Validity Act, for a colonial legislature to restrict or abolish the appeal unless specifically authorized to do so by a British act.

3

When independence is to be granted to a Commonwealth country, one of the most important questions to be dealt with at the outset is the inequality which arises from the existence of a power in the parliament of the United Kingdom to make laws for that country. The simple and straightforward course, in the eyes of a layman, would be for parliament to enact that this power is hereby abolished in respect of the Commonwealth country, and that it will never be exercised or revived again. Lawyers, however, have doubted the efficacy of this step. They hold that the power is inalienable and they demonstrate this by asserting that, since one parliament cannot bind its successor, a later parliament would always be at liberty to revive and exercise the power, whatever a predecessor might have declared or promised. Whether this view is sound is a matter for argument. None the less, the inequality has not so far been tackled by a head-on approach. Instead the legislation has attempted not to abolish the power but to ensure that, if it is ever exercised, it will be ineffective unless the legislature of the Member of the Commonwealth concerned consents to it. What has been attempted, in short, is not to abolish the power, but, in the words of the Imperial Conference of 1930, to find an 'appropriate method of reconciling the existence of this power with the established constitutional position'[13] of equality. A number of distinct but connected steps have been taken towards this end.

At first sight the obvious step would be to repeal the Colonial Laws Validity Act of 1865 in respect of those Commonwealth countries which were to attain equality of status. And this in fact was done for Canada, Australia, New Zealand, and South Africa by the Statute of Westminster,[14] and for Ceylon and

[12] 3 & 4 Wm. IV, c. 41, and 7 & 8 Vict., c. 69.
[13] Cmd. 3717. Adopting para. 54 of the *Report of the Conference on the Operation of Dominion Legislation*, 1929, Cmd. 3479.
[14] By s. 2 (1). Certain reservations were made in respect of their constitutions, which are explained below. See pp. 59 ff.

Ghana by their respective Independence Acts.[15] But this did no more than remove a declaration that the power existed and a rule of construction to determine when it should be deemed to have been exercised. With the repeal of the Colonial Laws Validity Act, it could be argued not only that the power of the parliament of the United Kingdom to make superior laws for the Commonwealth overseas still existed, but that the contention might be revived, which the act had been passed to negate, that repugnancy to English law (and not merely to acts of parliament extending to a colony by express words or necessary intendment) was a ground for invalidity of the acts of a Commonwealth country overseas. The mere repeal of the Colonial Laws Validity Act, therefore, while it had some significance, did not neutralize or nullify, much less abolish, the inequality.

If the inequality could not be abolished by law, why should it not be nullified by convention? The Members of the Commonwealth represented at the Imperial Conference of 1930 agreed to take this first step. They placed on record the following statement:

It would be in accord with the established constitutional position of all Members of the Commonwealth in relation to one another that no law hereafter made by the Parliament of the United Kingdom shall extend to any Dominion otherwise than at the request and with the consent of that Dominion.[16]

This declaration received the approval of the parliaments of all the Dominions; it was recited in the preamble to the Statute of Westminster in 1931, and the parliament of the United Kingdom thereby expressed its acceptance of it. It will be noticed that the convention proceeds upon the basis that the power exists; it does not say that it must never be exercised again in the future; it does not attempt to abolish it. It says that the power shall not be used unless the Dominion concerned requests and consents to the exercise.

Yet this convention did not alter the law. So a second step was taken. It was enacted as follows:

[15] Ceylon Independence Act, 1947, First Schedule, para. 1 (1); Ghana Independence Act, 1957, First Schedule, para. 1. No action was necessary for India and Pakistan since the Colonial Laws Validity Act did not apply to India.

[16] Cmd. 3717. Adopting para. 54 of the *Report of the Conference on the Operation of Dominion Legislation*, 1929, Cmd. 3479.

No Act of Parliament of the United Kingdom passed after the commencement of this Act shall extend, or be deemed to extend, to a Dominion as part of the law of that Dominion unless it is expressly declared in that Act that that Dominion has requested, and consented to the enactment thereof.

This provision occurs in section 4 of the Statute of Westminster and applies now to Canada, Australia, New Zealand, South Africa, and the United Kingdom. It applied to the Irish Free State or Eire until it withdrew from the Commonwealth in 1949. A substantially similar provision appears in section 1 (i) of the Ceylon Independence Act, 1947, and in section 1 (*a*) of the Ghana Independence Act, 1957.[17]

The enacted provision does not go so far in controlling the power of the parliament of the United Kingdom as the convention does. The convention lays down a rule to determine when the power may be exercised; the law lays down a rule to determine when the power has or may be deemed to have been exercised. If the parliament of the United Kingdom passed a law extending to a Dominion without the request and consent of that Dominion but inserted in the law a declaration that the request and consent of the Dominion had been obtained, it would have broken the convention, but it would not have broken the legal rule. The convention and the legal rule work together and neither is completely effective without the other.

The provisions of section 4 of the Statute of Westminster and section 1 of the Ceylon and of the Ghana Independence Acts have been misunderstood at times because it has been thought that their intention was to abolish or nullify the power of the parliament at Westminster to make laws extending to another Member of the Commonwealth. This was not their intention. They were enacted on the assumption that the parliament at Westminster had that power and that it could be exercised. They declared, as a rule of construction, that it would have been and should be deemed to have been exercised when the

---

[17] The request and consent required in the case of Australia is that of the parliament and government of the Commonwealth of Australia (s. 9 (3) of the Statute of Westminster); in the case of Ghana (s. 1 of the Ghana Independence Act, 1957) and of New Zealand (Statute of Westminster Adoption Act, 1947 [No. 38 of 1947]) it is the request and consent of the parliaments of those Members. For the other Members concerned, no mouthpiece is prescribed.

act in question contained a declaration that it had been passed at the request and with the consent of the Member concerned.[18]

It is as a rule of construction that the sections are best understood. It is useful to recall that it was 'practical considerations affecting both the drafting of bills and the interpretation of statutes'[19] which led the Imperial Conference of 1930 to recommend the inclusion of what became section 4 in the Statute of Westminster. The Colonial Laws Validity Act, 1865, had said that an act of parliament should be deemed to extend to a colony 'when it is made applicable to such Colony by the express words or necessary intendment of any act of parliament'. The Statute of Westminster and the Ceylon and the Ghana Independence Acts replace this rule by another. They say that an act of parliament shall be deemed to extend to the Members of the Commonwealth concerned when it contains a declaration that the Member concerned has requested and consented to it. The provisions of these sections are not directed to legislators but to judges; they are not a self-denying ordinance of the parliament of the United Kingdom (that self-denying ordinance is contained in the convention) but a direction to the courts in the Commonwealth to assist them in applying the law to the cases that come before them.[20]

4

It is understandable that these provisions did not appear, to some communities in the Commonwealth at any rate, to go far enough. Suppose, by inadvertence or by deliberate intention, an act was passed containing a declaration of request although no such request had been made. It would extend to the Member concerned. And then, even supposing that no issue of mistake or intention arose, was it not contrary to equality for a Member

[18] Examples of acts passed under the provisions of s. 4 of the Statute are the Abdication Act of 1936 so far as it extended to Canada, and the British North America Act, 1949 (No. 1); the New Zealand Constitution (Amendment) Act, 1947; and the Cocos Islands Act, 1955, and the Christmas Island Act, 1958, to both of which Australia requested and consented.

[19] Adopting para. 55 of the *Report on the Operation of Dominion Legislation* of 1929.

[20] The effect of section 4 was discussed by the High Court of Australia in *Copyright Owners Reproduction Soc. Ltd.* v. *E.M.I. (Aust.) Pty. Ltd.*, 1959 Argus L.R. 127.

to receive part of its law through the authority of the parliament of the United Kingdom and not through the authority of its own parliament? And could nothing be done about that by legal means? Must reliance be placed on convention alone?

Such a view seems to have been adopted by the parliament of the Union of South Africa and to have found expression in section 2 of its Status of the Union Act, passed in 1934.[21] It ran:

> The Parliament of the Union shall be the sovereign legislative power in and over the Union, and notwithstanding anything in any other law contained, no act of the Parliament of the United Kingdom and Northern Ireland[22] passed after the eleventh day of December, 1931[23] shall extend or be deemed to extend, to the Union as part of the law of the Union, unless extended thereto by an act of the Parliament of the Union.

This section purported to substitute, for South African courts at any rate, a new rule of construction in place of that enacted by the parliament of the United Kingdom in section 4 of the Statute of Westminster. The test for a South African court was not to be whether an act of the parliament at Westminster contained a declaration expressing the request and consent of South Africa, but whether an act of the South African parliament extended an act of the parliament of the United Kingdom to South Africa. And presumably it was to be immaterial to South African courts whether the extended act contained a declaration of request and consent or not.

The South African provision, too, seemed to adopt a different attitude towards an act of the parliament of the United Kingdom from that embodied in section 4 of the Statute of Westminster. Section 4 was based upon the acceptance of the proposition that an act of the parliament of the United Kingdom could of its own force and motion cross the seas to a Member of the Commonwealth and become part of its law. It did not need to be brought; it could come. And section 4 explained when it should be deemed to have made the journey. Section 2 of the Status Act does not proceed upon this assumption.

---

[21] No. 69 of 1934.

[22] The words 'of Great Britain' after 'United Kingdom' were omitted, presumably by mistake.

[23] The date of the commencement of the Statute of Westminster.

Without actually denying it, it puts forward another. It provides that any act of the parliament of the United Kingdom which South Africans want shall be brought to South Africa by its own parliament. It may be that it could come, but it is going to be brought. It will not come under its own steam in a United Kingdom ship; it will come as a passenger in a South African ship.

Doubts were raised about the capacity of the South African parliament to add this rule of construction to that already laid down in the Statute of Westminster by section 4 or to substitute it for it. It was held to constitute an amendment to section 4 of the Statute, and in the view of some authorities, notably Professor A. Berriedale Keith,[24] no power to amend the Statute had been conferred upon the parliaments of the Members of the Commonwealth to which it applied. For reasons which will be given later[25] the better opinion seems to be that section 2 of the Status Act was valid. But it is interesting to notice that when the Indian Independence Act came to be passed in 1947 care was taken to leave no room for doubts of this kind. The South African device of requiring the consent of the parliament of the Dominion was preferred to that of a declaration of the request and consent of the Dominion as in section 4 of the Statute of Westminster. Section 6 (4) of the Indian Independence Act runs:

No Act of Parliament of the United Kingdom passed on or after the appointed day shall extend or be deemed to extend to either of the new Dominions as part of the law of that Dominion unless it is extended thereto by a law of the legislature of the Dominion.

By this enactment the parliament of the United Kingdom substituted a new test by which it could be decided whether a British act extended to India or Pakistan. It was not a matter of express words or necessary intendment, nor a declaration of request and consent as in the Statute of Westminster and in the Ceylon and Ghana Independence Acts; it was a matter of producing an Indian or Pakistani act which extended the United Kingdom act to the Member concerned. The parliament at Westminster takes away from its acts their power, of their own

---

[24] See, for example, *Speeches and Documents on the British Dominions*, p. 305, n. 1.   [25] See below, pp. 33–34.

motion, to cross the seas to India. It stops them at the water's
edge, so to speak, and they can proceed no farther unless an
Indian vessel picks them up and takes them to India. In this
respect, indeed, the British acts are no different from the acts
of, say, the parliament of Norway. The Indian legislature may
enact that a Norwegian law should extend to India, if it chooses
to do so.

But there could still remain some ground for uneasiness, even
if the formula in the Indian Independence Act were adopted.
Supposing, to speak in extremes, and to forget politics and
remember only legalism, that the provisions were repealed by
the parliament of the United Kingdom. Or supposing, to take
a more moderate example, that a law were passed applying to
India by name and in express words which left no doubt that it
was intended to extend to India. Would not such an act amount
to an amendment, *pro tanto*, of section 6 (4) of the Indian
Independence Act, and thereby extend to India? And if this
may be supposed of the provision in section 6 (4), it may be
supposed also of section 4 of the Statute of Westminster. Supposing that section were repealed, or that a law was passed,
without a declaration of request and consent, but applying
in express words to a Dominion, would that not amount to
a repeal *pro tanto* of section 4 and therefore extend to the
Dominion?

Some authorities might dispute at the outset the possibility of
a repeal or amendment of section 6 (4) of the Indian Independence Act by the action of the parliament of the United Kingdom alone. They could argue that any such purported repeal
or amendment would itself fall under the provisions of section
6 (4). It would claim to extend to India (if not it would be ineffective) and by section 6 (4) could not do so without an act
of the parliament of India extending it thereto. The argument
might be put in another way by saying that section 6 (4) created
a new legislature so far as laws of the United Kingdom extending to India were concerned, a legislature consisting of the parliament of the United Kingdom and the parliament of India. No
such law could be passed without the concurrence of both. In
this respect section 6 (4) went further than section 4 of the
Statute of Westminster. The latter did not, in law, require the
concurrence of another legislature in addition to the parliament

of the United Kingdom; it merely required that parliament to declare that it had the concurrence.

It is impossible to say what interpretation a court in a Commonwealth Member would adopt if these issues were raised before it. The possibility is so remote that it may seem fruitless to consider it. A court in the United Kingdom would be faced with a decision whether it should prefer a later act of parliament to an earlier act when the two conflicted and it is difficult to see how it could avoid preferring the later act.[26] A court in the overseas Members concerned, however, might decide that since the British act had not been extended to that Member by an act of the parliament of that Member (as in the case of South Africa) or did not contain a declaration of request and consent (as in the case of Australia, Canada, and New Zealand), it was not part of the law of that Member, and therefore no question arose of preferring a later British act to an earlier British act.

5

It is possible, however, to meet the misgivings expressed about the effectiveness of section 6 (4) of the Indian Independence Act and section 4 of the Statute of Westminster by reference to powers which the parliament of the United Kingdom conferred upon the Members of the Commonwealth when dealing with legislative inequalities. The question is approached not from the negative but from the positive point of view of what the parliaments of the other Members of the Commonwealth may do.

Thus, in the Statute of Westminster, upon the repeal of the Colonial Laws Validity Act, it was positively enacted that the parliament of a Dominion not only was not fettered by acts of the parliament of the United Kingdom, but was empowered to amend or repeal such acts. The position was set out in section 2 (2) of the Statute as follows:

No law and no provision of any law made after the commencement of this Act by the Parliament of a Dominion shall be void or inoperative on the ground that it is repugnant to the law of England, or to the provisions of any existing or future Act of Parliament of

---

[26] But see H. R. Gray, 10 *University of Toronto Law Journal* (1953-4), pp. 69-70. His article on the sovereignty of parliament today is a valuable criticism of the assumption that parliament cannot bind itself.

the United Kingdom, or to any order, rule or regulation made under any such Act, and the powers of the Parliament of a Dominion shall include the power to repeal or amend any such Act, order, rule or regulation in so far as the same is part of the law of the Dominion.

This provision regulates the position of the parliaments of Canada, Australia, New Zealand, and South Africa. It was repeated also in the Ceylon Independence Act, 1947,[27] and in the Ghana Independence Act, 1957.[28] It permitted those parliaments to repeal or amend any existing acts of the parliament of the United Kingdom extending to the Members concerned, and in this way allowed them to get rid of past legislation which they did not wish to retain any longer. It was a matter of opinion whether the Statute of Westminster itself could be included within the term 'existing' act of parliament. If it could, then these parliaments might repeal or amend it in so far as it was part of the law of their countries. The better opinion seems to be that it does include the Statute, for the power conferred comes into operation 'after the commencement of this Act', and by that time the Statute is an existing act of parliament of the United Kingdom. Although the Ceylon and Ghana Independence Acts adopted the same form of words as in section 2 (2) of the Statute of Westminster, the Indian Independence Act, which was passed six months before the Ceylon Independence Act,[29] removed all doubt by referring to 'this or any existing or future Act of Parliament of the United Kingdom'. It is interesting that this difference of wording should occur in two acts passed within six months of each other, and that the more explicit and superficially liberal grant of power should appear in the earlier act and not in the later. It may be used perhaps as an argument for the view that the widest powers were intended to be conferred in both cases, and that the only difference between the two forms of words was a difference of draftsmen.

Our principal interest in the provisions, however, lies in the fact that they conferred power on the parliaments of these Members of the Commonwealth to repeal or amend 'future' acts of parliament of the United Kingdom. By virtue of this

[27] First Schedule, para. 1 (2).
[28] First Schedule, paras. 1 and 2.
[29] The Indian Independence Act received the royal assent on 18 July 1947, and the Ceylon Independence Act on 10 Dec. 1947.

power, then, it was surely open to the parliaments of these Members to repeal or amend any act of parliament of the United Kingdom which contradicted implicitly or explicitly those provisions whether of the Statute of Westminster or of the Indian, Ceylon, or Ghana Independence Acts which laid down the relationship between the parliament of the United Kingdom and the parliaments of the other Members. And indeed it would be possible for a parliament of a Member to enact that any act of the parliament of the United Kingdom which purported to repeal or amend section 4 of the Statute of Westminster or the appropriate section of one of the Independence Acts, as the case may be, should be void and of no effect as part of the law of that Member. In this way a Member by the use of powers given to it under one section of the Statute of Westminster or of an Independence Act might protect itself from losing the freedom which it had gained under other sections of the Statute or of the Independence Acts from being legislated for by the United Kingdom parliament.

It was possible to introduce a notion of this kind when considering the effect of section 2 of the Status Act of 1934 in South Africa.[30] To those who questioned the validity of this provision of the Status Act it was possible to answer that if it was a repeal or amendment by implication of the Statute, it was perfectly valid because the Union parliament was empowered to amend the Statute. But it was possible to take another line. It was possible to say that the Union parliament was repealing or amending in advance, under section 2(2) of the Statute of Westminster, any future acts of the parliament of the United Kingdom in so far as they purported to be part of the law of the Union unless and until such acts had been extended to the Union by its parliament.

6

Did the parliaments of the Members of the Commonwealth achieve equality with each other and in particular with the parliament of the United Kingdom as a result of the provisions of the Statute of Westminster and of the Independence Acts? If we put aside for the moment various provisions retained by Australia and Canada in regard to their constitutions, it would

[30] See above, p. 30.

seem possible to say that although there might still remain some doubts about whether the power of the parliament of the United Kingdom to legislate for the other Members had been abolished, its use had either been nullified or, in some cases, reconciled with equality of status. For India and Pakistan under the Indian Independence Act and for South Africa by a combination of the Status Act and the Statute, the power had at least been nullified; for Australia, Canada, and New Zealand, who accepted the provisions of section 4 of the Statute, and for Ceylon, Ghana, and Malaya under the similar provision in their Independence Acts, the power had been at least reconciled with equality.

And yet there were always possible nightmares for the nationalistic legalist, so long as there existed, even in paralysed form, some organ at Westminster that could make laws extending to other Members of the Commonwealth. After all, this power did not reside in the parliament of any other Member of the Commonwealth. How could one so organize one's constitutional position that no question could arise, even hypothetically, of law-making by Westminster for other Members of the Commonwealth?

One suggested solution was to cease to be part of the Queen's dominions, so that the enactments of the Queen in parliament should not be capable of extending to you. There were no doubt many reasons which led India to choose a republican form of government, but one consequence of its choice and perhaps one minor cause of its choice was that in so doing it ruled out any possibility that an act of the United Kingdom parliament could be construed to extend to India of its own force and validity. The parliament of India might, of course, choose to extend such an act to India, whether India was a republic or not, but in that respect the parliament of the United Kingdom was no different from the parliament of Norway or the parliament of any other country. Pakistan occupies a similar position. Nor is it necessary to become a republic in order to achieve this position. Malaya is a kingdom, but it is not a realm of Elizabeth II and is outside her dominions and therefore no court in Malaya or in any other Member of the Commonwealth would hold that an act of the parliament of the United Kingdom extended thereto, of its own force and authority.

India and Pakistan have gone further in this matter, however.

Not only have they declared themselves no longer part of the Queen's dominions, but they have adopted constitutions which clearly make a break with their legal system of the past. Their parliaments claim legislative power from the constitution and the constitution claims authority, not from the parliament of the United Kingdom (as does, for example, the Canadian or Australian or New Zealand constitutions) but from the people. The link with the parliament at Westminster is broken, and the Indian Independence Act is regarded not as the first chapter of a new constitutional history, but as the last chapter of the old. This theme will be considered in more detail later.[31] It is mentioned here to illustrate the way in which equality of status in legislative matters has been worked out to its logical conclusion by at least two Members of the Commonwealth.

7

The acquisition of equality of status in legislative power ensures actually or potentially equality of status in almost all other spheres. Inequalities may be removed by law as and when Members choose to do so. In these matters Members have differed and their positions in strict law have seldom been identical. It is necessary, therefore, to describe in some detail the situation of each of the Members in regard to the principal elements of inequality which did or still do exist.

Let us begin with the position about disallowance and reservation. Equality in respect of these powers has been achieved by the use of an interesting combination of constitutional convention and strict law. When the Imperial Conference of 1930 considered these powers it adopted certain constitutional conventions about their existence and exercise and these applied to Canada, Australia, New Zealand, South Africa, and the Irish Free State, as well as to the United Kingdom. So far as disallowance was concerned it was agreed in 1930 that 'the power of disallowance can no longer be exercised in relation to Dominion legislation'.[32] To adopt this convention was to nullify the power of disallowance but it was not to abolish it. It was agreed, therefore, that those Dominions which possessed the

[31] See Chap. IV.
[32] Adopting para. 23 of the *Report on the Operation of Dominion Legislation*, Cmd. 3479.

power to delete disallowance from their constitutions might do so, by following the prescribed procedure for constitutional amendment, while in the case of those Dominions which did not possess this power 'it would be in accordance with constitutional practice that, if so requested by the Dominion concerned, the government of the United Kingdom should ask Parliament to pass the necessary legislation'.[33] The principles laid down in 1930 are still recognized and have governed the action that has since been taken.

The position now is that disallowance finds a place in the constitutions of Australia,[34] Canada,[35] and New Zealand[36] alone among Members of the Commonwealth, although it is, of course, found in the constitutions of many of those Commonwealth countries which are not yet independent Members. The parliaments of Canada and New Zealand can remove disallowance whenever they wish, while in Australia the power can be removed by the ordinary process of constitutional amendment which involves action not only by the parliament of the Commonwealth of Australia, but also the holding of a referendum. No action is required, however, by the parliament of the United Kingdom. It may be mentioned, also, that the power of disallowance subsists in the constitutions of the six Australian states.[37] Although these states were not represented at Imperial Conferences and the resolutions passed there do not apply to them, yet it is difficult to conceive that while Australians considered as citizens of the Commonwealth of Australia are to enjoy equality of status, Australians considered as citizens of the separate states are not. The removal of disallowance from the state constitutions may be carried out by the ordinary process of constitutional amendment and if the consent of the United Kingdom should be required in strict law to the completion of this process, there can be no doubt that it will be given, in accordance with the convention adopted by the Imperial Conference of 1930.

While Australia, Canada, and New Zealand have been content to allow disallowance to survive in their constitutions,

[33] Ibid.
[34] Australian constitution, s. 59.
[35] British North America Act, 1867, s. 56.
[36] New Zealand Constitution Act, 1852, s. 58.
[37] 5 & 6 Vict., c. 76, and 13 & 14 Vict., c. 59.

South Africa has not. In 1934, by section 11 of the Status Act, disallowance was removed from the constitution of the Union.[38] When the Indian Independence Act was passed in 1947 it provided that disallowance should not apply to the two new Dominions of India and Pakistan.[39] Needless to say, disallowance finds no place in the constitutions of the Republic of India, or of the Republic of Pakistan, nor is it found in the constitutions of Ghana and of Malaya, which came into force in 1957.

There is, however, a limited sphere in which disallowance was provided for in the constitution of Ceylon of 1947 of which something should be said, for it illustrates a point of general application to other Members of the Commonwealth. This concerns the possibility of disallowance by the United Kingdom of laws passed by the legislature of a Member of the Commonwealth dealing with certain trustee securities. The Colonial Stock Act of 1900[40] had provided that the British Treasury might lay down conditions under which colonial stocks would be admitted as trustee securities in the United Kingdom. The third of these conditions laid down by the Treasury was that the country concerned must place on record a formal expression of its opinion that legislation which appeared to the government of the United Kingdom to alter any of the provisions affecting such trustee stock to the injury of the stock-holders or to depart from the original contract, might properly be disallowed. Naturally it was possible for the advantages of this act to be secured only by those countries for which the power of disallowance had been provided in their constitutions. The Irish Free State, for example, was not able to obtain these advantages because disallowance found no place in its constitution of 1922.

When, after the Imperial Conference of 1930, the removal of disallowance came to be contemplated as a consequence of the principle of equality of status, some consideration had to be given to the matter of colonial stocks. How could the legitimate safeguards required by the United Kingdom government to protect its own investors be reconciled with equality? In 1934, when the Union of South Africa decided to remove disallowance from its constitution, an alternative procedure was devised.

---

[38] Except as provided for in para. 20 of the schedule to the constitution affecting the native territories.

[39] s. 6 (3).   [40] 63 & 64 Vict., c. 62, s. 2.

By the Colonial Stock Act, 1934,[41] passed by the parliament of the United Kingdom, it was enacted that the third of the conditions prescribed by the Treasury under section 2 of the Colonial Stock Act, 1900, should be deemed to have been observed with respect to any stock issued by the government of a Dominion if, either the requirement therein specified had been complied with, or if two other requirements were complied with. The first requirement was that the government of the Dominion had undertaken that legislation which appeared to the government of the United Kingdom to alter any of the provisions affecting the stock to the injury of the stock holders or to involve a departure from the original contract in regard to the stock, should not be submitted for the royal assent except after agreement with the United Kingdom government, and that if attention was drawn to any such legislation after the passing thereof by the Dominion parliament, the Dominion government would take the necessary steps to ensure such amendments as might be requested by the government of the United Kingdom. The second requirement was that the above undertaking should have been confirmed by an act of the parliament of the Dominion. The Union of South Africa accepted this alternative procedure and it came into effect upon the removal of disallowance from the constitution under section 11 (2) of the Status Act.

In the case of Ceylon special provisions were inserted in the constitution by which disallowance might be exercised upon Ceylon laws which, in the opinion of the United Kingdom, made alterations to the injury of the stock holder or involved a departure from the original contract in respect of Ceylon stocks which were either specified in the second schedule[42] to the constitution or which might in the future be placed upon the list of trustee securities at the request of the government of Ceylon. The provisions of the Colonial Stock Act of 1934, however, extend to Ceylon[43] and it would therefore be open to the parliament of Ceylon to remove the provisions concerning disallowance from the constitution by the ordinary process of constitutional amendment, and to adopt the alternative procedure

---

[41] 24 & 25 Geo. V, c. 47, s. 1 (1).
[42] These were loans raised in London before 1939; when repaid, the provision relating to them becomes a dead letter. Jennings, *Constitution of Ceylon*, pp. 23 and 210.
[43] By the Ceylon Independence Act, 1947, Second Schedule, para. 4.

available under the act, as South Africa has done. When Ghana
and Malaya became independent in 1957, the provisions of the
act of 1934 were made applicable to them.[44] It is interesting to
notice that when the Federation of the West Indies was set up
in 1957, the power of disallowance was provided for in the constitution in respect of laws of the federal legislature only so far
as was necessary to safeguard the position of trustee securities
in terms of the Colonial Stock Act of 1900.[45] The power of disallowance in respect of laws made by the legislature of the
Federation of Rhodesia and Nyasaland, on the other hand, is
unqualified.[46]

The situation about reservation resembles that of disallowance in most respects. Australia, Canada, and New Zealand
alone among the Members of the Commonwealth retain it in
their constitutions. In all three constitutions[47] there is a power
in the hands of the Governor-General to reserve bills at his discretion, but it is established by constitutional convention that
the Governor-General would exercise this power only in accordance with the advice of his ministers. It was placed on record
at the Imperial Conference of 1930 that 'His Majesty's Government in the United Kingdom will not advise His Majesty the
King to give the Governor-General any instructions to reserve
Bills presented to him for assent'.[48] No inequality in relation to
the United Kingdom was involved, therefore, in the existence
of these powers. In Australia, however, a further requirement
of reservation exists in the constitution. Bills must be reserved
which limit the matters on which the Judicial Committee of the
Privy Council may be asked to grant special leave to appeal from
the High Court of Australia.[49] In the New Zealand Constitution
Act[50] it is required that bills altering the salary of the Governor
or the sums allocated to native purposes, both of which were set
out in the schedule to the act, must be reserved. And in the

[44] By the Ghana Independence Act, 1957, Second Schedule, para. 4, and the
Federation of Malaya Independence Act, 1957, First Schedule, para. 8.
[45] Constitution of the West Indies (S.I. No. 1364 of 1957), s. 52.
[46] Constitution of Rhodesia and Nyasaland (S.I. No. 1199 of 1953), s. 25.
[47] Australian constitution, ss. 58 and 60; B.N.A. Act, 1867, ss. 55 and 57; New
Zealand Constitution Act, 1852, ss. 56 and 59.
[48] Adopting para. 32 of the *Report on the Operation of Dominion Legislation*, Cmd. 3479.
[49] Australian constitution, s. 74.
[50] s. 65.

Australian states there is a statutory obligation to reserve bills making certain constitutional changes.[51]

It is clear that these powers exist only because the Members concerned are content to acquiesce. The parliaments of Canada and New Zealand can remove them from the constitutions whenever they choose; the Australian constitution can be amended to remove the powers by the ordinary process of constitutional amendment. Nor can it be imagined that any obstacle would be raised by the United Kingdom in the way of the Australian states removing reservation from their constitutions if they wished to do so.

So long as statutory requirements to reserve certain bills exist, however, it is clear that the Governor-General must reserve such bills. What would happen to them? It was agreed by the Imperial Conference of 1930 that it would not be in accordance with constitutional practice for advice to be tendered to His Majesty by His Majesty's Government in the United Kingdom in respect of any reserved bill whatsoever contrary to the views of the government of the Dominion concerned.[52] Thus if a bill has to be reserved, it will receive assent or be refused assent in accordance with the views of the government of the Member concerned. No inequality can thus arise. If, therefore, the Australian parliament passed a bill limiting the matters in which appeals by special leave could be taken to the Judicial Committee of the Privy Council, that bill would have to be reserved by the Governor-General, but when presented to Her Majesty, it would receive assent if the government of Australia so advised.

Such other powers of reservation as existed in relation to Members of the Commonwealth have now been abolished either by the Member concerned or by the action of the parliament of the United Kingdom. Certain provisions which amounted to obligatory reservation in the Merchant Shipping Act, 1894,[53] and the Colonial Courts of Admiralty Act, 1890,[54] were repealed so far as Australia, Canada, New Zealand, and South Africa were concerned by sections 5 and 6 of the Statute of Westminster, and for Ceylon and Ghana by the Ceylon and the

---

[51] Australian States Constitution Act, 1907 (7 Edw. VII, c. 7).
[52] Adopting paras. 32 and 33 of the *Report on the Operation of Dominion Legislation.*   [53] 57 & 58 Vict., c. 60, ss. 735 and 736.
[54] 53 & 54 Vict., c. 27, ss. 4 and 7.

Ghana Independence Acts.[55] The power of reservation in the Ceylon constitution was repealed by the Ceylon Independence Order-in-Council of 1947;[56] and the Indian Independence Act[57] removed reservation so far as the Dominions of India and Pakistan were concerned.

South Africa proceeded by stages. Its constitution had contained provisions empowering the Governor-General to reserve bills at his discretion; instructions had also been issued to the Governor-General of the Union to reserve classes of bills. The constitution itself also imposed upon the Governor-General a statutory duty to reserve bills limiting the matters in which an appeal by special leave to the Judicial Committee of the Privy Council might be granted. By section 64 of the constitution it was provided that all bills repealing or amending that section or any of the provisions of chapter iv of the act under the heading 'House of Assembly', and all bills abolishing provincial councils or abridging the powers conferred on them under section 85 of the act, should be reserved. And in paragraph 25 of the schedule to the act, the Governor-General was required to reserve bills to alter or amend that schedule (which laid down the conditions under which the South African government would administer the native territories if they were handed over to the Union). In 1934 the parliament of the Union, by the Status Act,[58] repealed all these powers of reservation with two important exceptions— that relating to bills limiting the appeal to the Privy Council and that relating to bills altering the terms of the schedule concerning the government of the native territories, if transferred to the Union. As the repeal involved an amendment of section 64 of the constitution, and as by the terms of this section such amending legislation must itself be reserved, the Status Bill was reserved by the Governor-General and assented to by the King on the advice of the Prime Minister of the Union[59]—the whole procedure being in accordance with the law and with the constitutional conventions of equality laid down in the Imperial Conferences of 1926 and 1930. In 1937 new instructions were issued by the King to the Governor-General of the Union on

[55] First Schedule, ss. 3 and 4, and First Schedule, paras. 4 and 5 respectively.
[56] s. 5.   [57] s. 6 (3).
[58] ss. 8, 9, and 11 (i).
[59] See Kennedy and Schlosberg, *Law and Custom of the South African Constitution*, p. 617.

the advice of the Prime Minister of the Union, and the opportunity was then taken to remove instructions to reserve from
the document.[60] It was not until 1950 that the requirement
to reserve bills limiting the appeal to the Privy Council was
removed from the constitution.[61] Reservation still remains in
respect of bills altering the schedule affecting the government
of the native territories, if transferred.

8

It is a mark of a sovereign, independent state that its legislature has power to make laws with extra-territorial effect. The
nature and extent of the power should not be misunderstood.
Extra-territorial legislation simply means legislation which
attaches significance for courts within the jurisdiction to facts
and events occurring outside the jurisdiction. This does not
imply that one state can pass laws for another state, or that
several systems of law will be in operation regulating a particular sphere within any given state. It means only 'that each
nation has the capacity to legislate outside the three mile limit
of its own territory, in respect of its own subjects, in such a way
as to make them amenable to the law, as administered in its own
courts, when they come within its jurisdiction'.[62]

Before the passing of the Statute of Westminster, in 1931, it
was generally held that the overseas countries of the Commonwealth lacked power, in some degree at any rate, to legislate
with extra-territorial effect. The origin, nature, and extent of
the doctrine was obscure and open to controversy.[63] Whether
it could be said to result in a position of inequality to the United
Kingdom might be disputed. In so far as the lack of power was
said to arise from the terms of a country's constitution and that

[60] The previous instructions had done no more than require the Governor-
General to reserve bills which, in fact, he was already required to reserve by
the provisions of the constitution.

[61] By Act No. 16 of 1950 which abolished the appeal itself.

[62] The Solicitor-General, in the debate on the Statute of Westminster Bill,
British House of Commons, 1931. See 260 *H.C. Deb.* 5 s., col. 263.

[63] Lord Sankey in *British Coal Corporation* v. *The King*, [1935] A.C. 500
at p. 520. See also *Macleod* v. *Attorney-General for New South Wales*, [1891]
A.C. 455, and *Croft* v. *Dunphy*, [1933] A.C. 156. For a full discussion of the
subject see D. P. O'Connell, 'The Doctrine of Colonial Extra-territorial Legislative Incompetence', in 75 *L.Q.R.* (1959), pp. 318 ff.

constitution was framed and enacted by the United Kingdom, and in so far as the lack of power resulted in its being necessary for a country to rely upon the parliament of the United Kingdom to legislate on its behalf with extra-territorial effect, to that extent it might be said that inequality of status arose or was illustrated by this difference in power between the parliaments at Westminster and overseas. In the result, it was decided by the Imperial Conferences of 1926 and 1930, that power to legislate with extra-territorial effect should be granted to the Dominions. Section 3 of the Statute of Westminster is as follows: 'It is hereby declared and enacted that the Parliament of a Dominion has full power to make laws having extra-territorial operation.' By virtue of this section Australia, Canada, New Zealand, and South Africa have power to legislate with extra-territorial effect. India, Pakistan, Ceylon, and Ghana all acquired the power in their respective independence acts.[64] Malaya has the power in its constitution.[65]

It should not be assumed that the countries of the Commonwealth which have not yet obtained equality of status are completely unable to make laws with extra-territorial operation. A great deal will depend upon the terms of their constitutions and upon the course of judicial interpretation. It is perhaps true to say, however, that in the absence of express words or necessary intendment in the constitution or other acts of the parliament of the United Kingdom applying to the country and granting power to make laws, the presumption would still be strong that the legislature of a non-self-governing country of the Commonwealth lacked power to legislate with extra-territorial effect.[66] It is an inconvenient position for countries which have some measure of self-government for 'it introduces a general uncertainty which can be illustrated by questions raised concerning fisheries, taxation, shipping, air navigation, marriage, criminal law, deportation, and the enforcement of laws against smuggling and unlawful immigration'.[67]

[64] Indian Independence Act, s. 6 (1); Ceylon Independence Act, First Schedule, s. 2; Ghana Independence Act, First Schedule, para. 3.
[65] Ninth Schedule, Federal List, 1 (g).
[66] See H. A. Smith, 1 *Canadian Bar Review*, at pp. 338–50, and A. B. Keith, to the contrary, in *Journal of Comparative Legislation* (1923), 3rd ser., vol. v, at p. 274.
[67] Para. 38 of the *Report of the Conference on the Operation of Dominion*

9

Equality has been discussed so far in connexion with the exercise of legislative power by Commonwealth countries. It is necessary to consider next the exercise of judicial power. One mark of the subordination of Commonwealth countries to the United Kingdom was the existence of an appeal to the Judicial Committee of the Privy Council. It was recognized and regulated in a series of acts of the parliament of the United Kingdom of which the Judicial Committee Acts of 1833[68] and 1844[69] are the most important. Appeals came to the Judicial Committee either by special leave of the Judicial Committee itself, or without such special leave. The former is usually called the appeal as of grace, and the latter the appeal as of right. The distinction appears to be that in the appeal as of grace the subject has the right to ask the Judicial Committee for special leave and the Judicial Committee has the right to grant or refuse leave. In the appeal as of right the subject has the right to appeal to the Judicial Committee without asking its special leave, and the Judicial Committee has the duty to admit and determine such an appeal.

In fact the right of the subject to appeal to the Judicial Committee without special leave has been restricted or abolished by act of the parliament of the United Kingdom or by order-in-council under the authority of such an act or by colonial laws passed under the authority of an act of the parliament of the United Kingdom. It is usual to find that the appeal without special leave is made subject, where it exists, either to the requirement that no such appeal shall lie unless the sum in dispute in the case is of a certain size, such as £500 or more; or unless leave to appeal is given by the court in the Commonwealth country.

Legislation, Cmd. 3479. It is interesting to notice that the constitution of the Federation of the West Indies of 1957 confers powers to legislate with extra-territorial effect upon the legislature of the Federation or of a territory of the Federation in regard to certain aspects of removing prisoners, regulating fisheries, and regulating immigration and providing for the safety of shipping. S.I. No. 1364 of 1957. Article 54 of the constitution. Similar powers are found in the constitution of Rhodesia and Nyasaland (S.I. No. 1199 of 1953), Second Schedule, Federal List, item 2.

[68] 3 & 4 Wm. IV, c. 41.
[69] 7 & 8 Vict., c. 69, s. 1.

So far as the appeal by special leave is concerned, the Judicial Committee regards itself as bound by certain rules. In regard to criminal cases the words of Lord Halsbury in *Riel* v. *The Queen* express the customary rule adopted by the committee. He said:

It is the usual rule of this Committee not to grant leave to appeal in criminal cases, except where some clear departure from the requirements of justice is alleged to have taken place.[70]

In respect of civil cases, the committee's rule was laid down already by Lord Fitzgerald in *Prince* v. *Gagnon* when he said:

... Their Lordships are not prepared to advise Her Majesty to exercise her prerogative by admitting an appeal to Her Majesty in Council from the Supreme Court of the Dominion, save where the case is of gravity involving matter of public interest or some important question of law, or affecting property of considerable amount, or where the case is otherwise of some public importance or of a very substantial character.[71]

The principle of equality clearly requires that Members of the Commonwealth should not be subject to the appeal to the Judicial Committee if they wish to be rid of it.[72] If they possess the power within their own constitutions to restrict or abolish the appeal, they are free to do so; if they lack this power, then the parliament at Westminster should enact the necessary legislation at their request and with their consent. If we wish to know whether a Member has power within its constitution to

---

[70] (1885), 10 A.C. 675 at p. 677. See also Lord Cave in *Nadan* v. *The King*, [1926] A.C. 482 at p. 495, and the cases there cited by him. Cf. *Knowles* v. *The King*, [1930] A.C. 366 at pp. 371–2, and more recently *Aladesuru* v. *The Queen*, [1956] A.C. 49 at p. 56; *Ng* v. *The Queen*, [1958] A.C. 173 at p. 183. On 28 July 1959 the Judicial Committee refused special leave to appeal from the High Court of Australia in *Stuart* v. *The Queen* and granted it in *Attorney-General for South Australia* v. *Brown* (both murder cases). *The Times*, 29 July 1959.

[71] (1882), 8 A.C. 103, at p. 105. Cf. also *Johnston* v. *Minister of St. Andrew's Church, Montreal* (1877), 3 A.C. 159; *Valin* v. *Langlois* (1879), 5 A.C. 115; *Montreal* v. *Ecclesiastiques de St. Sulpice* (1889), 14 A.C. 660; *Daily Telegraph* v. *McLaughlin*, [1904] A.C. 776; *Hull* v. *McKenna*, [1926] I.R. 402, Lord Buckmaster at p. 409.

[72] '... It is not consistent with the political conception which is embodied in the British Commonwealth of Nations that one Member of the Commonwealth should be precluded from setting up, if it so desires, a Supreme Court of Appeal having a jurisdiction both ultimate and exclusive of any other Member.' Lord Jowett L.C. in *Attorney-General for Ontario* v. *Attorney-General for Canada*, [1947] A.C. 127 at pp. 153–4.

restrict or abolish the appeal, we must, so the decided cases would seem to hold,[73] ask three questions. First of all, since the appeal is an exercise of the royal prerogative, has the Member been empowered to legislate upon that prerogative in this respect? It is accepted as a rule of construction by the courts that the power to legislate upon the prerogative has not been granted save by the express words or necessary intendment of an act of parliament of the United Kingdom or under its authority. Secondly, even if such power has been given, has the legislature of the Member a power to make laws repugnant to the various Judicial Committee Acts which have regulated the appeal? And thirdly, since the granting of special leave to appeal and the hearing of all appeals occurs in the United Kingdom, the seat of the Judicial Committee, has the Member power to make laws with extra-territorial effect? For without such a power it was doubted whether an attempt by a Member to limit or abolish the appeal could be effective.

Power to overcome all these three obstacles could be granted by the parliament of the United Kingdom to Members. Some of the litigation upon this subject arose through doubts about whether in fact Members did possess these powers. The decided cases make clear, also, what obstacles must be overcome if Commonwealth countries not yet independent are to achieve equality in the judicial sphere in due course.

Canada led the way by passing in 1888 an act[74] which purported to abolish the right of appeal in criminal cases with or without special leave of the Judicial Committee. In the case of *Nadan v. The King*[75] in 1926 it was decided by the Judicial Committee that the act was invalid because it failed to overcome two of the obstacles mentioned above. It conflicted with the Judicial Committee Acts of 1833 and 1844 and at that time Canada had no power to make laws repugnant to those acts, for the Colonial Laws Validity Act still applied to Canada. Secondly, Canada had no power, in regard to this matter at least, to make laws with extra-territorial effect. This decision was one powerful factor in leading the Imperial Conference of 1926,

---

[73] *British Coal Corporation* v. *The King*, [1935] A.C. 500; *Nadan* v. *The King*, [1926] A.C. 482 and cases there cited.
[74] 51 Vict., c. 43. Revised Statutes, 1906, c., 146, s. 1025.
[75] [1926] A.C. 482.

which met soon after the decision in *Nadan* v. *The King* was made known, to declare the equality of status of the Dominions and the United Kingdom and to set on foot an inquiry into the way in which the legal inequalities could be removed. When the Statute of Westminster was passed in 1931, the way seemed clear for Canada to abolish the appeal. The obstacle of the Colonial Laws Validity Act and of the lack of power to legislate with extra-territorial effect had beeen removed from Canada by sections 2 and 3 of the Statute of Westminster. The parliament of Canada therefore re-enacted the measure of 1888. When its validity came to be tested before the Judicial Committee in 1935 in the case of *British Coal Corporation* v. *The King*[76] the one point remaining to be decided was whether the parliament of Canada had power to legislate upon the prerogative in this respect. It was held[77] that the powers conferred upon the parliament of Canada by the British North America Act, 1867,[78] to regulate 'the criminal law, except the constitution of courts of criminal jurisdiction but including the procedure in criminal matters' and to provide for a general court of appeal for Canada, were sufficient, not by express words but by necessary intendment, to enable the parliament of Canada, in the absence of the two fetters already referred to, to restrict or abolish the prerogative power to grant special leave to appeal in criminal matters.

A final stage in the abolition of the appeal to the Judicial Committee from Canada was taken when in 1947 the Judicial Committee held valid[79] a Canadian bill[80] abolishing appeals whether in civil or criminal cases not only from the Supreme Court of Canada but also from the superior courts of the provinces. The bill's validity was based on section 101 of the British North America Act, which empowered the parliament to 'provide for the constitution, maintenance and organisation of a general court of appeal for Canada', 'notwithstanding anything in this

---

[76] [1935] A.C. 500. [77] Ibid., at pp. 516 ff.

[78] ss. 91 (27), 101.

[79] *Attorney-General for Ontario* v. *Attorney-General for Canada*, [1947] A.C. 127.

[80] The bill, No. 9 of 1939, received a first reading in 1939, and was referred thereafter to the Supreme Court of Canada, which upheld it by a majority. Leave to appeal from the Supreme Court's decision was granted by the Judicial Committee in 1940, but it was agreed between the parties to postpone the hearing of the appeal until after the war.

act'. It was true that section 92 (14) of the act gave to the provinces exclusive control over 'the administration of justice in the province' and that Lord Sankey had said in the *British Coal Corporation Case* that 'a most essential part of the administration of justice consists of the system of appeals'.[81] But the grant of power in section 101 was made 'notwithstanding anything in this act', and it must be held to prevail over section 92 (14) if there was any conflict between them. Sections 2 and 3 of the Statute of Westminster had removed the obstacles of repugnancy to the acts of 1833 and 1844 and the lack of power to legislate with extra-territorial effect. It remained only to decide, therefore, whether the powers granted in section 101 were wide enough to enable the parliament of Canada not only to deal with the prerogative but to deal with it in such a way that its exercise in relation to the provinces as well as to Canada as a whole might be restricted. In other words, it was necessary to show that section 101 conferred on the parliament of Canada a power to make recourse to the general court of appeal not only final but exclusive. The Judicial Committee held that it did. The parliament of Canada accordingly passed the Supreme Court Amendment Act in 1949[82] and appeals ceased to come to the Judicial Committee.

The appeal from South Africa was abolished in 1950. In the constitution of the Union, provision had been made for the existence of the appeal by special leave, but the appeal without special leave had been barred.[83] Power was given to the parliament of the Union to restrict or abolish the appeal by special leave, subject to reservation of any bill so doing.[84] By this explicit grant of power from the parliament of the United Kingdom, the parliament of the Union was clearly enabled to overcome the three obstacles to the abolition of the appeal which have been referred to above, and had been so authorized from 1910 when the constitution came into operation. The position was unaffected by the passing of the Statute of Westminster. When the Status Act was passed in 1934, reservation in respect of bills limiting the appeal was not removed from the constitution. When in 1950, therefore, the government of the Union decided to introduce a bill to abolish the appeal, it followed the

---

[81] At p. 520.
[83] s. 106.
[82] 13 Geo. VI, c. 37.
[84] Ibid.

procedure which had been available since 1910. The bill was reserved; it received the assent of the King upon the advice of His Majesty's ministers in the Union and it came into effect on 12 April 1950.[85] The appeal by special leave had, in fact, been very little used in the Union, which may explain why the government had not been in a hurry to abolish it.[86] But it certainly constituted in form at least a restriction upon the judicial autonomy of the Union and had it still existed when litigation arose, as it did in 1951, about the entrenched clauses of the constitution, no doubt special leave to appeal to the Privy Council would have been asked for.

Appeals from India and Pakistan were abolished in 1949 and 1950 respectively by acts in almost identical form passed by the Constituent Assemblies of these two Dominions under the powers conferred upon them by the Indian Independence Act of 1947. The Indian Act—entitled the Abolition of Privy Council Jurisdiction Act, 1949—came into effect on 10 October 1949, and the Privy Council (Abolition of Jurisdiction) Act, 1950, of Pakistan came into effect on 1 May 1950. In each case provision was made for the completion of appeals pending before the Judicial Committee, so that the last appeal was completed by the Judicial Committee from India on 6 February 1950, and from Pakistan on 20 June 1950.

Australia, New Zealand, Ceylon, Ghana, and Malaya still retain a system of appeals to the Judicial Committee, but they are all free to remove it whenever they think fit. So far as Australia is concerned, the appeal without special leave was barred by the Australian constitution[87] when it was enacted by the

---

[85] No. 16 of 1950.

[86] Leave to appeal had been granted three times only before 1934; in that year leave was given in *Pearl Assurance Co.* v. *Union Government*, [1934] A.C. 570. See *South African House of Assembly Debates*, vol. 28, Col. D. Reitz, col. 226. An agitation to abolish the appeal arose as a result of this case, but the government refused to act. In Jan. 1937 a private member's bill providing for the abolition of the appeal was introduced in the House of Assembly, but in the course of the debate it was made clear that though the government did not regard the Judicial Committee as a completely satisfactory court of appeal from the Union (General Smuts, the Minister of Justice, *House of Assembly Debates*, ibid., col. 247), it was not prepared to take action to abolish the appeal. The bill was defeated by 70 votes to 19. It is interesting to record that the bill was introduced by Mr. Swart who as Minister of Justice in Dr. Malan's government introduced the bill in 1950 by which the appeal was abolished. *House of Assembly Debates*, vol. 70, cols. 916 ff.   [87] s. 73.

parliament of the United Kingdom in 1900. Moreover, the appeal by special leave was restricted by section 74 of the constitution which ran:

No appeal shall be permitted to the Queen in Council from a decision of the High Court upon any question, howsoever arising, as to the limits *inter se* of the constitutional powers of the Commonwealth and those of any State or States, or as to the limits *inter se* of the constitutional powers of any two or more States unless the High Court shall certify that the question is one which ought to be determined by Her Majesty in Council. The High Court may so certify if satisfied that for any special reason the certificate should be granted, and thereupon an appeal shall lie to Her Majesty in Council on the question without further leave.

This power has been sparingly exercised by the High Court of Australia. A certificate has been granted in one case only.[88] The decision of the Judicial Committee in this case[89] and its decisions in certain earlier constitutional cases[90] tended to confirm opinions in favour of restricting appeals, so far as possible, both by legislation and by judicial decision. In particular, the Commonwealth parliament, in its amendments to the Judiciary Act,[91] has prevented any of the *inter se* questions referred to in section 74 from being dealt with by the Supreme Courts of the States of Australia otherwise than upon the condition that any appeal therefrom should be to the High Court only.

In addition to this express limitation upon the appeal by special leave, the constitution also empowered the parliament of the Commonwealth to pass laws limiting the matters in which special leave to appeal might be asked, subject to the reservation of any such laws[92]—a provision adopted later in the constitution of South Africa. The appeal could also have been abolished by the ordinary process of constitutional amendment, but this was more difficult than the passing of a bill through the parliament. Australia, then, has been free to restrict or abolish the appeal by special leave ever since the establishment of the Commonwealth

---

[88] *Colonial Sugar Refining Co. Ltd.* v. *Att.-Gen. for the Commonwealth*, 15 C.L.R. 182 at p. 234.
[89] [1914] A.C. 237.
[90] e.g. *Webb* v. *Outrim*, [1907] A.C. 81.
[91] Judiciary Act., 1903–27, ss. 38A–40A.
[92] s. 74.

in 1901. It has not in fact exercised the power. If it chose to do so now, the requirement of reservation would still apply, but the assent of the sovereign would be given upon the advice of the Australian government, not of the government of the United Kingdom, in accordance with the constitutional convention agreed upon by the Imperial Conference of 1930, and acted upon in the case of similar legislation by the parliament of the Union in 1934 and in 1950.

It is necessary to note, however, that the position of the states of Australia in law is different from that of the Commonwealth. The appeal with and without special leave still exists from the Supreme Courts of the states,[93] and their parliaments have no power to restrict or abolish it, for the relevant provisions of the Statute of Westminster do not apply to the states. They are not empowered to make laws with extra-territorial operation nor to override the Judicial Committee Acts of 1833 and 1844. If an Australian state wishes, therefore, to restrict or abolish the appeal, it will have to ask the United Kingdom to take the necessary action. The constitutional conventions governing such requests have not been explicitly laid down but in this matter, as in the cases of reservation[94] and disallowance,[95] it may be assumed that the principle of equality would be applied to Australians regarded as citizens of states in the same manner as to them regarded as citizens of the Commonwealth of Australia.

So far as Ceylon and Ghana are concerned, the powers granted to their parliaments by their Independence Acts and by their constitutions would appear to be wide enough to allow the legislatures to restrict or abolish the appeal, just as did India and Pakistan. In the meantime the appeal with or without special leave continues to exist for Ceylon and Ghana.[96]

New Zealand is in a similar position. Until it adopted the relevant sections of the Statute of Westminster in 1947 it was unable to restrict or abolish the appeal because it lacked power

---

[93] In their state jurisdiction, though not in the federal jurisdiction vested in them by the Commonwealth parliament.

[94] See above, p. 41.

[95] See above, p. 37.

[96] The appeal from Ghana is regulated by an Order-in-Council of 1957 passed after independence and at the request of the government of Ghana. S.I. No. 1361 of 1957.

to legislate with extra-territorial effect or to make laws repugnant to the Judicial Committee Acts. These two obstacles were removed by sections 2 and 3 of the Statute, and the powers of the New Zealand parliament to make laws for peace, order, and good government, it is submitted, are wide enough not by express words but by necessary intendment to authorize the making of laws affecting the prerogative in regard to appeals. No such legislation has yet been passed, but since it can be passed whenever the parliament of New Zealand wishes, the continued existence of the appeal cannot be said to infringe the principle of equality.

Arrangements for appeals to the Judicial Committee from the Supreme Court of the Federation of Malaya take an interesting form. As the Queen is not head of the state in Malaya, appeals lie to the Yang di-Pertuan Agong, the head of the state or king of Malaya, and he is authorized by the constitution of Malaya[97] to make arrangements with the Queen for the reference to the Judicial Committee of these appeals. As a result of the arrangements which were made and embodied in an Order-in-Council and in an act of the parliament of Malaya, appeals lie to the Yang di-Pertuan Agong and are referred by him to the Judicial Committee (*a*) in the case of any decision from which an appeal from the Supreme Court would have been entertained by the Judicial Committee (with or without special leave) immediately before Independence Day (31 August 1957), and (*b*) in the case of any decision as to the effect of any provision of the constitution of the Federation.

In cases where leave of the Supreme Court has not been obtained, application may then be made for special leave to appeal to the Yang di-Pertuan Agong, who shall then either grant or refuse permission in those cases as the Judicial Committee may recommend. In any case where a special leave to appeal is so granted, an appeal shall lie to the Yang di-Pertuan Agong, and shall be referred by him to the Judicial Committee. In order to avoid expense and delays, appeals and applications for leave to appeal shall be lodged in the Registry of the Judicial Committee. Reports and recommendations of the Judicial Committee shall be sent by the Registrar of the Privy Council to one of Her Majesty's Principal Secretaries of State for transmission

[97] Article 131.

to the Yang di-Pertuan Agong. On receipt of such a report or recommendation, the Yang di-Pertuan Agong shall make such order as may be necessary to give effect to it.

It has been thought worth while to describe these arrangements in some detail for they illustrate the way in which the position of the head of the state of Malaya is preserved and respected, while at the same time appeals can be made in practice direct to the Judicial Committee. These arrangements can be modified or abolished by the parliament of Malaya and the article of the constitution which authorizes them may be amended and repealed by the ordinary process of constitutional amendment—namely, a two-thirds majority of the total number of each house of the parliament of Malaya on the second and third readings of the bill proposing amendments.[98] The existence of the appeal from Malaya is therefore in no way a mark of its subordination to the parliament or government of the United Kingdom.

The application of the principle of equality to Commonwealth countries in regard to their relations with other states has two aspects. It requires the renunciation by the United Kingdom of its right to conduct the external relations of a Commonwealth country and it requires also the recognition by foreign countries of the right of the Commonwealth country to conduct its own external relations.[99] It involves, therefore, questions of international law and relations and not only of constitutional law and convention. Indeed there have been times in the development of Commonwealth relations when the obstacle to a Commonwealth country's undertaking the conduct of its external relations has been not the unwillingness of the United Kingdom to renounce its authority but the reluctance of foreign states to recognize the authority of the Commonwealth country to act in international relations. Such difficulties arose, for example, at the time of the Peace Conference of Paris in 1919, at the Washington Naval Disarmament Conference in 1921–2, and in connexion with the conclusion of the Halibut Fishery Treaty with the United States in 1923. And it may be noted that Ceylon, for example, had to wait for some

---

[98] Article 159 of the constitution of Malaya.
[99] See R. B. Stewart, *Treaty Relations of the British Commonwealth of Nations*, chaps. 6 and 7.

years after its independence was recognized by other Members of the Commonwealth before it was admitted to membership of the United Nations.

The history of the acquisition by Commonwealth countries of the power to conduct their external relations has been described in some detail elsewhere, and need not be recapitulated here.[1] It was a gradual and piecemeal development until 1939, and allowed plenty of scope for argument about the precise status of Members of the Commonwealth in international law at different times. For our purpose it is sufficient to state what the present position is, and in particular what obstacles have to be overcome or what inequalities removed if a Commonwealth country is to become responsible for its own external relations. It is as well to begin with a brief statement of the legal position.

A non-self-governing Commonwealth country has its relations with other states conducted on its behalf by the Queen acting upon the advice of Her Majesty's government in the United Kingdom. The Queen appoints and receives diplomatic representatives, appoints plenipotentiaries for the conduct of negotiations, and ratifies treaties. The documents which authorize these actions all require the participation of a minister of the United Kingdom if they are to be of legal effect. In some cases a seal must be affixed and this cannot be carried out unless a minister authorizes such action. When a Commonwealth country advances towards self-government in the conduct of external affairs, therefore, it must at some stage acquire the legal power to advise the Queen to execute documents on its behalf. The participation and intervention of a United Kingdom minister must give way to that of a minister of the Commonwealth country concerned. Arrangements may be made also for the delegation to the sovereign's representative in the Member of some or all of the sovereign's powers in external affairs.[2] So we

[1] See, for example, R. B. Stewart, op. cit.; P. J. Noel-Baker, *The Present Juridical Status of the British Dominions in International Law*; A. G. Dewey, *The Dominions and Diplomacy*; W. K. Hancock, *Survey of British Commonwealth Affairs, vol. i, Problems of Nationality, 1918–36*; N. Mansergh, *Survey of British Commonwealth Affairs, Problems of External Policy, 1931–39*, and ibid., *Problems of Wartime Co-operation and Post War Change, 1939–52*.

[2] As was done in Canada in 1947, for example, when new letters patent were issued constituting the office of Governor-General. Printed in Mansergh, *Documents and Speeches on British Commonwealth Affairs*, vol. i, p. 77.

find that at a certain stage Commonwealth countries pass laws establishing seals and authorizing the use of them by the sovereign or her representative upon the advice of the government of the Commonwealth country. Some Members of the Commonwealth have been content to leave these formal legal changes until a late stage in the development of their control over external relations, being satisfied with the exercise of power in practice while the formalities are carried through with the participation of a United Kingdom minister. Others have been anxious to bring the law into line with practice as soon as possible. Thus South Africa passed a Royal Executive Functions and Seals Act in 1934,[3] at the same time as the Status Act, and provided legal machinery through which all acts performed by the sovereign on behalf of South Africa could be carried through by the sovereign or by his representative solely upon the advice of South African ministers. Canada waited until 1939 before passing a Seals Act.[4]

So far as those Members of the Commonwealth of which the Queen is the head of the state are concerned, the conduct of external relations is carried through by instruments issued on the authority of or in the name of the Queen or her representative in the Member concerned and upon the advice of her ministers in that Member. This stage may have been reached gradually, by the working of constitutional convention first and thereafter by the passing of laws, as in the case of Canada or Australia or New Zealand, or it may have been carried out by a sweeping grant of power by legislation as in India, Pakistan, Ceylon, or Ghana. Thus, in the Indian Independence Act of 1947[5] it is declared that, as from an appointed day, 'His Majesty's Government in the United Kingdom have no responsibility as respects the government of any of the territories which, immediately before that day, were included in British India'. And in the Ceylon Independence Act, similarly, it was declared that 'As from the appointed day His Majesty's government in the United Kingdom shall have no responsibility for the government of Ceylon'.[6] Thereafter all acts of the sovereign on behalf

[3] No. 70 of 1934.
[4] 3 Geo. VI, c. 22. For the Canadian position see Thomas Franck, 32 *Canadian Bar Review* (1954), pp. 1084 ff.
[5] s. 7 (i) (a).
[6] s. 1 (2).

of Ceylon in external or internal affairs would be carried out on the advice of the Ceylon government. The Members of the Commonwealth of which the Queen is not the Head of the state —India, Pakistan, and Malaya—do not, of course, conduct their external affairs through the Queen but through their own head of state. Similar documents are used, however, and provisions for seals and other forms of authentication are made.

III · AUTONOMY

I

'They are autonomous communities.' This is the way in which the founder Members of the Commonwealth described themselves in the report of the Imperial Conference of 1926. The very essence of autonomy is the capacity to adopt and adapt your own constitution, regulating and amending the framework of your government as you think necessary. How do the Members of the Commonwealth stand in this respect? The prospect of independence raised, in fact, a number of difficult problems which deserve careful discussion. They continue to harass constitution makers in the Commonwealth to this day.

Put briefly, the grant of autonomy raises the whole question of the authority and supremacy of the constitutions of Members of the Commonwealth, once those constitutions lose any superior status they may have enjoyed as acts of the parliament of the United Kingdom or as instruments made under the authority of such acts. It means that the communities concerned must consider carefully what form of government they wish to live under, what checks or safeguards, if any, they wish to impose upon their political institutions, and in particular upon their parliaments. Shall there be special safeguards for the liberty of the subject or for minority communities? And if these safeguards and checks are to be effective, what constitutional provisions are needed to secure it? It had been possible in the past to rely upon the overriding supremacy of legislation by or under the authority of the parliament at Westminster. When this goes, what takes its place? Problems of this kind are of far greater importance than the hypothetical discussions about whether or not the autonomy granted by the parliament of the United Kingdom could be withdrawn, which have been mentioned in the last chapter.

These questions arose in an interesting way when the discussions were proceeding which later led to the enactment of the Statute of Westminster. It had been agreed among Members of the Commonwealth at the Imperial Conference of 1926 that the principle of equality should govern their relations and it followed as one consequence of this that the parliaments of the overseas Members should be empowered to repeal or amend acts of the parliament of the United Kingdom extending to them. To this end the clause which was to become section 2 of the Statute of Westminster was drafted, which proposed that the Colonial Laws Validity Act of 1865 should be repealed, and that the powers of the parliament of a Dominion should include the power to repeal or amend any act of the parliament of the United Kingdom in so far as the same was part of the law of the Dominion.

But the repeal of the Colonial Laws Validity Act did more than merely remove the rule of construction, contained in sections 1, 2, and 3 of that act, by which an act of a colonial legislature was void if it was repugnant to an act of the parliament of the United Kingdom (or any order made under such an act), which extended to the colony by express words or necessary intendment. The Colonial Laws Validity Act contained some other important provisions, and in particular it laid down in section 5 certain requirements about the powers and procedure in amending colonial constitutions as follows:

Every colonial legislature shall have, and be deemed at all times to have had, full power within its jurisdiction to establish courts of judicature, and to abolish and reconstitute the same, and to alter the constitution thereof, and to make provision for the administration of justice therein; and every representative legislature shall, in respect to the colony under its jurisdiction, have and be deemed at all times to have had, full power to make laws respecting the constitution, powers, and procedure of such legislature; provided that such laws shall have been passed in such manner and form as may from time to time be required by any act of parliament, letters patent, order-in-council, or colonial law for the time being in force in the said colony.

Now the constitutions of Canada and Australia, for example, were contained in acts of the parliament of the United Kingdom. These constitutions divided legislative power between the parliaments of Canada and of Australia, on the one hand, and the legislatures of the provinces of Canada and the states of Australia on the other, in such a way that this division could not be altered by any of these legislatures or parliaments acting alone. This was an essential principle of the federal system of government which had been established by the constitutions. In Canada the constitution—the British North America Act, 1867, and certain subsequent acts of the parliament of the United Kingdom[1]—could be altered only by that parliament; in Australia, the constitution could be altered by a process set out in the constitution[2] which involved in addition to the approval of the two houses of the Commonwealth parliament, the consent in a referendum of a majority of all the electors voting and of a majority of the electors in a majority of the six states; the Constitution Act itself—of which the constitution was section 9—could be altered only by the parliament of the United Kingdom, which could also, of course, as a matter of law, alter the constitution itself if it chose to do so. It was of fundamental importance to Canada and Australia that the constitution should be supreme over the legislatures. Before the passing of the Statute of Westminster it was clear that these constitutions were supreme and what is more that they were supreme, if for no other reason, because they were acts of the parliament of the United Kingdom. While nationalism, therefore, might wish to see the removal of the supremacy of British acts over laws made in Canada or Australia, federalism saw in the supremacy of British acts the safeguard of the system of government.

For, it was argued, if the Colonial Laws Validity Act was repealed, and if the parliaments of Canada and Australia were empowered to repeal or amend British acts extending to them, then these parliaments could alter those particularly important British acts, the constitutions as set out in the British North America Act, 1867, and the Australian Commonwealth Constitution Act, 1900. And would not the parliaments be free to amend the constitutions by a simple act of parliament once there had been abolished, with the repeal of the Colonial Laws Validity Act, that provision in section 5 of the act which had said that constitutional amendments should be passed only 'in such manner and form as may from time to time be required by any act of parliament . . . for the time being in force in the said

---

[1] For a discussion of what acts make up the constitution of Canada, see P. Gérin Lajoie, *Constitutional Amendment in Canada*, chap. 1.

[2] s. 128.

colony'?[3] And if this were so, these parliaments could unilaterally alter the division of powers between themselves and
the provinces and states within their countries, and so convert
the federal system into a centralized, unitary system. Now
whether this would be a desirable thing or not, it was a separate
question from that of securing equality between the parliaments
of Canada and Australia on the one hand and the parliament of
the United Kingdom on the other. The method of altering the
federal constitutions of these countries was an important question, but it should be dealt with separately. So far as Australia
was concerned, a method of alteration entirely within the hands
of Australians themselves was available. Canadians in 1931 had
not yet agreed upon an appropriate method of amendment and
therefore they still relied upon the parliament at Westminster.

Whether or not these misgivings were justified, Canada and
Australia were resolved to maintain the supremacy of their constitutions and to base that supremacy upon the status of the
constitutions as acts of the parliament of the United Kingdom.
Accordingly, at the request of Canada and Australia, reservations were inserted in the Statute of Westminster which were
designed to ensure that the legal position so far as their constitutions were concerned was unchanged by any provision in the
Statute which extended the powers of the parliaments of Canada
and Australia.

Thus, so far as Canada was concerned, although by sections
2 and 7 (2) of the Statute, the Colonial Laws Validity Act was
repealed in so far as it applied to the parliament of Canada and
the legislatures of the provinces of Canada, it was provided in
section 7 (1) of the Statute that 'nothing in this Act shall be
deemed to apply to the repeal, amendment, or alteration of the
British North America Acts, 1867 to 1930, or any order, rule or
regulation made thereunder'.[4] And to make clear that the division of powers between the parliament of Canada and the
legislatures of the provinces was unaltered by anything in the
Statute, it was further provided, in section 7 (3), that 'the powers

---

[3] *Attorney-General for New South Wales* v. *Trethowan*, [1932] A.C. 526;
[1930] 31 S.R. (N.S.W.) 183; [1931] 44 C.L.R. 394.
[4] The expression British North America Acts, 1867 to 1930, had been statu-
torily defined. It covered the British North America Acts of 1867, 1871, 1886,
1915, 1916, and 1930. It did not include the Parliament of Canada Act, 1875, or
the British North America Act, 1907.

conferred by this Act upon the Parliament of Canada or upon the legislatures of the Provinces shall be restricted to the enactment of laws in relation to matters within the competence of the Parliament of Canada or of any of the legislatures of the Provinces respectively'. This meant that the parliament and the legislatures could make laws only on those matters which the constitution of Canada placed within their competence, but that if in so doing they should make a law which was repugnant to an act of the parliament of the United Kingdom extending to Canada or to a province (other than the British North America Acts, 1867 to 1930) the Canadian or provincial act would not be void for repugnancy to the British act.

Similar but more elaborate provisions were inserted in the Statute to safeguard the position of the states of Australia. In section 8 of the Statute it was provided that 'nothing in this Act shall be deemed to confer any power to repeal or alter the Constitution or the Constitution Act of the Commonwealth of Australia . . . otherwise than in accordance with the law existing before the commencement of this Act'. There followed in section 9 (1) a clause declaring that 'nothing in this Act shall be deemed to authorise the Parliament of the Commonwealth of Australia to make laws on any matter within the authority of the States of Australia not being a matter within the authority of the Parliament or Government of the Commonwealth of Australia'. No proposal had been made that the repeal of the Colonial Laws Validity Act should be extended to the states of Australia as had been done for the provinces of Canada. Consequently it was not necessary in this section to provide that the parliaments of the states of Australia should be confined to matters within their authority.

So anxious were the states of Australia that nothing in the Statute of Westminster should alter their status in relation to the parliament of the Commonwealth of Australia that they secured the insertion in the Statute of yet another safeguard, designed this time to protect them not from the powers granted to the parliament of the Commonwealth of Australia in section 2 of the Statute, but from certain consequences which they feared might follow from section 4 of the Statute. By this section, it may be recalled, no future act of the parliament of the United Kingdom would extend to a Dominion unless it contained a declaration that it was passed at the request and with the consent of that Dominion; and in the case of Australia this meant[5] the request and consent of the parliament and government of the Commonwealth of Australia. It was objected that this might be held to mean that the concurrence of the parliament and government of the Commonwealth might be required to any request by a state of Australia to the parliament of the United Kingdom for legislation in respect of some matter within the competence of that state. It should be explained that the states of Australia, unlike the provinces of Canada, are largely responsible for the administration of the criminal law. For the efficient conduct of this administration extra-territorial powers were necessary, and as the state parliaments in general lacked these powers, laws had been passed by the parliament of the United Kingdom, such as the Fugitive Offenders Act[6] and the Territorial Waters Jurisdiction Act,[7] to assist in the regulation of these matters. It might conceivably be necessary in the future for a state to ask the parliament of the United Kingdom to legislate further on these topics or others within the competence of the states.[8] Might it not be argued then that such a request needed the concurrence of the parliament and government of the Commonwealth? There was a good deal of force in this view and it was resolved therefore to introduce into the Statute a clause making it clear that nothing in section 4 of the Statute should be held to require the request and consent of the parliament and government of the Commonwealth to such legislation otherwise than in accordance with the constitutional practice prevailing before the passing of the Statute.[9]

New Zealand is a unitary and not a federal state, and it lacked therefore this particular concern which was shown in Canada and Australia for the preservation of the supremacy of the constitution. None the less, it was anxious to maintain the existing position and it therefore associated itself with Canada and Australia by securing the insertion in the Statute of Westminster of a provision that 'nothing in this Act shall be deemed to

---

[5] By s. 9 (3) of the Statute of Westminster.
[6] 44 & 45 Vict., c. 69.   [7] 41 & 42 Vict., c. 73.
[8] It was admitted that it would be difficult to imagine a case where it might be necessary. See *Australian Commonwealth Parliamentary Debates*, vol. 132, p. 1085.
[9] It appears as s. 9 (2).

confer any power to repeal or alter the Constitution Act of the Dominion of New Zealand otherwise than in accordance with the law existing before the commencement of this Act'.[10] At the time of the passing of the Statute, it could be maintained that the parliament of New Zealand under the provisions of the New Zealand Constitution Act of 1852,[11] as amended in 1857,[12] was empowered to amend all the Constitution Act except certain specified sections. Of these it may be worth mentioning the section establishing the parliament itself (s. 32); regulating the time or place of its meeting, its prorogation and dissolution, the taking of an oath or the making of an affirmation by its members (ss. 44, 46, 47); empowering the parliament to make laws and defining that power (s. 53); providing for the appropriation and issue of public moneys (s. 54); providing for the governor's power to assent, refuse assent, or reserve bills duly passed by the parliament and for the disallowance of acts (ss. 56–59); and defining the terms 'Governor' and 'New Zealand'—the latter including a definition of the boundaries of the colony (s. 80). Yet at the same time it must be recalled that by section 5 of the Colonial Laws Validity Act, the New Zealand parliament had obtained 'full power to make laws respecting the constitution, powers and procedure of such legislature'; and it might be reasonably maintained that this grant of power enabled it to make almost any alteration it pleased in the constitution[13] though it is doubtful whether it was sufficient to remove all the restrictions imposed by the act of 1857.

The ironical position was reached, therefore, that if section 2 of the Statute was made to apply to New Zealand without qualification, and if thus the Colonial Laws Validity Act ceased to apply to New Zealand, a question could arise whether the parliament of New Zealand could amend the constitution as freely as before. Might it not be argued that the prohibitions in the act of 1857 were revived? In excluding its Constitution Act from the operation of section 2 of the Statute, New Zealand retained wide powers of constitutional amendment, preserved the *status quo*, and postponed for the time being the problems

[10] s. 8—which applied to Australia also.
[11] 15 & 16 Vict., c. 72.
[12] By 20 & 21 Vict., c. 53, s. 2.
[13] R. O. McGechan in *New Zealand and the Statute of Westminster* (ed. J. C. Beaglehole), pp. 100–3, favoured this view.

about powers of amendment that might be raised when the Colonial Laws Validity Act ceased to apply to the constitution.

These sections which were inserted in the Statute of Westminster on behalf of Canada, Australia, and New Zealand had as their common object the preservation of the status of their constitutions as acts of the parliament of the United Kingdom extending to the Members concerned by express words, and possessing supremacy over laws made by any legislatures in these Members by virtue of the rule of repugnancy laid down in the Colonial Laws Validity Act. So reluctant, indeed, were Australia and New Zealand to agree to the repeal of the Colonial Laws Validity Act at all that they arranged for the insertion in the Statute of Westminster of a section postponing the application of sections 2–6 of the Statute to them until they adopted it, a step which was not taken by Australia until 1942[14] and New Zealand until 1947.[15] During this period, indeed, certain acts of the parliament of the United Kingdom were passed which extended to Australia and New Zealand by virtue of the Colonial Laws Validity Act, though their application to these Members was in fact with their consent and at their request.[16] This request and consent, however, was not recited in the acts because section 4 of the Statute did not yet apply to Australia and New Zealand.

2

It is time to ask now whether these safeguarding clauses in the Statute of Westminster were really necessary. Would the constitutions of Canada and Australia have ceased to be supreme over the parliaments of Canada and Australia and the legislatures of the provinces of Canada, if sections 7, 8, and 9 of the Statute had not been passed? In other words, did the supremacy of these constitutions depend upon the fact that they were made at Westminster or upon the terms of the constitutions themselves?

[14] By the Statute of Westminster Adoption Act, No. 56 of 1942. The adoption was dated back to 3 Sept. 1939.

[15] Statute of Westminster Adoption Act, No. 38 of 1947, which came into effect, and the adoption also, on 25 Nov. 1947.

[16] For example, the Whaling Industry (Regulation) Act, 1934, the Emergency Powers (Defence) Act, 1939, the Prize Act, 1939, and the Army and Air Force (Annual) Act, 1940, applied to Australia and New Zealand. The Geneva Convention Act, 1937, extended to Australia.

It is clear that the framers of the Statute of Westminster, and particularly the governments and parliaments concerned in Canada and Australia, believed that, in the absence of safeguards, there was at least a strong presumption that the parliaments of Canada and Australia would acquire a power which they did not already possess to alter the constitutions of their countries. The powers of the parliament of a Dominion, said section 2 (2) of the Statute, shall include the power to repeal or amend any existing or future Act of parliament of the United Kingdom in so far as the same is part of the law of the Dominion. It did not say any existing Act except the Constitution. It seemed to suggest that, once it was established that an act was an act of parliament of the United Kingdom, the powers of the parliament of a Dominion were immediately attracted to it so as to be able to repeal or amend it. And if it were objected that, in the Australian constitution, for example, a special process of constitutional amendment had been laid down, which the parliament of Australia must surely be bound to follow, it was possible to answer that, with the repeal of the Colonial Laws Validity Act and particularly of section 5 of that act, there had disappeared the requirement that a parliament in amending a constitution must pass its laws in such manner and form as may from time to time be required by act of parliament of the United Kingdom.

This line of argument has much to commend it. It is worth stating the other side. Might it not be true that what was done by section 2 (2) of the Statute of Westminster was not to increase the area of the powers of the parliament of a Dominion beyond those laid down in its constitution, but to provide that any act passed by the parliament of a Dominion within the area of its powers should not be void through repugnancy to an imperial act extending to the Dominion. This interpretation of section 2 (2) was explained by Mr. Justice Dixon (as he then was)[17] in an article in the *Australian Law Journal*[18] in these words:

It does not necessarily mean that the Parliaments of the Dominions shall have an independent power of repealing or amending Imperial Statutes operating in the Dominion simply because they are

[17] Later Sir Owen Dixon, Chief Justice of the High Court of Australia.
[18] 10 *Australian Law Journal*, Supplement, p. 101.

Imperial Statutes. It would be more natural to regard it as doing no more than removing from the legislative power of the Dominion the restriction on its exercise which the existence of an Imperial Statute might impose. So regarded it would not enlarge the ambit of the powers of a Dominion Parliament. It would leave them no more and no less extensive than it found them. But it would increase the strength of the power operating within the same limits so that all the law relating to the subject matter of the power, including provisions of Imperial Statute, would be liable to amendment by the exercise of the power.

If this view of section 2 (2) of the Statute of Westminster were adopted, how would it affect the position of the parliaments in the Dominions concerned in relation to their constitutions in the absence of the safeguarding sections 7, 8, and 9? Take the case of Australia to begin with. Suppose the parliament of the Commonwealth passed a measure purporting to alter the constitution, say by adding some subject to the list of the powers upon which the parliament could make laws, that this bill received the royal assent, and that the High Court of Australia was invited to pronounce upon the validity of this bill. The court would observe that this measure purported to amend the constitution, that amendments to the constitution to be valid must be passed in a particular manner, laid down in section 128 of the constitution, that this measure had not been passed in that manner, and that it was not therefore an amendment at all. And as it was not an amendment, no question could arise of whether it was or was not repugnant to an act of parliament of the United Kingdom. The test of repugnancy arises only in relation to a law of the parliament of the Commonwealth.

A similar argument can be advanced in relation to a law passed by the parliament of the Commonwealth which does not purport to amend the constitution but which is alleged to conflict with the constitution on the ground, say, that it deals with a subject not placed by the constitution within the ambit of the powers of the parliament of the Commonwealth. Here it is open to the court to say that although the measure is an act of parliament, passed in the prescribed manner—unlike the purported amendment discussed above—it is not a valid act because it is *ultra vires* the parliament of the Commonwealth. Here again the test of repugnancy does not arise, for the act fails on the ground of *ultra vires*.

On this approach to the question, the constitution of Australia remains supreme over the parliament of the Commonwealth, but not because it is an act of the parliament of the United Kingdom. It is supreme because it is the constitution, and as such must be construed as logically prior to any measure passed by the parliament which owes its existence and powers to the constitution. The supremacy of the constitution is based upon logic, not upon its origin. On this line of argument, the constitution of Australia would have remained supreme even if the safeguarding sections 8 and 9 of the Statute of Westminster had not been inserted. It is true that, with the repeal of the Colonial Laws Validity Act, there would have been removed the safeguard in section 5 of that act that a law amending a constitution must be passed 'in such manner and form as may from time to time be required by any Act of Parliament'. But the courts would themselves have in effect restored the rule by their construction of the nature and meaning of the constitution.

Could the same line of argument be applied to the constitution of Canada? If section 7 of the Statute of Westminster had not been enacted, would the parliament of Canada have remained confined in its legislative powers to the area already allotted to it before the passing of the Statute? In particular, would it have remained unable to amend the British North America Act, 1867? Here again it is necessary to look at the constitution and to see what law-making powers it confers upon the legislatures it creates. In the British North America Act of 1867 the parliament of Canada is authorized 'to make laws for the peace, order and good government of Canada in relation to all matters not coming within the classes of subjects by this Act assigned exclusively to the Legislatures of the Provinces'. If the parliament of Canada should enact a measure which fell within the classes of subjects assigned exclusively to the legislatures of the provinces, it would be *ultra vires* and a court would hold it invalid on that ground. The question of repugnancy, again, would not arise. It would seem, therefore, that if the test of repugnancy had been abolished by the Statute of Westminster so far as the British North America Act of 1867 was concerned, the parliament of Canada would still have been prevented from making laws upon subjects assigned exclusively to the provinces—and, it may be added, the legislatures of the provinces would have been confined to these subjects. So far as the division of legislative powers in the constitution was concerned, therefore, the constitution would have remained supreme, not in virtue of its being an act of the parliament of the United Kingdom, but in virtue of its being a constitution.

But the position of the Canadian parliament is not identical with that of Australia in these matters. It does not follow from what has been said so far that the Canadian parliament would not have been able to alter the British North America Act at all, if section 7 had not been inserted in the Statute of Westminster. Before the passing of the Statute the parliament of Canada was unable to alter the British North America Act. If section 7 had not been inserted in the Statute, it can be argued that while the parliament of Canada would not have been able to make any law which conflicted with section 92 of the British North America Act—the section which enumerated the powers of the legislatures of the provinces—it would have been able to make laws which conflicted with other sections of the British North America Act. Thus section 50 of the act lays down that the House of Commons of Canada shall continue for five years (subject to earlier dissolution by the Governor-General) and no longer. If the parliament of Canada had enacted a law amending or repealing this section, it would not be a law on a subject assigned exclusively to the provinces; it would therefore be a valid act, though it would conflict with section 50 of the British North America Act; but if the test of repugnancy had been abolished, then the act would not be void. On this argument, therefore, if section 7 had not been inserted in the Statute, the powers of the parliament of Canada would have been altered except in so far as its law-making powers had been restricted by the terms of the constitution itself as in section 92. In the case of Canada, therefore, the supremacy of the constitution arose, in some measure, from the fact that it was an act of the United Kingdom parliament and would have been destroyed if the superior status of such an act had been removed under the terms of the Statute of Westminster. The supremacy of the constitution could survive the repeal of the restriction of repugnancy only if the actual terms of the constitution imposed limitations upon the scope and manner of the law-making powers of the legislature. In these circumstances the question of repugnancy did not arise.

The differences between Canada and Australia in these matters arose from the difference in the terms in which law-making powers were granted to the parliaments in their respective constitutions. It leads to the conclusion that if in Canada and Australia it was intended that the position of the constitution in relation to the parliament should remain unchanged by the enactment of sections 2–6 of the Statute of Westminster, then it was necessary for section 7 to be inserted in the Statute in respect of Canada, but that it was not necessary to insert section 8 in the Statute in respect of Australia.

None the less these safeguarding sections were inserted. The Australian constitution remains unaffected by the passing of the Statute of Westminster. In the case of Canada, a change in the amending power has been made since 1931, and a word should be said about it. In 1949 the parliament of the United Kingdom passed the British North America (No. 2) Act, 1949,[19] section 1 of which ran as follows:

Section ninety-one of the British North America Act, 1867, is hereby amended by renumbering Class 1 thereof as Class 1A and by inserting therein immediately before that Class the following as Class 1:—

1. The amendment from time to time of the Constitution of Canada, except as regards matters coming within the classes of subjects by this Act assigned exclusively to the legislatures of the Provinces, or as regards rights or privileges by this or any other Constitutional Act granted or secured to the legislature or the government of a province or to any class of persons with respect to schools or as regards the use of the English or the French language or as regards the requirements that there shall be a session of the Parliament of Canada at least once each year, and that no House of Commons shall continue for more than five years from the day of the return of the Writs for choosing the House; provided, however, that a House of Commons may in time of real or apprehended war, invasion or insurrection be continued by the Parliament of Canada if such continuation is not opposed by the votes of more than one-third of the members of such House.

[19] 12, 13, & 14 Geo.VI, c. 81.

This amendment to the British North America Act, 1867, like others that had been passed since the Statute of Westminster,[20] was enacted by the parliament of the United Kingdom as a result of an address to the King passed by the two houses of the parliament of Canada. Since the Statute did not apply to it there was no declaration of request and consent under section 4 of the Statute, though in fact the act was passed at the request of the Senate and House of Commons of Canada and would not have been passed otherwise.[21] It confers a considerable power of constitutional amendment on the parliament of Canada and it is interesting to notice that this power is a power to amend 'the Constitution of Canada', not just the British North America Acts, 1867 to 1930. It will be for the Supreme Court of Canada to say, in case of dispute, whether or not any amendment made under this power is an amendment of the constitution.[22]

What is the position of the British North America Act, 1949 (No. 2), in relation to the parliament of Canada? Could it be amended by the parliament of Canada? The answer would seem to be that as the act inserts a new section into the British North America Act, 1867, this new section becomes part of the act of 1867 and is thus protected by section 7 of the Statute of Westminster. If it is to be amended, it must be amended by the parliament of the United Kingdom acting, in accordance with constitutional convention, on an address by the Senate and House of Commons of Canada. What would be the position, however, if section 7 of the Statute was not there? The answer to this question is not free from doubt. There seems good reason to believe that, in the absence of section 7, the parliament of Canada would be free to amend the constitution of Canada except as regards matters coming within the classes of subjects assigned

---

[20] Namely the British North America Acts of 1940 (3 & 4 Geo. VI, c. 36); 1943 (6 & 7 Geo. VI, c. 30); 1946 (9 & 10 Geo. VI, c. 63); and 1951 (14 & 15 Geo. VI, c. 32).

[21] The British North America Act, 1949 (No. 1) (12 & 13 Geo. VI, c. 22), which provided for the incorporation of Newfoundland as the tenth province of Canada is an exception. It contains a declaration of request and consent in terms of s. 4 of the Statute because it was an act which, although incidentally involving amendment of the British North America Act of 1867, was primarily concerned with giving force of law to the terms upon which Newfoundland joined Canada. To a large extent, therefore, it fell outside the provisions of s. 7 of the Statute.

[22] See F. R. Scott, 8 *University of Toronto Law Journal* (1949–50), pp. 201–7.

exclusively to the legislatures of the provinces in section 92. It may be, however, that a court would construe the whole of the restrictions upon the power of constitutional amendment conferred in the act of 1949 as still binding and restricting the law-making powers of the parliament of Canada. In either case the interpretation would rest upon the narrow construction of section 2 (2) of the Statute of Westminster. If the wider view was taken then the whole constitution would be open to amendment by the parliament of Canada.

3

It is instructive to consider the question also from the point of view of those Members of the Commonwealth which deliberately chose not to adopt provisions similar to sections 7, 8, and 9 of the Statute of Westminster when they attained equality of status. Thus, in 1931, the Irish Free State and the Union of South Africa both decided that they did not wish any special safeguards to be inserted in the Statute of Westminster in respect of their constitutions and they accepted the full powers which the Statute conferred. The Colonial Laws Validity Act was repealed in respect of these two members and with it went any special safeguard which section 5 of the act might be thought to contain. New Zealand acquired the same position when, in 1947, it not only adopted the Statute of Westminster but also at the same time secured the passage by the parliament of the United Kingdom, under the provisions of section 4 of the Statute, of the New Zealand Constitution (Amendment) Act[23] which removed from the parliament of New Zealand all restrictions upon its power to amend its Constitution Act of 1852. So also in 1948, when Ceylon obtained independence, and in 1957 when Ghana obtained independence, the Colonial Laws Validity Act was repealed in respect of them, so that no reliance could be placed upon it in considering the extent and nature of the supremacy of their constitutions. What consequences followed for the authority of their constitutions?

Consider first the case of the Irish Free State. The unqualified

---

[23] 11 Geo. VI, c. 4. It was passed as a result of the New Zealand Constitution (Request and Consent) Act, No. 44 of 1947, passed by the parliament of the Dominion.

grant of power by the Statute of Westminster to the Free State was not passed through the parliament of the United Kingdom without a protest. Amendments were moved, notably by Colonel Gretton in the House of Commons,[24] and by Lord Danesfort in the House of Lords,[25] to provide that nothing in the Statute should be deemed to apply to the alteration, amendment, or repeal of the Irish Free State (Agreement) Act, 1922 (which gave force of law to the treaty), or so much of the Government of Ireland Act, 1920, as continued to be in force in Northern Ireland. The object of these amendments was to ensure that the Free State legislature should possess no greater power to amend the Free State constitution after the passing of the Statute than it had before. That is to say, it was intended to confer upon the Free State the same status in this respect as Canada, Australia, and New Zealand desired under the Statute.

The effect of the Statute was tested in the Judicial Committee of the Privy Council in *Moore's Case* in 1935[26] when the validity of an act of the Oireachtas[27] purporting to abolish the appeal to the Judicial Committee was questioned. In its judgment the board said:

Before the passing of the Statute of Westminster it was not competent for the Irish Free State Parliament to pass an Act abrogating the Treaty because the Colonial Laws Validity Act forbade a Dominion Legislature to pass a law repugnant to an Imperial Act. The effect of the Statute of Westminster was to remove the fetter which lay upon the Irish Free State Legislature by reason of the Colonial Laws Validity Act. That legislature can now pass Acts repugnant to an Imperial Act. In this case they have done so.[28]

The language used by the board here is ambiguous, and as a result the effect of its decision has given rise to controversy. Article 50 of the constitution of the Irish Free State had given power to the Oireachtas to make 'amendments of this Constitution within the terms of the Scheduled Treaty'. Was this a restriction on the area of the powers of the Oireachtas? If it was, then the effect of the repeal of the Colonial Laws Validity

---

[24] 260 *H.C. Deb.* 5 s., col. 303.
[25] 83 *H.L. Deb.* 5 s., col. 231.
[26] *Moore* v. *Attorney-General of Irish Free State*, [1935] I.R. 472, [1935] A.C. 484.   [27] No. 45 of 1933.
[28] [1935] A.C. 484 at 498.

Act depended on the interpretation of section 2 of the Statute of Westminster. On the narrower interpretation, the Statute confines a legislature within the area of its powers; on the wider interpretation it enabled it to extend the area. The Judicial Committee did not discuss the question of area. It could be argued that it did not regard the Oireachtas as confined in area and that, as a result, it did not find it necessary to consider the narrower or the wider interpretation of the meaning of section 2. Its argument appears to have been: the Oireachtas is confined to making amendments within the terms of the scheduled treaty; if it alters the scheduled treaty in an appropriate respect, then it can amend the constitution accordingly. And this is what it has done.

Whatever view is taken of the reasoning of the judgment, it is clear that it decided that the effect of the repeal of the Colonial Laws Validity Act, so far as the Irish Free State was concerned, was that a safeguard which restricted constitutional amendments was removed. The manner of amendment had not been changed, but some parts of the constitution which could not be altered before 1931, because the Colonial Laws Validity Act prevented it, were now alterable because the act had been repealed.

The case of South Africa raised a different set of considerations. While the Union was not troubled with the conservative scruples of some other unitary Dominions, nor with the specific legal conflicts of the federal Dominions, it possessed some of the political conflicts of a unified rather than of a united state. In consequence the constitution of the Union contained certain safeguards to protect the rights of the original colonies which went to make up the Union. By section 152 of the South Africa Act, 1909, the parliament of the Union was empowered to repeal or alter any of the provisions of the act, subject to the proviso that no provision of the act, for the operation of which a definite period of time was prescribed, should be repealed or altered during that period; and further that no repeal or alteration of section 152 itself, or of sections 33 and 34 (until the number of members of the House of Assembly had reached the limit therein prescribed or until a period of ten years had elapsed after the establishment of the Union, whichever was the longer period), or of sections 35 and 137, should be valid unless the bill had been passed by both houses of parliament sitting together, and at the third reading had been agreed to by not less than two-thirds of the total number of members of both houses. These sections thus safeguarded were referred to as the 'entrenched clauses' of the South Africa Act. The general effect of section 152 was that difficulties were placed in the way of an amendment of those portions of the act which regulated the proportionate representation of the original four colonies in the House of Assembly (ss. 33 and 34); which safeguarded the continuance of the native franchise in Cape Province (s. 35); and which guaranteed the equality of the English and Dutch languages (s. 137). Section 152 was itself safeguarded also, in order that the requirements therein contained for a two-thirds majority in a joint session might not themselves be repealed by a simple majority in separate sessions.

It was feared that the unqualified extension of section 2 of the Statute to the Union parliament would destroy the legal safeguard provided in section 152, and that the Union parliament would be empowered to repeal or alter any section of the South Africa Act, including section 152, by the process of ordinary legislation. A section of opinion in the Union, consequently, desired the insertion of some reservation in the Statute in so far as the 'entrenched clauses' were concerned. However, when in the South African parliament during the debates in 1931 on the resolution requesting the passage of the Statute by the United Kingdom parliament, the question of a safeguard was raised, notably by General Smuts, the leader of the Opposition,[29] the government were unwilling to accept this proposal. But, by agreement between General Hertzog, the Prime Minister, and General Smuts, the resolution requesting the passage of the Statute was agreed to 'on the understanding that the proposed legislation will in no way derogate from the entrenched provisions of the South Africa Act', these words being an amendment by General Smuts. The view of the government and its supporters might be stated in the words of Dr. Stals in the House of Assembly: '. . . I think that no one in the House, or in the Union, doubts the moral obligation of the Parliament and the people to respect the basic principle in our constitution, and

[29] See *House of Assembly Debates*, vol. 17, cols. 2397–2403, and 2736–63; *Senate Debates*, 1931, cols. 479–87.

therefore it appears to me to be unnecessary to include a provision for securing it.'[30]

This resolution had no legal force, but it could have become
a constitutional convention. In this connexion it is interesting to
notice that the Speaker of the House of Assembly gave it as his
view in 1934 'for the guidance of honourable members' that 'if it
is desired to amend or repeal any of the entrenched clauses, then
the procedure laid down in the South Africa Act must be followed', and that this procedure was followed by the Union parliament when legislation abolishing the Cape native franchise,
provided for in 'entrenched' clause 35 of the South Africa Act,
was passed in 1936.

In the years that followed, however, the fears of those that
doubted the efficacy of the entrenched clauses seemed justified.
In 1937 the Appellate Division of the Supreme Court of South
Africa in the case of *Ndlwana* v. *Hofmeyr*[31] appeared to have
adopted the view that the Union parliament was no longer
bound to follow the special procedure laid down in section 152
of the South Africa Act. In 1950 the government of the Union
adopted the same view in introducing legislation to abolish
the Cape coloured franchise and the Speaker of the House of
Assembly reversed the ruling of his predecessor, basing his
opinion on the decision of 1937.

It may be added that this view was adopted by many com-
mentators upon the Statute.[32] In 1952, however, the Appellate
Division decided in the case of *Harris* v. *The Minister of the
Interior*[33] that in spite of the passing of the Statute of Westminster, the entrenched sections were still binding and that any
attempt to alter them contrary to the procedure laid down in
section 152 was void. The main lines of the court's decision may
be stated.

The Appellate Division held that the Colonial Laws Validity
Act was not relevant to a consideration of the effectiveness of

---

[30] *House of Assembly Debates*, vol. 17, col. 2739. Senator Malan expressed
the same view, *Senate Debates*, 1931, col. 484.

[31] [1937] A.D. 229.

[32] Wade and Phillips, *Constitutional Law*, 4th ed., pp. 425–6; A. B. Keith,
The Dominions as Sovereign States, p. 177; H. J. May, *The South African
Constitution*, pp. 32–33; K. C. Wheare, *The Statute of Westminster and
Dominion Status*, 4th ed., pp. 240–2.

[33] 1952 (2) A.D. 428.

the entrenched sections. They noted that section 152 of the South Africa Act gave to the Union parliament a power to amend any section of that act, provided of course that the provisions of section 152 itself were followed.

A repeal or alteration of the South Africa Act [they held] enacted by an Act of the Union Parliament in accordance with the provisions of section 152 would be repugnant to the provisions so repealed or altered. Those provisions are, it is true, contained in a British Act of Parliament, namely, the South Africa Act, but that repugnancy is specifically authorised by that very British Act which is a later Act than the Colonial Laws Validity Act and must therefore in case of conflict over-ride the earlier Act. Section 2 of the Colonial Laws Validity Act could, therefore, have no application to a repeal or an amendment of the South Africa Act.[34]

With the conclusion stated here the author has no quarrel. It must be conceded that if the Union parliament, acting in terms of the South Africa Act, should amend any part of that act, section 2 of the Colonial Laws Validity Act would have no material upon which to operate. But would it not be preferable to state this by asserting not that amendments to the South Africa Act, duly passed, were valid though repugnant but that they were valid because not repugnant? Surely an authorized amendment is not repugnant to the South Africa Act but consistent with it? The point is more than a matter of words, but it need not detain us here, for there is no disagreement about the inapplicability of section 2 of the Colonial Laws Validity Act so far.

But what about amendments to the South Africa Act passed contrary to the provisions of section 152? Would they not be void by virtue of section 2 of the Colonial Laws Validity Act and by virtue of section 5 also? The court's answer to this question is that it is not necessary to bring the Colonial Laws Validity Act into the matter at all. There is section 152 which lays down the manner and form in which the act may be altered; it governs the situation and the Colonial Laws Validity Act need not be invoked. That was the position before the passing of the Statute. It follows therefore that the repeal of the Colonial Laws Validity Act by the Statute made no difference to the position. Section 152 was there before and it was there afterwards.

[34] 1952 (2) A.D. 428 at p. 461.

It must be conceded, of course, that the Statute of Westminster did not repeal section 152. But did it not weaken the effectiveness? Might not the repeal of the Colonial Laws Validity Act coupled with the words of section 2 (2) of the Statute of Westminster mean that section 152 was now on the same footing in South African law as any other law in the Union? And here we move on to the second ground upon which it seemed proper to conclude that the entrenched clauses were no longer effective. If we consider the concluding words of section 2 (2) of the Statute—'the powers of the Parliament of a Dominion shall include the power to repeal or amend any such Act, order, rule or regulation in so far as the same is part of the law of the Dominion'—does that not mean that the Statute made a positive grant of power to the Union parliament to alter the South Africa Act just as if it were any other act of the Union parliament, and could it not therefore alter section 152 without following the special procedure laid down there?

The court's answer to this contention was that when section 2 (2) of the Statute of Westminster refers to 'a law made by a Dominion, such law means in relation to South Africa a law made by the Union parliament functioning either bicamerally or unicamerally in accordance with the requirements of the South Africa Act'.[35] The court here gives its authority to a line of argument which was set out with great cogency by Professor D. V. Cowen in his *Parliamentary Sovereignty and the Entrenched Sections of the South Africa Act* (1951), and it may be added that for the clearest and most convincing statement of that argument Professor Cowen's book still stands alone. Shortly stated the argument is that, although it is accepted that there are no limits to the power of the Union parliament to amend the South Africa Act and to amend or abolish the entrenched sections, and although it might be argued that section 2 (2) of the Statute of Westminster relieved the Union parliament of all legal restrictions imposed upon it by any British law, the prior and fundamental question was: 'What is the Union parliament?' Granted that an act of the Union parliament is always valid, when is the Union parliament to be deemed to have passed an act of parliament? And the answer to this question, says the court, is that whereas in relation to most matters the Union

---

[35] At p. 462.

parliament consists of the Governor-General and the two houses sitting separately and it is deemed to have passed an act when the consent of all three of these elements is obtained, in relation to matters contained in the entrenched sections the Union parliament consists of the Governor-General and the two houses sitting together and it is deemed to have passed an act when the consent of the Governor-General and of two-thirds of the two houses sitting together is obtained.[36] If the proper procedure is not followed no act of parliament has been passed; and therefore the provisions of the Statute of Westminster relating to the powers of the Union parliament do not begin to apply.

This is a strong argument. Moreover, it is equally effective in meeting the contention that the repeal of the Colonial Laws Validity Act abolished the efficacy of the entrenched sections as it is in disposing of the argument based upon the words in section 2 (2) of the Statute of Westminster. For a measure passed contrary to the entrenched sections would not be an act of parliament at all and therefore no question of repugnancy would arise and the provisions of the Colonial Laws Validity Act would not come into operation. Their repeal by the Statute of Westminster does not therefore affect the question of the entrenched sections. It is upon this ground rather than upon the ground adopted by the court that it seems preferable to establish the proposition that the Colonial Laws Validity Act may be disregarded.

It seems clear that in the discussions of the effect of the Statute of Westminster upon the entrenched sections which went on before the judgment of the Appellate Division, a fundamental question had been steadily ignored, namely: What is the parliament of the Union? It had been assumed that the parliament of the Union was the three elements of Governor-General, Senate, and House acting separately and that it was to such a parliament and its acts that the Colonial Laws Validity Act and the Statute of Westminster exclusively referred so far as the Union was concerned. This, it should be admitted, was an unwarranted assumption, ignoring as it did the provisions of the constitution

[36] And this does not exhaust the possibilities. For s. 63 of the South Africa Act provides that a case of deadlock between the two houses shall be decided by a joint sitting with a simple majority. This provision strengthens the view that the South Africa Act does not conceive of the parliament of the Union as an exclusively bicameral body.

of the Union which created the law-making authority of the Union, and determined its structure and mode of legislating no less than its powers. The procedure referred to in the entrenched sections was part of the definition of the Union parliament and was not a limitation upon the powers of an exclusively bicameral parliament. The Colonial Laws Validity Act and the Statute of Westminster affected the powers of the Union parliament but they did not affect its definition; they regulated the effect of an act of the Union parliament but they did not determine when it should be deemed to have passed an act. So it was that, in the judgment of the court, a measure passed contrary to the entrenched sections, both before the passing of the Statute and since, is of no effect not because it is an invalid act, but because it is not an act of parliament at all.

It may be worth while to mention two further considerations which were used to support the view that the passing of the Statute of Westminster destroyed the efficacy of the entrenched sections. The first was that whereas saving clauses were inserted in the Statute in respect of the Canadian, New Zealand, and Australian constitutions no such clauses were inserted in respect of the constitution of the Union. It seemed reasonable to assume that these saving clauses were inserted because it was thought that without them the parliaments of Canada, Australia, and New Zealand would have obtained an unrestricted power to alter the constitutions of these Dominions and this result was not desired by those Dominions. Here again, however, as the court has pointed out, whatever may have been the need for such saving clauses in the case of Canada, Australia, and New Zealand, no such clauses were needed for the Union. The parliament of the Union had power to amend the South Africa Act in any particular before the passing of the Statute; no increase upon the area of its powers could be granted by the passing of the Statute. Nor did the Statute make any change in the rules which determined how parliament should express its will. '"Parliament"', said the court, 'means Parliament functioning in accordance with the South Africa Act.'[37]

The second consideration which seemed to confirm the view that the entrenched clauses lacked force was the decision of the Appellate Division itself in 1937 in the case of *Ndlwana* v.

[37] At p. 465.

Hofmeyr. That case the court itself now overruled in its decision in *Harris's Case*. It pointed out that its predecessors had evidently assumed—as many students of the subject had done before and since—that the parliament of the Union could mean only the Governor-General and the two houses sitting separately, and that any document produced by that body and purporting to be an act of parliament must be accepted by the court as such. But, said the court in 1952, 'this Court is competent to enquire whether, regard being had to the provisions of section 35, an act of Parliament has been validly passed'.[37a] It was true, no doubt, to say, as the court had done in *Ndlwana* v. *Hofmeyr*, that 'Parliament's will, as expressed in an Act of Parliament, cannot now in this country as it cannot in England be questioned by a Court of Law whose function it is to enforce that will not to question it'.[38] But that statement, true as it is, does not conclude the matter. It is necessary to go farther and ask whether the document that purports to be an act of parliament expressing the will of parliament is in reality such. This is what the court did in *Harris's Case*, thus bringing the discussion down to the fundamental question. It was because the court in *Ndlwana* v. *Hofmeyr* had not addressed itself to this prior question that the argument in its judgment was largely irrelevant.

The court's judgment makes it clear that the validity of the entrenched clauses and their priority in determining what is an act of parliament in the Union depend in no way upon their being part of a superior Imperial Act. Their priority depends not upon origin but upon logic. The efficacy of the provisions in the South Africa Act describing how parliament is constituted and how it legislates for different purposes follows from the nature of a constitution, and it would so follow even if laws made by the parliament of the United Kingdom had never had the power to prevail over colonial laws repugnant to them. The judgment in *Harris's Case* does not assert the imperial supremacy of British law over South African law; it asserts the logical priority of a constitution over the institutions which it has created and whose nature and powers it describes and determines.[39]

[37a] At p. 470.   [38] At p. 237.
[39] See D. V. Cowen, 'Legislature and Judiciary', 15 *Modern Law Review*

4

It is tempting to exaggerate the effect of the decision in *Harris's Case* and to apply it without qualifications to the constitutional situation in other Members of the Commonwealth. It is important to emphasize, therefore, that it is a decision upon the meaning of a certain part of the South African constitution by a South African court. The relation, in other Commonwealth Members, between the constitution and the legislature will depend upon the terms of the constitution and the position in each Member will have to be separately considered. We have seen already that there is good ground for the belief that the repeal of the Colonial Laws Validity Act in relation to the Australian constitution would have had an effect quite different from its repeal in relation to the Canadian constitution.

What *Harris's Case* did assert, however, was that if a constitution is to be validly altered, the procedure laid down for the alteration of the constitution must be followed. This is not a very startling proposition. It is difficult to see how it can be gainsaid. It is, indeed, just what the Colonial Laws Validity Act itself said, when it spoke of the requirement that alterations 'shall have been passed in such manner and form as may from time to time be required by any act of parliament, letters patent, order-in-council, or colonial law for the time being in force in the said colony'. When the Colonial Laws Validity Act itself no longer exists as part of the law of a Member of the Commonwealth, the rule that constitutions may be amended only in the prescribed manner and form still stands as a rule of common sense and logic. And it is applied in countries where no question can arise of the constitutions being an act of the parliament of the United Kingdom. Its classic statement is in the judgment of Chief Justice Marshall, of the Supreme Court of the United States, in the case of *Marbury* v. *Madison*[40] when he said:

The Constitution is either a superior paramount law, unchange-

(1952), p. 282, and 16 *Modern Law Review* (1953), p. 273, for a careful discussion of the issues raised in the case. See also Geoffrey Marshall, *Parliamentary Sovereignty in the Commonwealth*; D. V. Cowen, 'The Entrenched Sections of the South Africa Act', in 70 *South African Law Journal* (1953), p. 238; H. R. Gray, 'The Sovereignty of Parliament Today', in 10 *Toronto Law Journal* (1953), p. 54.
[40] 1 Cranch 137, 2 L. Ed. 60 (1803).

able by ordinary means, or it is on a level with ordinary legislative acts, and, like other acts, is alterable when the legislature shall please to alter it. If the former part of the alternative be true, then a legislative act contrary to the Constitution is not law; if the latter part be true, then written constitutions are absurd attempts, on the part of the people, to limit a power in its own nature illimitable.

Courts in Members of the Commonwealth find themselves faced with a decision between alternatives of this kind when they come to interpret the effect of constitutions whose authority, after the grant of autonomy, certainly owes nothing to the Colonial Laws Validity Act or to the supremacy of legislation by the parliament at Westminster. And there is no doubt that, so far at least, they have followed the line of reasoning illustrated as well by *Marbury* v. *Madison* as by *Harris's Case*. It is worth while to glance at the provisions in the constitutions of certain of the Members which impose restrictions on the legislature.

In the Ceylon constitution of 1947, the parliament of Ceylon is empowered to alter the constitution provided that no amending bill 'shall be presented for the Royal Assent unless it has endorsed on it a certificate under the hand of the Speaker that the number of votes cast in favour thereof in the House of Representatives amounted to not less than two-thirds of the whole number of members of the House (including those not present)'. In addition the parliament of Ceylon was forbidden to pass laws which

prohibit or restrict the free exercise of any religion; or make persons of any community or religion liable to disabilities or restrictions to which persons of other communities or religions are not made liable; or confer on persons of any community or religion any privilege or advantage which is not conferred on persons of other communities or religions; or alter the constitution of any religious body except with the consent of the governing authority of that body, provided that, in any case where a religious body is incorporated by law, no such alteration shall be made except at the request of the governing authority of that body.[41]

These safeguards of the rights of communities and religions could be repealed or amended by the parliament of Ceylon,

[41] s. 29.

provided it followed the prescribed procedure for amendment of the constitution. So long as they stand in the constitution, laws in contravention of them are void to the extent of the contravention.[42] And so long as the prescribed procedure for constitutional amendment is there, it must be followed; if it is not followed, the purported amendment is not law.

The constitution of Malaya similarly provides that no amendment may be made unless it has been passed in each house of parliament at the second and third readings by at least a two-thirds majority of the total number of members of that house.[43] The constitution contains also a substantial declaration of fundamental liberties,[44] including the liberty of the person, the prohibition of slavery and forced labour, and protection against retrospective criminal laws and repeated trials. All persons are declared to be equal before the law and no discriminating legislation shall be passed unless expressly authorized by the constitution. No citizen shall be banished or excluded from the federation. Every citizen has the right to freedom of speech, to assemble peaceably and without arms, and to form associations, subject, however, to the requirements of security, public order, morality, and the like. Freedom of religion is guaranteed. Property may not be compulsorily acquired without adequate compensation. And there are detailed expositions and qualifications of these rights. Any law which is inconsistent with the constitution is void to the extent of the inconsistency.

So also in the constitution of Ghana of 1957 there were similar provisions both for safeguarding rights and for prescribing a method of amending the constitution.[45] No bill for amending the constitution should be presented for the royal assent unless it had endorsed on it a certificate from the Speaker of the Assembly that it was passed at its third reading by not less than two-thirds of the whole number of members of the Assembly. Moreover, bills which sought to amend certain sections of the

---

[42] In 1952 the Ceylon Supreme Court was asked to declare the Ceylon Citizenship Act of 1948 and the Ceylon (Parliamentary Elections) Amendment Act of 1949 invalid in so far as they purported to deprive Indians in Ceylon of the franchise. The Supreme Court upheld the acts in *Mudanayake* v. *Sivagnanasunderam* (1952), 53 N.L.R. 25, and the Judicial Committee of the Privy Council agreed in *Pillai* v. *Mudanayake*, [1953] A.C. 514.

[43] s. 159.   [44] Part II of the constitution, ss. 5–13.

[45] ss. 31–33.

constitution or which proposed to abolish or suspend a regional assembly or diminish the functions or powers of a regional assembly required not only to be passed by the two-thirds majority as specified above, but required also a certificate that they had been referred to the regional assemblies and had been approved by not less than two-thirds of the total number of regional assemblies. Alterations to the boundaries of regions required the support of certain specified majorities in the regional assemblies concerned.

In addition to these provisions—which were set out in great detail in the constitution—it was laid down also that 'no law shall make persons of any racial community liable to disabilities to which persons of other such communities are not made liable'. 'Subject to such restrictions as may be imposed for the purposes of preserving public order, morality or health, no law shall deprive any person of his freedom of conscience or the right freely to profess, practise or propagate any religion.'

Here again the safeguards rested upon the procedure for constitutional amendment. They could be repealed or reduced by constitutional amendment but the proper procedure must be followed. To ensure this, the Ghana Independence Act of 1957 provided that notwithstanding the provisions of the act which granted the fullest autonomy to Ghana 'the constitutional provisions shall not be repealed, amended or modified otherwise than in such manner as may be specified in those provisions'.[46] These rules regulating constitutional amendment were repealed, however, in December 1958, by the Constitution (Repeal of Restrictions) Act, which made it possible, henceforth, for amendments to be made by a simple majority of the Assembly and made it unnecessary for regional assemblies to consent to changes. The position in Ghana thus became like that in New Zealand.

In 1947 the parliament of New Zealand obtained power to alter, suspend, or repeal at any time all or any of the provisions of the New Zealand Constitution Act of 1852.[47] At the same time by adopting the Statute of Westminster, it removed the application of the Colonial Laws Validity Act from New

[46] 5 & 6 Eliz. II, c. 6, First Schedule, para. 6.
[47] By the New Zealand Constitution (Amendment) Act, 1947, 11 & 12 Geo. VI, c. 4.

Zealand legislation. In 1950, in pursuance of these powers, the parliament abolished the upper house and so became a single-chambered legislature. The question arises, therefore, whether the parliament of New Zealand like that in Ghana is now completely unfettered by the constitution and whether, even if it wished to do so, it could impose fetters upon itself or its successors. Have we in New Zealand and Ghana examples of the sovereign legislature whose characteristic is that it cannot bind itself?

This question has been considered in New Zealand, more particularly in the course of discussions about the setting up of a new second chamber to replace that abolished in 1950. Could the position and powers of such a second chamber be safeguarded against hasty abolition? Could some procedure for constitutional amendment be made binding upon the parliament of New Zealand?[48] And the questions became of greater importance when in 1956 the single-chambered parliament of New Zealand passed an electoral act[49] in which it was provided, by section 189, that certain sections of the act relating to the duration of parliaments, the fixing of electoral boundaries, the age of voting, and the secrecy of the ballot should require, for their repeal or amendment, either a three-quarters majority of the total membership of the house of representatives or approval at a referendum. By oversight or intention, however, no special procedure was required for the repeal of section 189 itself.

Some observations may be offered about the position. In the first place it must be emphasized that *some* rules regulate the process of law-making in New Zealand and Ghana. The principal rule is that, to make an act of parliament of New Zealand and Ghana requires the assent not only of the house of representatives but also of the Governor-General. A bill which had received the assent of the house only would not be law. This rule could be changed, but it could be changed only by the procedure laid down for making the law at that time.

Suppose that the parliaments of New Zealand and Ghana make new rules about the procedure which must be followed

---

[48] See E. K. Braybrooke, *Political Science*, Mar. 1951, and K. J. Scott, ibid., Mar. 1954: also an extract from the Report of the New Zealand Constitutional Reform Committee of 1952 printed in Geoffrey Marshall, *Parliamentary Sovereignty in the Commonwealth*, at pp. 262–6.

[49] No. 107 of 1956.

in law-making. Must they not be followed so long as they exist, and must they not be changed, if they are to be changed, by the procedure laid down at the time? There may be scope for argument about what the rules are, what obstacles have been created, and how far they extend. But if rules of procedure are there, it is submitted that they must be followed. If they are not followed, what is produced is not an act of parliament at all. This proposition is illustrated, of course, in *Harris's Case* and lies at the basis of the judgment in that case. It qualifies, or at least clarifies, the assertion that a legislature cannot bind itself. A legislature can bind itself to follow a future procedure and it can rid itself of the obligation to follow that procedure only by the enactment of a new rule in accordance with that procedure. This does not contradict the proposition that a later act of parliament prevails over an earlier act. This is true. But a measure which has not been passed in accordance with the prescribed procedure is not an act of parliament and the question of its prevailing over an earlier act does not arise.

If this line of reasoning is accepted, it follows that the parliaments of New Zealand or Ghana could impose restrictions upon their future procedure in law-making; they could establish a second chamber and entrench its status and powers; they could safeguard certain rights or institutions. They could achieve this through prescribing by law certain procedures which must be followed in law-making. If they were not followed, no law would have been made, just as surely as, on the present rules, no law is made unless the assent of the Governor-General is obtained.

In the case of the New Zealand electoral act of 1956, a difficulty arises from the fact that the entrenching section 189 is not itself entrenched. If no special procedure is required to amend section 189, then by ordinary legislation it can be repealed and with it go the special rules which were to apply to the amendment of other sections. But if section 189 itself was also entrenched,[50] it would seem that section 189 itself and the sections to which it referred could not be amended save by following the procedure laid down in section 189. Unless that procedure was followed no act of parliament would have been passed.

---

[50] This is usual in entrenching clauses. See, for example, s. 152 of the South Africa Act, 1909.

What has been said about the position of the New Zealand and Ghana parliaments in relation to the amendment of their constitutions, and to the procedure of law-making, applies obviously to all other parliaments of the Members of the Commonwealth in so far as they might wish to restrict their procedure in law-making. And it is clear that some most interesting issues arise about the meaning of the historic concept of the sovereignty of the parliament of the United Kingdom.[51] A full discussion of these questions belongs to the study of the constitutional structure of the individual Members of the Commonwealth concerned, rather than of the Commonwealth as a whole. They have been introduced in this chapter to illustrate and explain in an introductory way the nature and consequences of the principle of autonomy which is a fundamental principle of the constitutional structure of the Commonwealth.

[51] See Geoffrey Marshall, op. cit. See also H. R. Gray, 'The Sovereignty of Parliament Today', 10 *University of Toronto Law Journal* (1953-4), pp. 54 ff.; Sir Owen Dixon, 'The Common Law as an Ultimate Constitutional Foundation', 31 *Australian Law Journal* (1957) at pp. 240 ff.

IV · AUTOCHTHONY

I

Autonomy is one fundamental principle in the constitutional structure of the Commonwealth. But for some Members of the Commonwealth it is not enough to be able to say that they enjoy a system of government which is in no way subordinate to the government of the United Kingdom. They wish to be able to say that their constitution has force of law and, if necessary, of supreme law within their territory through its own native authority and not because it was enacted or authorized by the parliament of the United Kingdom; that it is, so to speak, 'home grown', sprung from their own soil, and not imported from the United Kingdom. They assert not the principle of autonomy only: they assert also a principle of something stronger, of self-sufficiency, of constitutional autarky or, to use a less familiar but accurate word, a principle of constitutional *autochthony*,[1] of being constitutionally rooted in their own native soil.

The working out of these ideas has produced some radical changes in the constitutional structure of the Commonwealth. They were of great importance in the making of the constitutions of India and Pakistan, and it is for this reason that those constitutions were not discussed in the previous chapter in relation to the principle of autonomy. And there is good reason to believe that in other Members of the Commonwealth autochthony will become a characteristic of their constitutional arrangements.[2]

The issues involved were very clearly and forcefully pre-

---

[1] From the Greek αὐτόχθων—'sprung from that land itself' (*O.E.D.*).

[2] This could be expressed in Kelsen's language by saying that each Member of the Commonwealth will be seeking a separate *Grundnorm*, and that the days of the common *Grundnorm* are numbered. I do not discuss the subject in these terms, partly through incompetence but chiefly because the late R. T. E. Latham pursued this interesting little animal as profitably as it can be done in his brilliant supplement entitled 'The Law and the Commonwealth' to W. K. Hancock, *Survey of British Commonwealth Affairs, 1918–36*, vol. i, and published separately in 1949.

sented when the constitution for the Irish Free State came to be drafted in 1922. Although the Republic of Ireland, the successor to the Irish Free State, ceased to be a member of the Commonwealth in 1949, the principles which its founders asserted, though rejected by other Members of the Commonwealth at the time, came to have a strong influence on the course of the development of the constitutional structure of the Commonwealth, particularly after 1945. It is clear also, that this influence is by no means exhausted. It is worth while therefore to explain the attitude they adopted and the steps they took to get it accepted.[3]

The Irishmen who framed the constitution in Dublin in 1922 believed that they were acting on behalf of the people of an independent republic and that the constitution which they drew up obtained force of law through the approval of the representatives of those people. They described themselves as the Third Dáil Eireann. Their view is expressed in the preamble to the Constitution of the Irish Free State (Saorstat Eireann) Act which these representatives passed[4] and which runs as follows:

Dáil Eireann sitting as a Constituent Assembly in this Provisional Parliament, acknowledging that all lawful authority comes from God to the people and in confidence that the National life and unity of Ireland shall thus be restored, hereby proclaims the establishment of the Irish Free State (otherwise called Saorstat Eireann) and in the exercise of undoubted right, decrees and enacts as follows:

And in section 1 it enacts that the constitution scheduled to the act shall be the constitution of the Irish Free State.

The view of the government and parliament of the United Kingdom, on the other hand, was that the power to establish the Irish Free State and to give it a constitution with force of law lay with the parliament of the United Kingdom alone. They did not recognize Ireland as an independent country but as a part of the United Kingdom whose parliament alone could grant self-government. When, therefore, the Irish representatives in Dublin had concluded their work and embodied it in the Constitution of the Irish Free State (Saorstat Eireann) Act, the parliament of the United Kingdom proceeded to pass what

[3] See V. T. H. Delany, 'The Constitution of Ireland: Its Origin and Development', in 12 *University of Toronto Law Journal* (1957–8), p. 1.
[4] On 25 Oct. 1922, and referred to as No. 1 of 1922.

it described as the Irish Free State Constitution Act.[5] This act is entitled 'An Act to provide for the Constitution of the Irish Free State' and begins:

> Whereas the House of the Parliament constituted pursuant to the Irish Free State (Agreement) Act, 1922,[6] sitting as a Constituent Assembly for the settlement of the Constitution of the Irish Free State, has passed the Measure (hereinafter referred to as 'the Constituent Act'), set forth in the Schedule to this Act, whereby the Constitution appearing as the First Schedule to the Constituent Act is declared to be the Constitution of the Irish Free State. . . .

And in section 1 it enacts that the constitution set forth in the first schedule to the Constituent Act shall, subject to the provisions to which the same is by the Constituent Act made subject, be the constitution of the Irish Free State, and shall come into operation on being proclaimed by His Majesty.

The view expressed by the parliament of the United Kingdom was that the Constituent Assembly was a 'House of Parliament' not Dáil Eireann; that its authority came from the Irish Free State (Agreement) Act, not from 'God to the people' nor from 'undoubted right'; that its deliberations were directed to the 'settlement' not the enactment of a constitution; that it passed a 'Measure', not an act, though that measure might be referred to as 'The Constituent Act'; and that it merely 'declared' the scheduled constitution to be the constitution of the Irish Free State, it did not enact it. On the British view, indeed, the Assembly had no power to enact a constitution; it had not been authorized to do so by the Irish Free State (Agreement) Act. All that the house of parliament did was to 'prepare' a constitution in accordance with the practice which had been followed already in Canada, Australia, and South Africa, and in the Australian colonies. Mr. Lloyd George, the Prime Minister of the United Kingdom, expressed this view in his speech in the House of Commons in introducing the Irish Free State Constitution Bill: 'Here we are going to follow the example which has been set in the framing of every constitution throughout the Empire.[7] The constitution is drafted and decided by the Dominion, the

---

[5] 13 Geo. V (sess. 2), c. 1. Received the royal assent on 5 Dec. 1922.

[6] An earlier act of the parliament of the United Kingdom, 12 Geo. V, c. 4. Assented to on 31 Mar. 1922.

[7] An exaggeration.

Imperial Parliament taking such steps as may be necessary to legalise these decisions.'[8]

This difference of opinion about the legal basis of the constitution of the Irish Free State persisted throughout the history of the Free State. It was reflected in particular in the attitude of the courts in the Free State and in the United Kingdom towards the constitution. The Supreme Court of the Irish Free State, more particularly in the case of *The State (Ryan)* v. *Lennon,*[9] decided in 1934, spoke of the constitution as 'the fundamental structure upon which the State was set up by the Third Dáil Eireann sitting as a Constituent Assembly. The Dáil thereby formulated the system or principles, and created the organs of government of the State.'[10] On the other side was the completely opposing view expressed by the Judicial Committee of the Privy Council in the case of *Moore* v. *The Attorney-General for the Irish Free State*, decided in 1935.[11]

In their opinion [said Lord Sankey] the Constituent Act and the Constitution of the Irish Free State derived their validity from the Act of the Imperial Parliament, the Irish Free State Constitution Act, 1922. This Act established that the Constitution, subject to the provisions of the Constituent Act, should be the Constitution of the Irish Free State and should come into operation upon being proclaimed by His Majesty, as was done on December 6, 1922. The action of the House of Parliament was thereby ratified; apart from such ratification that body had no authority to make a Constitution. . . .[12]

These views were clearly irreconcilable. The one took its start from an Irish legislature possessed of supreme authority to enact a constitution in exercise of its undoubted right, and regarded the acts of the parliament of the United Kingdom as valid and necessary only in so far as they gave force of law in the United Kingdom to the changes consequential upon the

---

[8] 149 *H.C. Deb.* 5 s., col. 42.   [9] [1935] I.R. 170.
[10] *Per* Kennedy C.J. at p. 203. FitzGibbon J. in the same case said that he was not disposed to quarrel with the statement 'that the Constitution was proclaimed in the name of the people by Dáil Eireann as an act of supreme authority, which it alone had the right to do, because it was the mouthpiece of the people, requiring and receiving no royal assent'. Ibid., at p. 226. See also Kennedy C.J. in *Lynham* v. *Butler*, decided in 1927. [1933] I.R. 74.
[11] [1935] A.C. 484; [1935] I.R. 472.
[12] [1935] A.C. 484 at p. 497.

recognition by the United Kingdom of the establishment of the Irish Free State. The other takes its start from the parliament of the United Kingdom as the only source of legal authority, and regards the Irish assembly and its measures as legally valid in the United Kingdom or in the Irish Free State only in so far as they derive such force of law from acts of the parliament of the United Kingdom. The argument proceeds on parallel lines.

2

This conflict of view about the legal basis of the constitution of the Irish Free State continued so long as the constitution itself existed. So far as the principle of autonomy was concerned, however, as distinct from the principle of autochthony, the British view was more favourable, if anything, to the Free State than the Irish view. For when the Statute of Westminster was passed in 1931, it gave full powers to the parliament of the Free State to repeal or amend any act of the parliament of the United Kingdom which extended to the Free State, and this included— so the Judicial Committee of the Privy Council decided in *Moore's Case*—the Irish Free State Agreement Act and the Irish Free State Constitution Act and its schedules. The parliament of the Free State was able therefore to remove any provisions of the agreement to which it objected and any inequalities in the agreement or in its constitution which had been imposed upon it in 1922.[13] On the Irish view, however, the Articles of Agreement and the constitution had been enacted by the Third Dáil, which had stipulated that no amendment might be made to the constitution which conflicted with the Articles of Agreement, and there was no body—certainly not the parliament of the United Kingdom—which was able to remove this restriction upon constitutional amendment which the Third Dáil had imposed.

These arguments were brought to an end when the constitution of the Irish Free State of 1922 was superseded in 1937 by the constitution of Eire. In the enacting of this constitution great care was taken that it should not only be but also be seen to be 'home grown' in legal theory and practice. In the first

[13] 'The Statute of Westminster gave to the Irish Free State a power under which they could abrogate the Treaty. . . .' *Moore's Case*, [1935] A.C. 484 at p. 499.

place, the draft constitution, prepared by Mr. De Valera's
government, was presented to the Dáil, but it was not enacted
by it. The Dáil was invited to discuss the draft, to amend it, and
to approve it, but to go no further. Thereafter it was submitted
to the people in a referendum, and their approval constituted
the enactment of the document.[14] It was thus impossible to argue
that the constitution obtained force of law through the authority of the Dáil which in turn had got its authority from the
Statute of Westminster and the Irish Free State Constitution
Act, 1922—both acts of the parliament of the United Kingdom.
On the contrary the constitution was an act of the people, as
declared in its preamble: 'In the Name of the Most Holy
Trinity, from whom is all authority and to whom, as our final
end, all actions both of men and states must be referred, We,
the people of Eire . . . Do hereby adopt, enact, and give to ourselves, this Constitution.'

Two points about these events deserve notice. The first is
that, on the Irish as well as on the British view of the legal basis
of the constitution of the Irish Free State, the enactment of the
constitution of 1937 caused a break in Irish constitutional history. There was a gap or break in legal continuity. Whether the
Dáil owed its authority to the Irish people or to the parliament
of the United Kingdom, it did not enact or purport to enact the
constitution of 1937. It showed to other Commonwealth countries a method of making a break with the past, and of conduct-
ing what, in law, was a revolution, not an amendment or revision
of the constitution of 1922. The second point is that Ireland
carried out these steps while still within the Commonwealth. It
showed the other Commonwealth countries that you could
adopt a home-grown constitution without being obliged to
leave the Commonwealth.

3

This desire to have a 'home-grown' or autochthonous constitution has been felt by other countries of the Commonwealth
as they have approached independence, but not by all. But the
same problem arises of how the parliament of the United King-

---

[14] The Plebicite (Draft Constitution) Act, 1937 (No. 16 of 1937), referred
to a 'draft constitution approved by Dáil Eireann'.

dom can grant autonomy to a Commonwealth country without at the same time granting it a constitution or authorizing its legislature to enact a constitution. If independence has been achieved in a peaceful way, as a result of agitation and negotiation but not through insurrection as in Ireland, it is most natural that the new constitution of the new independent Member of the Commonwealth should be, if not made, certainly legalized or given its hall-mark or trade-mark in the United Kingdom.

The cases of India and Pakistan provide some interesting illustrations of the problem. When India obtained independence in 1947 it was arranged that, pending the drawing up of a new constitution, it should continue to be governed under the Government of India Act, 1935,[15] as adapted to the new situation. It is clear, therefore, that until 26 January 1950, when the new constitution of India came into effect, India was governed under a constitution which owed its force of law to the parliament of the United Kingdom, and in particular to two acts of that parliament, the Indian Independence Act of 1947 and the Government of India Act of 1935. Pakistan was in a similar position from 1947 until its new constitution came into effect in 1956. What is the status of the new constitutions? The preamble to the Indian constitution of 1950 runs: 'We, the people of India, having solemnly resolved to constitute India into a sovereign democratic republic . . . in our constituent assembly, this twenty sixth day of November, 1949, do hereby adopt, enact, and give to ourselves this Constitution.' The preamble to the constitution of the Islamic Republic of Pakistan runs: 'We the people of Pakistan in our Constituent Assembly this twenty ninth day of February 1956 and the seventeenth day of Rajah, 1375, do hereby adopt enact and give to ourselves this Constitution.' Although this constitution was suspended in 1958, the course of events leading up to its enactment is worth some small study, for it is founded upon principles of enduring importance in the development of the constitutional structure of the Commonwealth.

Here is a claim that the constitution has been enacted by the people. And as if to make it clear and manifest that there was a break with the past, each constitution contained an article which repealed the Indian Independence Act, 1947, and the

---

[15] 25 & 26 Geo. V, c. 42.

Government of India Act, 1935,[16] upon the coming into effect of the new constitution. It is true that, unlike the people of Eire, the peoples of India and Pakistan were not asked to express their opinion of the draft constitutions; they did not actually enact them as did the people of Eire. They acted through their constituent assembly, rather in the same way as the Irish people were claimed to have acted through the Third Dáil in 1922. Yet the Indian and Pakistani documents claim that the people, not the constituent assembly, enacted the constitution; the people 'in', not 'through' or 'by' their constituent assembly. It is a fiction, of course, but it is not necessarily therefore bad law. Let us examine the cases of India and Pakistan separately.

Could it be argued that, in spite of what appears in the preamble of the Indian constitution, it owes its legal force none the less to the authority of an act of the parliament of the United Kingdom? It seems clear that this could have happened. For the Indian Independence Act of 1947 conferred full powers to make laws upon the legislature of the new Dominion of India[17] and provided that for the purpose of making provision as to the constitution of the Dominion the powers of the legislature of the Dominion should be exercisable in the first instance by the Constituent Assembly of the Dominion.[18] But did it happen? There is room for difference of opinion.

In the first place it could be argued that if the Constituent Assembly had passed the constitution and the Governor-General of India had assented to it, then undoubtedly the constitution would have had force of law, and would have derived this force of law from the powers conferred by the Indian Independence Act of 1947. This certainly did not happen. Though the Constituent Assembly itself passed the constitution, the Governor-General did not assent to it. He was not asked to assent to it. On the view of the members of the Constituent Assembly his assent was not required to complete the enacting process. How did they arrive at this view? To understand it we must go back to 1946 when arrangements for setting up the Constituent Assembly were first discussed.

A mission from the British cabinet led by Lord Pethick-

---

[16] Article 395 of the constitution of India and Article 221 of the constitution of Pakistan.
[17] s. 6.   [18] s. 8 (i).

Lawrence, then Secretary of State for India, visited India in 1946. After discussions it issued a final statement on 16 May 1946,[19] in the course of which it set forth a scheme for a Constituent Assembly to draw up a constitution for India. It would be elected indirectly by members of the provincial assemblies which had been set up under the provisions of the Government of India Act, 1935. The statement also said that there would have to be what it called a 'treaty' between the Union Constituent Assembly and the United Kingdom 'to provide for certain matters arising out of the transfer of power'. On 20 May a letter was sent to Lord Pethick-Lawrence on behalf of the Congress Working Committee and in the course of it the question of the status and power of the proposed Union Constituent Assembly was raised.[20] The relevant passage is as follows:

The Assembly itself, when formed, will in my Committee's opinion be a sovereign body for the purpose of drafting the constitution unhindered by any external authority, as well as for entering into a treaty. . . . The Constituent Assembly being a sovereign body for the purpose of the constitution its final decisions will automatically take effect.

Here was a claim that the Constituent Assembly should be regarded as having complete authority to enact the constitution, as sovereign in its own right, dependent on no outside body to authorize its actions either before or after its labours were concluded. To this claim Lord Pethick-Lawrence returned an answer. 'When the Constituent Assembly has completed its labours', he wrote, 'His Majesty's Government will recommend to Parliament such action as may be necessary for the cession of sovereignty to the Indian people. . . .'[21] This was, no doubt intentionally, a little vague. It did not actually say that the constitution could not come into effect until given force of law by the parliament of the United Kingdom. It might imply it, but it was conceivable that the steps necessary to cede sovereignty might not actually include the legalizing of the constitution.

Whatever was meant, however, the Indian Independence Act of 1947 gave full powers to the Constituent Assembly to enact

---

[19] See A. C. Banerjee, *The Making of the Indian Constitution*, vol. i, pp. 137–50.

[20] Ibid., p. 162.   [21] Ibid., p. 165.

the constitution. But did it mean that the assent of the Governor-General was necessary to complete the process of enactment? From the start, the Constituent Assembly proceeded upon the assumption that it did not. Whenever it produced constitutional measures (and it should be remembered that a great number of such measures had to be passed in the early years of independence before the constitution was completed) it regarded them as coming into force upon their signature not by the Governor-General, to whom they were not presented, but by the President of the Constituent Assembly. His signature was not regarded as assent but as authentication, as certifying that the measure which he signed was that which in fact the Assembly had passed.

Alongside these arrangements for the enactment of constitutional measures, there were distinct and different arrangements for the enactment of ordinary legislation. The members of the Constituent Assembly, sitting as a legislature, passed bills upon non-constitutional subjects, and these were submitted to the Governor-General for his assent. There were in fact two bodies —or, if you like, one body with two distinct functions.[22] The rules of procedure when constitutional measures were being discussed were different from those when ordinary measures were being discussed. The debates were reported in separate *Hansards*. The enactments were published separately in the volumes of statutes.

The question now arises: Did the Indian Independence Act of 1947 make the assent of the Governor-General an essential part of the process of enacting all legislation, constitutional or non-constitutional? If it did, then all the constitutional measures, including the constitution itself, passed by the Constituent Assembly, were not in fact enacted, and did not obtain force of law under the authority of the Indian Independence Act. They derived their force of law, if they had it, from elsewhere—from the people, from the Constituent Assembly itself as a sovereign body (on the Congress view), or from both. This is what the Congress Working Committee had wished to see happen right from the start and the procedure followed by the Constituent Assembly clearly was intended to assert this principle. The

[22] Compare the discussion in *Shankari Prasad* v. *Union of India* (1952), S.C.R. 89 where the Supreme Court of India considered the amending power under the new constitution of India.

similarity in aim and procedure between the Indian Constituent Assembly and the Third Dáil is apparent. There is just this difference. Whereas the parliament of the United Kingdom passed an act[23] which claimed to give force of law to the constitution of the Irish Free State, no such British act was passed purporting to give force of law to the Indian constitution. In the end no British validating act proved to be part of what Lord Pethick-Lawrence had vaguely referred to as 'such action as may be necessary for the cession of sovereignty to the Indian people'.

But now, supposing that the Indian Independence Act of 1947 did *not* require the assent of the Governor-General for the completion of the process of enacting laws, or at any rate of enacting constitutional laws? Might it not be that the act gave powers to the Constituent Assembly to enact constitutional laws, including the constitution, without bringing the Governor-General into the process at all? Perhaps the Constituent Assembly in dispensing with the Governor-General's assent was following the provisions of the Independence Act, not departing from them? If this is so, we reach the interesting conclusion that the Constituent Assembly did indeed enact the constitution, and did so under the authority of the powers conferred upon it by an act of the United Kingdom parliament, namely, the Indian Independence Act of 1947. The fact that the constitution itself declares at the outset that the people of India enacted it, is, in law, a mere flourish, for the constitution was enacted when the final vote was taken by the Constituent Assembly.

Whether or not the Governor-General's assent to bills, particularly constitutional bills, was required, was not in fact raised in the courts of India, but it was raised in Pakistan in 1954 and 1955, and very fully discussed in constitutional cases of the first importance.[24] It is not necessary for our purpose to go at all fully into the details of these cases.[25] What is apparent from a reading of them is that it is by no means certain that the Indian Independence Act required the assent of the Governor-General in order that the process of enacting constitutional measures should be

[23] The Irish Free State Constitution Act, 1922. See above, p. 91.
[24] See below, pp. 101 ff.
[25] The reader is referred to Sir W. I. Jennings, *Constitutional Problems in Pakistan*, where the judgments are printed in full and discussed acutely.

completed. Suffice it to say that if the Federal Court of Pakistan
is correct—and in my opinion it is—then the assent of the
Governor-General of India was required if the constitution of
India was to receive force of law under the authority of the
Indian Independence Act.[26] It did not receive that assent. Its
coming into force, therefore, makes a break in India's constitutional history and in the constitutional relations of the United
Kingdom with India, comparable with the break that occurred
in 1937 when the Irish constitution was adopted. If, on the other
hand, the Federal Court was not correct, and if the Indian Independence Act gave full power to the Constituent Assembly
to enact the constitution, without requiring the assent of the
Governor-General, then, ironically, it cannot at the same time
be claimed that the constitution owes its force of law ultimately
to the people of India or to the Constituent Assembly. It owes
its force of law, in the last resort, to the parliament of the United
Kingdom.

The decisions of the courts of Pakistan are not binding upon
India. We do not know what view would have been taken of
the matter if it had been raised in a case before the Supreme
Court of India or if it had been taken on appeal to the Judicial
Committee of the Privy Council from the Federal Court of
Pakistan or from the Supreme Court of India before that appeal
had been abolished. There is sufficient resemblance, however,
in the procedure adopted by the two countries, which both owe
their existence to the Indian Independence Act of 1947, to make
it possible to claim that the decisions in Pakistan are, at the least,
relevant to the forming of an opinion about the position in India.
So far as the position of the constitution of Pakistan is concerned, however, the decisions are of binding force and it is
worth while saying a little about it.

Whereas the Constituent Assembly of India produced a constitution by the end of 1949, so that it could come into full effect
on 26 January 1950, the Constituent Assembly of Pakistan, after
seven years, had still not completed the process. A draft constitution was at last ready in October 1954, and was to have been

[26] It may be mentioned that s. 6 (3) of the Indian Independence Act begins:
'The Governor General of each of the new Dominions shall have full power to
assent in His Majesty's name to any law of the legislature of that Dominion....'
But, it was asked, was the Constituent Assembly the legislature of the
Dominion?

reported to the Constituent Assembly on 27 October.[27] On 24 October, however, the Governor-General issued a proclamation announcing that 'the constitutional machinery had broken down', declaring a state of emergency and asserting that 'the Constituent Assembly as at present constituted has lost the confidence of the people and can no longer function'. This proclamation was taken as purporting to dissolve the Constituent Assembly. The president of the Assembly, Moulvi Tamizuddin Khan, claimed that the Governor-General had no power to dissolve the Assembly and petitioned the Sind Chief Court to issue a writ of mandamus under section 223 A of the Government of India Act, 1935. Section 223 A had been inserted in the act by the Constituent Assembly which had passed in 1954 the Government of India (Amendment) Act. This amendment, like all other constitutional measures which the Constituent Assembly had passed, had not been submitted to the Governor-General for his assent, for the Pakistan Constituent Assembly had followed the same procedure in law-making as had the Indian Constituent Assembly. When the case came before the Sind Chief Court, the Advocate-General of Pakistan raised the point, among others, that the Government of India (Amendment) Act of 1954 was invalid on the ground that it had not received the assent of the Governor-General. Moulvi Tamizuddin Khan succeeded in the Sind Chief Court,[28] but the Federation of Pakistan appealed to the Federal Court which declared that the Sind Chief Court had acted without jurisdiction since section 223 A (upon which its claim to jurisdiction was founded) was not part of the law of Pakistan, since it had not received the assent of the Governor-General.[29] Many other and more intricate and important constitutional issues were raised in these cases before the Sind Chief Court and the Federal Court, but for our purpose the chief and almost only point of importance is that of the necessity or otherwise of the assent by the Governor-General to constitutional measures by the Constituent Assembly.

It seems clear that the Constituent Assembly proceeded

[27] See the account in K. Callard, *Pakistan: A Political Study*.
[28] *Moulvi Tamizuddin Khan* v. *Federation of Pakistan*, P.L.R. 1955 Sind 96.
[29] *Federation of Pakistan* v. *Moulvi Tamizuddin Khan*, P.L.R. 1956 W.P. 306. Printed in Jennings, op. cit., pp. 79–238.

throughout on the assumption that the royal assent was unnecessary for enacting constitutional bills. It passed a rule of
procedure on 24 February 1948 that 'when a bill is passed by
the Assembly a copy thereof shall be signed by the President'.
On 22 May 1948 it substituted for this rule the following:
'When a bill is passed by the Assembly, a copy thereof shall be
signed by the President and it shall become law on being published in the official Gazette of Pakistan under the authority of
the President.' Neither of these rules purport explicitly to
abolish the royal assent, though the second might be thought to
come near it.[30] If it does attempt to do so, it must fail, if only
because it did not itself receive the royal assent. None the less,
it is difficult to escape the conclusion that the Constituent
Assembly meant by implication to substitute authentication by
the President for assent by the Governor-General, although the
terms of the rule did not expressly repeal the power of the
Governor-General to assent. The words of the rule, coupled
with the fact that assent was not sought, bring out the attitude
of the constitution makers fairly clearly into the open.

It is not necessary to describe the confusion which followed
the judgment of the Federal Court, whereby forty-four acts
were deemed to be invalidated,[31] nor the steps that were taken
in an attempt to overcome these difficulties.[32] In the outcome
the Federal Court expressed the opinion[33] that the Governor-
General had had power to dissolve the Constituent Assembly,
and that he had power to summon a new Constituent Assembly.
This new Constituent Assembly met on 7 July 1955, and completed its labours on 29 February 1956. The constitution, as
approved by the Assembly and as authenticated by the President
of the Assembly, was thereupon presented to the Governor-
General for his assent and assented to on 2 March 1956. In the
outcome, therefore, Pakistan, at the last critical stage, followed
a different procedure from India. And it is difficult to see how
any other action could have been taken in the light of the
decisions, so recently and deliberately given by the Federal

---

[30] This argument was advanced in the Federal Court in *Tamizuddin Khan's
Case*, but rejected by the court. See Jennings, op. cit., pp. 134-6.

[31] Including the Privy Council (Abolition of Jurisdiction) Act of 1950.

[32] Jennings, op. cit., pp. 5-6.

[33] In a *Special Reference* made by the Governor-General, Jennings, ibid.,
pp. 257-349.

Court. While, therefore, the constitution describes itself as enacted by the people of Pakistan, it was in fact and in law enacted by the Constituent Assembly with the assent of the Governor-General and it derived its force of law, therefore, from the Indian Independence Act of 1947. It would be open to a Pakistani court, of course, to say that it would look no further than the preamble to the constitution and to declare that the constitution is enacted by the people and owes its force of law to them. Yet to adopt that view would be to ignore or forget some important events in the constitutional history of Pakistan, and some important differences in the procedure adopted by India and Pakistan in the preparation and enactment of their respective constitutions.

4

If we accept the view that the constitution of India of 1950 does not owe force of law to the Indian Independence Act and that India achieved constitutional autochthony with the enactment of this constitution, our discussion of the supremacy and authority of the constitution proceeds on rather different lines from that adopted in the previous chapter in regard to the constitutions of other Members of the Commonwealth. Yet fundamentally there is a resemblance, for in all cases where the Colonial Laws Validity Act or the rules which it declared are no longer applicable, the authority of the constitution cannot arise from any supposed superiority in law made at Westminster.

In the Indian constitution, however, the source of legal authority is declared to be the people, who, in their constituent assembly, did adopt, enact, and give to themselves the constitution. Such limitations as the constitution imposes upon the organs its creates are imposed by the people, and may be altered or abolished only in the manner in which the people prescribe. The legislature, in particular, did not impose these limitations upon itself or upon other institutions of the state.

The constitution of India does in fact impose a variety of limitations upon legislatures. Part III contains a comprehensive declaration of fundamental rights—the right to equality, the right to freedom, the right against exploitation, the right to freedom of religion, cultural and educational rights, the right

to property, and the right to constitutional remedies. Inevitably
many of these rights are declared subject to qualifications, as, for
example, Article 25 (1) which states that 'subject to public order,
morality and health and to the other provisions of this Part,
all persons are equally entitled to freedom of conscience and
the right freely to profess, practice and propagate religion'. An
unqualified declaration of rights is incompatible with government. To the extent, however, that the constitution defines
them, rights are guaranteed and the Supreme Court of India has
the power to issue directions or orders or writs, whatever may
be appropriate, for the enforcement of any of the rights conferred by Part III.[34] In this matter it is clearly intended that the
will of the people as expressed in the constitution is supreme
over the legislature or any other institution of the state. Article
13 (2) declares: 'The State shall not make any law which takes
away or abridges the rights conferred by this Part and any law
made in contravention of this clause shall, to the extent of the
contravention, be void.'

A second important limitation upon legislatures embodied in
the constitution is the division of powers between the parliament of the Union and the legislatures of the component states
which make it up. These are set out in some detail in a Union
List, a State List, and a Concurrent List.[35] The division is by no
means unambiguous or rigid, and in this part of the constitution,
as in others, there is provision for the assumption of power by
the government of the Union in certain circumstances such as
an emergency. Subject to these extensive qualifications, however, limits are imposed and here again the courts have power
to determine whether or not limits have been transgressed. And
an appeal lies to the Supreme Court in any case which involves
a substantial question of law as to the interpretation of the constitution. In a succession of cases the Supreme Court has exercised this power.

In considering how far the people have imposed effective and
extensive checks upon the institutions of government which
they set up in their constitution, we must look not so much at
the courts as at the nature of the power to amend the constitution and in particular the limitations embodied in it. Amendments to the constitution[36] require a special process, which does

[34] Article 32.   [35] Part XI and Seventh Schedule.   [36] Article 368.

not, incidentally, involve recourse directly to the people. Subject to certain excluded topics (which will be mentioned later) an amendment to the constitution 'may be initiated only by the introduction of a bill for the purpose in either house of parliament, and when the bill is passed in each house by a majority of the total membership of that house and by a majority of not less than two-thirds of the members of that house present and voting, it shall be presented to the President for his assent and upon such assent being given to the bill, the constitution shall stand amended in accordance with the terms of the bill'.

If, however, the proposed amendment deals with certain specified sections of the constitution—affecting, for example, the election of the President, the judiciary, and the allocation of powers and the regulation of relations between the Union and the component states—or if it deals with the amending process itself, then the amending bill requires in addition to the consent of the two houses of parliament as set out above, the assent also of the legislatures of not less than half of the states of the Union.[37]

It is clear that the amendment of the constitution of India must be carried out according to the procedure laid down in it and that any act of a legislature which conflicted with the constitution must give way to it. On the other hand it is also clear that the limitations upon the legislatures, and in particular the fundamental rights declared in Part III, are capable of being modified or abolished by constitutional amendment. So far as the fundamental rights are concerned, indeed, they can be altered by the parliament of the Union, provided the appropriate majorities can be obtained.[38] But whatever the extent of the area over which the constitution is supreme, that supremacy and the authority of the constitution is based upon something which, whether it is to be called a *Grundnorm* or not, is Indian.

5

Up to 1960 no other Members of the Commonwealth had followed the example set by the Irish Free State, by India, and

[37] Not all the states, but the principal states, as prescribed in the terms of the article.
[38] The nature of the amending power was discussed in *Shankari Prasad* v. *Union of India, supra.*

by Pakistan[39] of endeavouring to establish their constitutions upon a basis of autochthony and to demonstrate that they owe their legal force in no way to the parliament of the United Kingdom or to any other external source whatever. This does not mean that the subject was not discussed nor that steps may not be taken in the future to follow the examples of India and Pakistan. Certainly the belief in national independence is not weaker in these other Members, and some such as Ceylon and Ghana may soon take action. If others take no action, their reasons may be that they are not interested in technicalities of law when they have the substance of power, or that they gain some useful advantages from these technicalities, or that the controversy which might arise from undertaking a revision or re-enactment of the constitution would do more harm than good.

In the case of the Federation of Malaya there was perhaps some room for argument about the extent to which the constitution had force of law throughout the federation as a result solely of the operation of the Federation of Malaya Independence Order-in-Council[40] and of the Independence Act.[41] Although the Order-in-Council says that the federal and state constitutions 'shall have the force of law'[42] from certain fixed dates, it claims to extend 'to the Settlements of Penang and Malacca and, so far as Her Majesty has jurisdiction therein, to the other territories of the Federation of Malaya'.[43] The wording adopted here recognizes the fact that although the two settlements were part of Her Majesty's dominions, the other territories of the federation were not—they were states with the Rulers of which the Crown had made agreements and whose consent had been sought and obtained to the terms of the new constitution. Indeed this constitution had been prepared by a constitutional commission which had itself been appointed in the name of the Queen and their Highnesses the Rulers and its report was addressed to the Queen and the Rulers.[44] Moreover the Federation of Malaya Independence Act of 1957, which

[39] The constitution of Pakistan was suspended at this time.
[40] No. 1533 of 1957. S.I. 1957, Part I, pp. 832 ff.
[41] 5 & 6 Eliz. II, c. 60.   [42] s. 2.
[43] s. 1 (2).
[44] Report of the Federation of Malaya Constitutional Commission, 1957, London, H.M.S.O. Colonial No. 330.

gave approval to the conclusion by the Queen and the Rulers of such agreement as appeared to the Queen to be expedient for the establishment of the Federation of Malaya as an independent sovereign country within the Commonwealth, was careful to provide that 'any such Agreement shall be conditional upon the approval of the new Federal Constitution by enactments of the existing Federal Legislature and of each of the Malay States; and that upon such approval being given Her Majesty by Order-in-Council may direct that the said Federal and State Constitutions shall have the force of law within the said Settlements, and, so far as She has jurisdiction in that behalf, elsewhere within the Federation . . .'.

It might be claimed, therefore, that the constitution of the Federation has force of law as a result of the approval not only of the Queen in Council but also of the Rulers. The question is how far the vague phrase 'so far as Her Majesty has jurisdiction therein' can take you. Was the jurisdiction sufficient to bring the constitution into full effect as a matter of law? If so the references in the Order-in-Council to the consent of the Rulers and to the terms of the agreement made between them and the Queen, though politically important, do not affect the legal position. If not, then it seems that the constitution owes its force of law to the authority both of the Queen in Council and to the Rulers. It is another question, of course, whether the Queen-in-Council or parliament could, if they had wished, have imposed the constitution upon the Rulers or could have abrogated the agreements unilaterally. That is a doubtful question of law. The fact is, however, that they did not. They proceeded throughout by seeking and obtaining the consent of the Rulers. In the outcome, then, there is room for doubt whether the constitution of Malaya draws its authority solely from the parliament and Privy Council of the United Kingdom as does Ghana and some other Members of the Commonwealth. On the other hand the type of procedure followed in India or Pakistan was not followed in Malaya and the constitution does not therefore rest its authority upon the same sort of basis as those of India or Pakistan. The reason for this is no doubt partly that the constitution of Malaya was drafted by the Constitutional Commission and not by a constituent assembly. Moreover, whereas in India and Pakistan the constitution-making occurred after independence was granted, in Malaya it preceded the granting of independence, and it was necessary therefore for the appropriate authorities in the United Kingdom to take action which, at one and the same time, conferred independence and brought the new constitution into effect.

Although other Members of the Commonwealth may not feel obliged to follow the methods adopted by Ireland and India in seeking to establish the autochthony of their constitutions, it must not be assumed that they accept without question the view that their own constitutions are not rooted in their own soil. The Australians might argue that, irrespective of the fact that the Australian constitution obtained force of law in 1900, through its being enacted by the parliament of the United Kingdom, it possesses force of law today through its acceptance by Australians for sixty years or more. To explain why they accept it would be a complicated matter. But, in the eyes of Australians, their constitution was framed by their representatives in a series of conventions in Australia, it was accepted by these representatives, legalized at Westminster, and thereafter provided the framework of the system of government for the country. It can be altered by Australians when they think fit. If, by some means, the constitution could be deprived of its quality of a British act, Australians would still regard it as having force of law. If the constitution obtained its life in the seed bed at Westminster, and was transplanted to Australia, it has struck root in the Australian soil, and it owes its life now to Australia and not to Britain.

The same sort of view could be expressed about the constitutions of Canada, South Africa, or New Zealand, for example. As Professor D. V. Cowen wrote, in dealing with the case of South Africa:

People have regulated their lives under the South Africa Act; they have elected parliaments in accordance with its provisions; those parliaments have been constituted and have functioned in terms of it. And, finally, the courts in their day to day work, have acted, and continue to act, on the assumption that the South Africa Act is South African law. In short, the South Africa Act continues in force in the Union by the habit of observance.[45]

And he goes on to quote with approval Bryce's observation:[46]

[45] 15 *Modern Law Review* (1952), at p. 295.
[46] *Studies in History and Jurisprudence*, vol. ii, p. 57.

The question, Who is legal Sovereign? stands quite apart from the questions, Why is he Sovereign? And Who made him Sovereign? The historical facts which have vested power in any given Sovereign, as well as the moral grounds on which he is entitled to obedience, lie outside the questions with which law is concerned; and belong to history, or to political philosophy, or to ethics; and nothing but confusion is caused by intruding them into the purely legal questions of the determination of the Sovereign and the definition of his powers.

This point of view may satisfy nationalism in some Members of the Commonwealth. For them it may be enough that, whatever the legal origins of their constitution, it is now thoroughly domiciled in their country, it is theirs, and they can do what they think with it. It is enough that their constitution is Australian law, Canadian law or New Zealand law or South African law, unalterable from outside (unless, as in the case of Canada, they choose to ask for alterations). It does not matter how it came to be law.

For others, however, nationalism is not satisfied with this position. They feel uneasy that part of the explanation why their constitution is law is that it was enacted by or under the authority of the parliament of the United Kingdom. It suggests inequality. If a court in South Africa were asked why it regarded the South Africa Act as law, it could, if it chose to answer, reply that it is law because it is law; or that it is law because South Africans accept it as law. But it could also answer, it is submitted, that it is law because it was enacted by the parliament of the United Kingdom. That would not be an incorrect answer. And the same is true of courts in Australia, New Zealand, or Canada, for example. The South Africa Act is undoubtedly South African law, just as the Australian constitution is Australian law, and the British North America Acts, 1867 to 1951, are Canadian law. But they are so not because they were made in South Africa or Australia or Canada, but because they were made in the United Kingdom in terms that extended them to South Africa, Australia, and Canada as part of the law thereof.

Is there no way of dealing with this position, short of adopting the method of a break in legal continuity favoured by Ireland and India. One suggestion is that, in the case of South Africa, for example, all that is needed is that the Union parliament should re-enact the South Africa Act and declare it to be the constitution of the Union in virtue of the sovereignty of the Union or of the Union parliament, and to obtain authority from no other source whatever. And it might go further and require all courts so to interpret the force and authority of the constitution. But can it not be said that the parliament of the Union gets its authority to re-enact the South Africa Act and to make these declarations from the Statute of Westminster and from the South Africa Act itself, and does not the line lead back once more to Westminster?

The only satisfactory reply to this argument, from the point of view of someone who wishes to deny that the line goes back unbroken to Westminster, is to maintain that in fact the Statute of Westminster itself cut the line from Westminster to Capetown, that the painter was cut, so to speak, at the Westminster end. This view of the effect of the Statute of Westminster is held by some in South Africa.[47] It is maintained that the effect of the Statute of Westminster was to renounce for ever the power of the parliament of the United Kingdom to make laws for South Africa and at the same time to give to the parliament of the Union full power to make laws for South Africa. This took away the British quality from at least all future acts of the Union parliament and enabled it to create an entirely South African constitution. On this view of the effect of the Statute of Westminster, South African nationalism could be satisfied with a constitution either re-enacted by the Union parliament or, if it was thought proper, submitted to the people in a referendum on the authority of the Union parliament. There is no need to make a break in continuity on the Indian or Irish model; the break was made in 1931 by the Statute of Westminster.

In Canada there has been some discussion of ways in which the constitution could come formally under Canadian control, and in particular of the appropriate amending powers which might take the place of the present reference of certain amendments to Westminster. Professor F. R. Scott suggested[48] that if

[47] 'There is little doubt that in the eyes of the South African courts the Statute of Westminster has resulted in a formal break in the continuity of the South African legal system. . . .' D. V. Cowen, 15 *Modern Law Review* (1952) at p. 294, n. 47. See also at p. 292.

[48] 'The Redistribution of Imperial Sovereignty' in *Transactions of the Royal Society of Canada*, xliv (ser. 3, s. 2, 1950), 33–34.

Canada was to end once and for all her legal dependence on the
United Kingdom, there should be enacted a Canadian Indepen-
dence Act by the United Kingdom parliament, at the request of
Canada. This act would recite that

as from the 'appointed day' (which might well be July 1 so as to
coincide with an existing national holiday) the new constitution of
Canada would take effect and thereafter all jurisdiction heretofore
vested in the Parliament of the United Kingdom in and over Canada
would cease. The constitution itself would contain a declaration of
sovereignty in the Canadian people and a provision that no United
Kingdom statutes would in future have the force of law in Canada
unless adopted by the Canadian parliament.

In this proposal, once more, there lies the difficulty—for
those who find it a difficulty—that the new constitution takes
effect in virtue of an act of the British parliament and although
all authority is thereafter renounced, and the painter is cut from
the Westminster end, the fact remains that it was by the action
of the parliament at Westminster that this situation has come
to pass. In the Canadian proposal, as in the South African, the
turning of the constitution into a Canadian or a South African
document is by the grace or the authority or the self-denial or
the renunciation of the United Kingdom. Surely, it might be
said, no more is required. If it is abdication—and in the South
African and Canadian views it would be—thereafter the constitutions are rooted in the native soil.

But with the examples of India and Ireland in mind, it will
not be surprising if nationalism demands even greater certainty.
If this is to be achieved, then some break of legal continuity
must be made. There are various methods by which this can be
done. The simplest perhaps is for the houses of the parliament
in the Member of the Commonwealth to prepare and pass a constitution and not to present it for the royal assent, providing in
the document that it should come into effect on a certain date
and supersede the existing constitution. Or a specially elected
or selected constituent assembly might prepare and pass the
constitution and provided it did not do so under powers conferred by an act of the legislature which had received the royal
assent, and did not submit the constitution for the royal assent,
then it could claim that the constitution was enacted on its
own authority. Or a constitution, prepared by the houses of a

parliament or by a constituent assembly, could be submitted for the approval of the people and could come into effect subject to that approval. And there are a number of other procedures that might appropriately be adopted. The essential point underlying all of them is that such action as is taken must not be taken under the authority of an act of parliament of the United Kingdom. What procedure would be appropriate would depend upon political conditions in the Commonwealth country concerned. It is clear, however, that a simple method of making the break— the refraining from presenting the measure for the royal assent —is available which allows for full consultation with the electorate or with elected representatives, and with minority interests and which could be combined with any procedure for the preparation of the document which was thought necessary in the country concerned.

At the same time some arrangement would have to be made to ensure that the courts would accept this new constitution, to avoid the difficulties that might arise if they acted as the Federal Court of Pakistan acted in 1955. Here the Irish constitution offers a useful suggestion. Article 34 provides that every judge shall, on appointment, make a declaration to uphold the constitution and the laws and that any judge who declines to do so shall be deemed to have vacated his office. A provision of this kind, or alternatively a provision that the question of the validity of the constitution should not be entertained in any court, or both, would surely suffice to remove difficulties.

At the same time it should be emphasized that this procedure does not involve a Member of the Commonwealth in ceasing to be a part of the Queen's realms, or in becoming a republic, nor does it necessarily involve the invocation of the people as a legislator. Although these steps were taken by India, they are not essential to the process of establishing a constitution which does not derive its authority from Westminster. While Canada, Australia, and New Zealand, therefore, might wish to establish their own home-grown constitution, they are not required to take the further steps of ceasing to be one of the Queen's realms —a step which, on the other hand, might appeal to South Africa, Ghana, or Ceylon.

And although traditionalists may regret the breaking of a legal link, which in practice means very little, nationalists will welcome a step which places their country's constitution and laws on a footing comparable to that enjoyed by the other sovereign independent states in the world. It must be expected, therefore, that Members of the Commonwealth will, as a rule, take steps quite soon after they achieve their independence through a constitution made in Britain, to embody that constitution and proclaim that independence in a document which they can claim owes its validity and authority to no outside country or institution but to themselves alone.

V · MEMBERSHIP

I

In the report of the Imperial Conference of 1926 the United Kingdom, Canada, Australia, New Zealand, South Africa, Newfoundland, and the Irish Free State described themselves as 'freely associated as Members of the British Commonwealth of Nations'.[1] While nobody at the time questioned the meaning of the term 'Member', nobody questioned the right of these countries in the Empire to call themselves 'Members' if they chose. In the years that have intervened, however, the meaning of membership of the Commonwealth has had to be investigated. What is involved in membership? How do you become a Member? How do you cease to be a Member? Who decides these things? The answers to these questions are by no means certain. In this chapter an attempt is made to set out some of the considerations that are involved.

It may be useful to begin by asking what were the characteristics which the original Members of the Commonwealth exhibited. The first was equality of status, their being in no way subordinate to the United Kingdom or to each other. By this characteristic they were marked off from the other countries in the British Empire. If you were a subordinate country in the Empire, then you were not a Member of the Commonwealth.

But while equality of status marked Members off from other countries in the Empire, it did not mark them off from other independent countries outside the Empire. If Canada was equal in status to the United Kingdom, so also was the United States. Equality of status merely placed these countries of the Empire on an equal footing with other sovereign, independent states. Membership involved something more than this. The second characteristic of Members was that, again in the words of the Report of 1926, they were 'within the British Empire'. As a consequence of this, or as an illustration of it, they described themselves as 'united by a common allegiance to the Crown'. By this characteristic they were marked off from foreign coun-

[1] Cmd. 2768, p. 14.

tries. What precisely was meant by 'common allegiance to the Crown' it was not easy to say. At the least it meant that government was carried on in each of the Members in the name of the King; their governments were His Majesty's governments. 'Allegiance' was a legal concept, and it had a place of particular importance in regard to questions of citizenship and to the law of treason. What it involved for the citizens of a Member was regulated, however, by the law of that Member.

The two characteristics of membership so far described would probably have been enough in the years after 1926 to enable someone to decide whether a country was a Member of the Commonwealth or not. Was the country within the British Empire, that is, did its citizens owe allegiance to the Crown? If so—and it would not always be easy to answer this question— is the country in no way subordinate to other countries in the Commonwealth?

There were, however, two other characteristics which Members exhibited. The first is a development which seems to have grown out of the declaration of common allegiance to the Crown, but it is distinct from it. It finds its expression in the preamble to the Statute of Westminster in words that were adopted by all the Members of the Commonwealth at the Imperial Conference of 1930: 'Inasmuch as the Crown is the symbol of the free association of the Members of the British Commonwealth of Nations, and as they are united by a common allegiance to the Crown. . . .' Here are two distinct ideas. The idea of common allegiance is mentioned separately; but, in addition to it, is the idea of the Crown as a symbol of the free association of the Members. This latter idea does not involve common allegiance in the legal sense of that word. All Members might accept the Crown as a symbol of their association—just as they might accept a flag or a flower—but not all might embody in their law the notion of allegiance to the Crown. And what did Crown mean? Did it mean what the King wore on his head or did it mean the King or did it mean the King acting on the advice of ministers or what? The answers to these questions were far from clear. The important point was that a distinction had been made between allegiance to the Crown and the Crown as a symbol of the association, though the importance of this distinction was not obvious at the time it was made.

A final characteristic of Members was that they were under an obligation to co-operate, or, as the Report of 1926 put it, 'free co-operation is its instrument'. How far this obligation extended is a separate question,[2] but that the Members were expected to co-operate is undoubted. It was as much a mark of membership as was equality of status, common allegiance, and the acceptance of the Crown as the symbol of association. It showed itself in membership, above all, of the Imperial Conference, the institution where the opportunity was offered for co-operation at the highest level.[3]

2

In the years that have passed since the Report of 1926 and the enactment of the Statute of Westminster, some modifications have been introduced into the meaning of membership. Yet a great deal of what was fundamental in 1926 still remains fundamental now. What makes a country eligible for membership of the Commonwealth now?

In the first place an essential prerequisite is equality of status, that is to say independence. No country is eligible unless it is fully self-governing. But what about allegiance? Must it now be able to claim that it owes allegiance to the Crown? The answer is No. It was placed beyond doubt when in 1949 the Members of the Commonwealth decided that India might continue to be a Member although it proposed to adopt a republican constitution in which the notion of allegiance to the Crown formed no part. It might be argued that the Members of the Commonwealth had gone some way towards this position when in 1937 they decided that Eire's adoption of a new constitution which contained no explicit reference to the Crown and under which scarcely any notion of allegiance to the Crown could be found, did not effect a fundamental alteration in the position of Eire as a Member of the Commonwealth.[4]

But while allegiance has disappeared as a test of eligibility,

[2] See Chap. VI.
[3] But membership of the Imperial Conference was not a distinguishing characteristic of Members of the Commonwealth, for India and Southern Rhodesia attended these meetings and they both lacked equality of status.
[4] Statement issued on 24 Dec. 1937. Printed in Mansergh, *Documents and Speeches on British Commonwealth Affairs*, vol. i, pp. 366-7.

the notion of the Crown as the symbol of the free association of Members has not. For in 1949 India 'declared and affirmed' her 'desire to continue her full membership of the Commonwealth of Nations and her acceptance of the King as the symbol of the free association of its independent member nations and as such the Head of the Commonwealth'. A full discussion of the implications of this symbol of association in the Commonwealth is undertaken in a later chapter.[5] It is enough to note here that one of the marks of a Member of the Commonwealth today is that it accepts the Crown or the Queen—both terms are used— as a symbol of its association with other Members. This is the position of all the Members, but some also owe allegiance to the Crown—whatever in law that may mean for each Member's citizens—as, for example, Australia, Canada, New Zealand, South Africa, Ceylon, and Ghana.[6] India, Pakistan, and Malaya, however, recognize the Queen only as a symbol of their association with the other Members in the Commonwealth.

The third condition of eligibility is the acceptance of the obligation to co-operate. It is interesting to notice that in 1936 when the Irish Free State was defining its relation to the monarchy, it described the King as the symbol not of the association of the nations of the Commonwealth but of their co-operation.[7] Though this is exceptional, it is clear that the obligation to co-operate is one of the things which membership involves. It was reiterated in 1949, for example, when India's republican constitution was envisaged and again in 1956 when Pakistan's republican constitution was similarly considered, by Members of the Commonwealth declaring themselves to be 'freely co-operating in the pursuit of peace, liberty and progress'.

A country is eligible for membership of the Commonwealth, therefore, if it has equality of status, if it is ready to accept the Queen as the symbol of its association, and if it is ready to accept

[5] Chap. VII.

[6] The last three have already announced their intention to become republics in due course.

[7] Mr. Costello, then in opposition, was quick to point out in the Dáil, during the debate on the legislation, that the Members of the Commonwealth did not recognize the Crown as the symbol of their co-operation but of their association. It was a debating point but none the less a point. See extract from his speech (64 Dáil Debates, cols. 1432–40) printed in Mansergh, op. cit., vol. i, p. 328.

the obligation to co-operate with the other Members. Is that all? Is there any requirement about form of government? Must Members be parliamentary democracies or at least striving to become parliamentary democracies? Can a dictatorship be a Member of the Commonwealth? The answer to this is that there is in fact no prerequisite laid down about the form of government which would or would not make a country eligible for membership. It is clear, of course, that its form of government must be such that it could claim to have equality of status or independence, and that it could accept the Queen as a symbol and that it could co-operate. But except in so far as these conditions for eligibility affect a form of government, no hard and fast rule is laid down. That is not to say that certain forms of government make co-operation easier or harder for Members or that it would be improper or impolitic for Members to take into consideration the form of government in a country before admitting it to membership. These are indeed most important considerations. So far, however, no rules on these subjects have been adopted. And indeed Pakistan continues as a Member of the Commonwealth, though its form of government is not parliamentary to say the least.

Or again, is one condition of eligibility that the country seeking membership shall already be within the Commonwealth, though not a Member of it? Can new Members come from outside? The answer to this is that up to now all Members of the Commonwealth have attained membership after a period as dependent countries of the Commonwealth. They have grown up to adult status. And there are good reasons for saying that Members so recruited are likely to be good Members. But there is no rule laid down which would prevent the introduction into the Commonwealth of new Members from outside, provided, of course, that they fulfilled the three criteria of eligibility already mentioned. Whether in general or in a particular case new Members from outside would be desirable is a political question of very great importance. From the point of view of the constitutional structure of the Commonwealth it is not excluded.

It is sometimes asked if a Member of the Commonwealth could continue to be a Member if it joined itself with a foreign country. Discussion of the subject arose from reports of a proposed closer association of Ghana and Guinea. On the existing rules of the Commonwealth, the answer is clear. If a Member joined with a foreign country in a union so close that the Member ceased to be a separate independent country, then it could no longer be a Member of the Commonwealth. It would lack equality of status or independence. If, therefore, Ghana and Guinea, say, formed a federal union and established a common government responsible for their external affairs and relations with other states, Ghana would no longer be a separate, independent state, and consequently no longer eligible to be a Member of the Commonwealth. If, on the other hand, Ghana and Guinea formed a loose confederation or league, under which, by whatever name it was called, each country maintained relations with other states, then Ghana undoubtedly would be eligible to continue as a Member of the Commonwealth. A very close association of the two states, with joint arrangements for defence, economic development, and external affairs might prove compatible with Ghana's membership of the Commonwealth. The test to apply, undoubtedly, would be whether, as a result of the arrangements, Ghana was still an independent state.

The question whether, if Ghana and Guinea formed a federation, say, under a common government, the Union of Ghana and Guinea could become a Member of the Commonwealth is, of course, a different matter. It would be a new state, it would be independent, and if it were willing to accept the obligations of membership, then its admission would be considered upon the same footing as that of any other country outside the Commonwealth.

Although the question has been discussed in terms of Ghana and Guinea, the same principles apply, of course, to any proposal that the United Kingdom, for example, should join a European federation. If it became a state in a European federation and ceased to be an independent country, it could not continue to be a Member of the Commonwealth. But a looser link with European states would clearly be compatible with continued membership of the Commonwealth. These, it must be emphasized, are the qualifications for membership as they now stand. But new situations and new needs would bring new rules. For in the Commonwealth, Members decide what they want to do, and then bring the rules up to date.

3

Granted then that a country is eligible for membership of the Commonwealth, and that it is willing to become a Member and to accept the symbol and the obligations of Members, what happens?[8] How does it get in? The short answer is that a country can become a Member of the Commonwealth if the other Members agree to accept it as such. A few points should be made in this connexion.

First of all it is not enough that a country, even a country in the Commonwealth, should be eligible and willing for membership. It is necessary also for the other Members to agree to admit it to membership. This means that a country in the Commonwealth might achieve equality of status with the United Kingdom, and all the other Members, by the conferring upon it of full self-government but that it would not become a Member of the Commonwealth unless the other Members admitted it. If they did not admit it, then the country would be an independent nation within the Commonwealth but not a Member of it. This possibility was not immediately foreseen in the years after 1926. It was more or less taken for granted that as the countries of the Commonwealth advanced to self-government, they would automatically become Members. If any doubts were cast upon this idea, they arose from a fear that these countries when they became independent might not wish to remain in the Commonwealth. They might want to leave it, as, for example, did Burma upon the grant of independence in 1948. There was a tendency to assume that if a country obtained independence and wished to remain in the Commonwealth, all other Members would be delighted to have it as a Member.

Misgivings started to arise, however, when the possibility began to be seen of independence being granted to Commonwealth countries in Africa, and in particular over the case of Ghana. The Union of South Africa doubted the wisdom of the policy of the United Kingdom in granting independence to African countries and raised the question whether it was proper for one Member of the Commonwealth alone to present others with the *fait accompli* of an independent Commonwealth

[8] See some interesting observations by S. A. de Smith in an article on the independence of Ghana, 20 *Modern Law Review* (1957), pp. 352 ff.

country claiming to be recognized as a Member of the Commonwealth. If this went on, would not the United Kingdom alone
be determining who the new Members of the Commonwealth
were to be, and was not this a matter for all the Members to
determine? The point was valid, and it was accepted by the
United Kingdom.

Some remarks by Dr. Malan, the Prime Minister of South
Africa, express the point strongly. He said:

Well, here we encounter a preposterous absurdity in existing
Commonwealth relations. The Commonwealth is a closed group,
all free and equal, and consequently one would expect that with the
admission of new Members all would also have an equal say, because
such a development might affect the whole being and character of
the group. But what do we find? Acting of her own accord and
without consultation with or approval of the other group Members,
England recently added India, Pakistan and Ceylon to the Commonwealth; and now she intends to continue the process without
limitation. As colonies, the territories do indeed belong to England,
but as potential Members of the Commonwealth, there are others
who are equally concerned with their position and who ought to
have an equal say as to whether they should be admitted. This absurdity should be resolved without further delay.[9]

The attitude of the United Kingdom was expressed in an
answer by Mr. P. C. Gordon-Walker, Secretary of State for
Commonwealth Relations, to a question in the House of Commons, on 7 June 1951.[10] He said:

Whilst the United Kingdom government alone carry the responsibility for internal constitutional developments in Colonies dependent upon the United Kingdom, we recognise the interest of the
governments of other Members of the Commonwealth, and it is
our practice to keep them informed of major developments in that
sphere. Were any question of admission to full and independent
membership of the Commonwealth to arise, all existing Members
would, following past practice, be consulted. . . . We must make
quite clear the distinction between the grant of responsible self-
government within the Commonwealth, which is a matter for the
United Kingdom government and the territory concerned, and for

[9] Statement made at Capetown on 23 Feb. 1951 and published in *Die Burger*
on 24 Feb. Reprinted in Mansergh, op. cit., vol. ii, pp. 1287–8.
[10] 488 *H.C. Deb.* 5 s., col. 1199. Reprinted in Mansergh, op. cit., vol. ii,
pp. 1288–9.

them alone, and the question of becoming a full Member of the Commonwealth, which is of course a matter for all Members of the Commonwealth. All steps towards responsible self-government within the Commonwealth are a matter between us and the territory concerned, and we must make that distinction quite clear and abide by it.[11]

How does this distinction work? There can be no doubt that so far as the admission of India, Pakistan, and Ceylon to full membership was concerned, the existing Members of the Commonwealth were consulted and gave their assent. Statements were made in June 1947 on behalf of the governments of Canada, Australia, New Zealand, and South Africa[12] welcoming the proposals made by the United Kingdom to grant independence to India.[13] And again at the Conference of Prime Ministers in 1949 there was the explicit declaration by the other members that they 'accept and recognise India's continuing membership in accordance with the terms of this declaration'. The same statement was made at the Conference of Prime Ministers in 1955 concerning Pakistan's membership of the Commonwealth when it should become a republic. Moreover the approach of India towards full membership was a long and familiar process, foreshadowed in the declaration by Mr. Montagu, Secretary of State for India in 1917, when he spoke of 'the progressive realisation of self-government in India as an integral part of the British Empire'. India had been a member of the Imperial Conference since those days and there had been plenty of opportunities for other Members of the Commonwealth to express their views about her constitutional development had they wished to do so.

Consultation was carried out similarly in the case of Ceylon and the final grant of independence was recognized and approved by the Conference of Prime Ministers in 1948 when they took the opportunity to record 'their recognition of Ceylon's independence and to affirm that Ceylon enjoys the same sovereign independent status as the other self-governing

[11] Similar statements were made by Mr. Churchill as Prime Minister on 16 June 1952 (502 *H.C. Deb.* 5 s., cols. 778–80); by the Minister of State at the Colonial Office, Mr. Hopkinson, on 28 Apr. 1954 (526 *H.C. Deb.* 5 s., cols. 1625–6); and by the Under-Secretary of State for Commonwealth Relations, Lord John Hope, on 11 Dec. 1956 (562 *H.C. Deb.* 5 s., cols. 239–40).

[12] General Smuts was Prime Minister at the time.

[13] Extracts are reprinted in Mansergh, op. cit., vol. ii, pp. 702–5.

countries of the Commonwealth which are members of the United Nations'.[14] Again in 1956 when Ceylon expressed its intention to adopt a republican form of government, and its wish to remain a Member of the Commonwealth thereafter, Members of the Commonwealth were consulted and expressed their acceptance of republican Ceylon as a Member of the Commonwealth in the future.

At the same time it is not at all clear that in the granting of independence to India, Pakistan, and Ceylon, there was necessarily any full and constant consultation between the United Kingdom and the other Members, nor that they were asked specifically in advance whether they consented to the admission of the independent countries to membership. It was perhaps assumed that, if they did not raise objections, they would consent. On some matters such as, for example, the defence arrangements made between Ceylon and the United Kingdom, it would seem that some particularly interested Members—Australia and New Zealand—were fully consulted beforehand and their agreement obtained.[15] But whatever may have been the procedure, it was clear that with the prospect of independence being granted to the Gold Coast, South Africa at least was uneasy, and Dr. Malan perhaps regretted the decisions that had been taken in 1947 about India, Pakistan, and Ceylon. It was not surprising, therefore, that when, in 1956, Mr. Lennox Boyd, Secretary of State for the Colonies, announced the terms upon which independence would be granted to the Gold Coast, he was careful to make a distinction between the grant of independence and the grant of membership of the Commonwealth. 'If a general election is held,' he said, 'Her Majesty's government will be ready to accept a motion calling for independence within the Commonwealth passed by a reasonable majority in a newly elected legislature and then to declare a firm date for this purpose. Full membership of the Commonwealth is, of course, a different question, and is a matter for consultation between all existing Members of the Commonwealth.'[16]

In the outcome consultation between the existing Members led to agreement that Ghana should be accepted as a Member

[14] Mansergh, ibid., vol. ii, p. 759.
[15] See Lord Addison's statement, 152 H.L. Deb. 5 s., col. 1205.
[16] 11 May 1956, 552 H.C. Deb. 5 s., col. 1558.

of the Commonwealth,[17] and in the communiqué issued after a meeting of Commonwealth Prime Ministers, held in London from 26 June to 5 July 1957, it was recorded that the conference welcomed the admission of Ghana as a full Member of the Commonwealth. Agreement was reached similarly to the conferment of full membership on Malaya when later in 1957 it would obtain independence. The process of consultation had produced unanimous consent.

4

But what is the rule? Is it necessary to obtain the unanimous consent of existing Members of the Commonwealth before a new Member can be admitted? In the statements that have been quoted so far from United Kingdom sources, it will be noted that 'consent' is not mentioned. All that is mentioned is 'consultation'. Nothing has been said about whether unanimity is required or whether a majority will do or whether one white ball will exclude. And nothing official has ever been laid down on this point by Members of the Commonwealth. All that is laid down is the obligation to consult.

If we want to investigate the subject further we must approach it from a different point of view. Oddly enough, some light on the rules (if there be any) regulating the admission of new Members to the Commonwealth can be gained by considering the rules (if there are any) regulating the secession of old Members from the Commonwealth. What is the position about this? For a long time after 1926 there was uncertainty about whether Members of the Commonwealth had or had not the right to secede. They had described themselves as 'freely associated'. Surely that must mean that they were free, if they wished it, to dissociate. Or did it mean no more than that of their own free will they had agreed to associate but that there was in fact no right or power to divorce? Any doubt that remained was removed, so far at any rate as the United Kingdom was concerned, when in 1944 Sir Stafford Cripps took to India a plan for the conferment of Dominion Status on India at the end of the war. In the course of his discussion of the plan at

[17] Announcement by Mr. Macmillan, Prime Minister of the United Kingdom, 565 H.C. Deb. 5 s., col. 605.

a press conference in New Delhi, he was asked by a reporter: 'Will the Indian Union be entitled to disown its allegiance to the Crown?' He replied: 'Yes. In order that there should be no possibility of doubt, we have inserted in the last sentence of paragraph (c) (ii) the statement: "but will not impose any restriction on the power of the Indian Union to decide in the future its relations to the other member States of the British Commonwealth." The Dominion will be completely free either to remain within or to go without the Commonwealth of Nations.'[18]

When later the term independence came to be used to describe the status of the new Dominions of India, Pakistan, and Ceylon, it was clear that the right to secede must be recognized as part of this status. And the legal powers granted to the new Members of the Commonwealth obviously extended to the enactment of an act of secession if they chose to do so. Though the legal measures necessary in each Member of the Commonwealth would differ in detail (and might perhaps involve in the case of Australia or Canada the assistance of the parliament of the United Kingdom) it is accepted that part of the status of membership of the Commonwealth is a unilateral right to secede.

How does this affect the procedure for admitting new Members to the Commonwealth? It means that if an existing Member is unwilling to accept a proposed new Member and votes against it, it is at liberty, if it wishes, to leave the Commonwealth. Other Members must decide whether they prefer to lose an existing Member or to lose a prospective Member, bearing in mind that if an independent Commonwealth country is refused membership, it will probably decide itself to leave the Commonwealth. The existing Members have a sanction in their threat to secede; so have the prospective new Members. It would be possible, therefore, for a new Member to be admitted to the Commonwealth by a majority vote, on the understanding that the Member or Members who objected to the proposed new Member could, if they chose, secede from the Commonwealth. It would not be necessary for them to do so logically; they could content themselves with registering their dissent and accept the majority decision. If, however, this did not suit them, secession is available to them. There is, therefore, considerable reason for

[18] Recorded in Sir R. Coupland, *The Cripps Mission*, p. 31.

Members of the Commonwealth to consult each other about proposed new Members so that unanimity may be achieved,[19] but at the same time it is open to Members to argue that the loss of one existing Member (say) is a small price to pay for the acquisition of several new Members.

The notion of an independent Commonwealth country remaining in the Commonwealth if it ceased to be or failed to become a Member is probably unlikely to be of practical importance. As, however, the distinction between independence within the Commonwealth and membership has been drawn, it is worth noticing certain possibilities. Thus a country like Canada could conceivably, as a result of its disagreement with the other Members of the Commonwealth, declare that it wished no longer to be a Member, but at the same time that it wished to preserve its link with the Queen, to remain a kingdom and one of the Queen's Realms. It would, in these circumstances, surely be within the Commonwealth, and a Commonwealth country. It would not, however, recognize for itself the Queen as the Head of the Commonwealth, for the Queen as Head of the Commonwealth is the symbol of the free association of its independent Member nations, and that for Canada, in these circumstances, would not be applicable. So also if a Commonwealth country was granted independence and wished to continue to be one of the Queen's Realms but was refused admission as a Member of the Commonwealth, it could, if it wished, remain within the Commonwealth, recognizing the Queen as the head of its government but not as Head of the Commonwealth. Put shortly, while existing Members of the Commonwealth may say that an independent Commonwealth country cannot be a Commonwealth Member they may not say that it cannot be a Commonwealth country. Only the independent country itself may do that.

[19] It would seem most important that consultation should occur well in advance of the grant of independence. Consultation, to be effective, must be full and prior. Yet the words of the government spokesman in the House of Commons in the discussion on the Ghana Independence Bill suggest that consultation with other Members about the admission of Ghana as a Member would be undertaken after the passing of the bill (562 *H.C. Deb.* 5 s., cols. 239–40). It may be presumed that he was referring to a formal approach to other Members. S. A. de Smith concluded from this statement that the United Kingdom 'was clearly of the opinion that consultation was not obligatory before the Bill became law'. 20 *Modern Law Review* (1957), pp. 353–4.

5

But is there not a big assumption concealed here? If there is a right of secession, is there not also a right of expulsion? Cannot the Members of the Commonwealth rid themselves of a Member of whom they disapprove? It is not quite clear, and there has, of course, been no official agreement upon the subject. But it would seem likely that Members could declare that in future some existing Member would no longer be recognized by them as a Member. The consequence would be that they would no longer feel obliged to co-operate with the 'expelled' Member and that they would not invite it to take part in the Commonwealth institutions such as the Prime Ministers' Conference through which co-operation is carried out. It is true that the 'expelled' Member could refuse to admit that it was expelled and could claim that it remained a Member of the Commonwealth and continued to recognize the Queen as the symbol of its association as a Member with the other Members. The situation might be ridiculous, but it would not on that account necessarily prove unworkable. Moreover, the 'expelled' Member, if it was a realm of the Queen, would continue to be within the Commonwealth.

Yet it may be doubted whether in fact existing Members have the right strictly speaking to expel another Member. They might achieve their object, perhaps, by themselves seceding from the existing Commonwealth and forming a new Commonwealth, without the 'objectionable' Member, and leaving the excluded Member to be the sole Member of the old Commonwealth. In the outcome there could be two Commonwealths with the Queen as Head of both.

Though these speculations may seem fanciful, they are not really inconceivable, nor are the issues which they raise unimportant. Their importance can be appreciated better perhaps if one recalls that differences of opinion between Members of the Commonwealth can be acute and it is by no means to be assumed that, if talk of expulsion arose, it would be a simple question of all Members save one being in agreement and that one being liable to expulsion. A much more evenly balanced division might occur, and two rival parties might claim themselves to be and to form the true Commonwealth. What is certain, however, is that these questions are susceptible more of political than of legal or constitutional treatment.

VI · CO-OPERATION

I

THE Members of the Commonwealth declared in the Report of the Imperial Conference in 1926 that 'free co-operation is its instrument'. This statement is as true today as it was in 1926. It should be remembered that this instrument is not that which Lionel Curtis favoured when he advocated the idea and adopted the name of a 'Commonwealth'. His aim was federation, and the instrument of a federation is a government with power to decide and to execute in matters of common concern. Co-operation falls far short of government. When federation was rejected, however, co-operation between sovereign, independent states was the most that could be expected.

Co-operation is a vague, loose word. It is customary, in the discussion of Commonwealth affairs, to use along with it 'communication' and 'consultation'.[1] It is perhaps worth while to say something about the meaning of these terms. 'Co-operation' is the widest; it means working or acting together. It implies freedom on the part of those who act or work together; co-operation is usually thought of as voluntary co-operation. This is certainly the meaning attached to it in the case of Members of the Commonwealth.

Acting or working together can occur at various stages. It is possible to agree that you will work together to the extent of exchanging information with each other on matters of common concern. This may well be described as 'communication'. Or you may go further than this and agree not merely to tell each other what you know and what you are doing or proposing to do but also to ask each other's opinion about it. This may well be described as 'consultation'. It is clear that 'consultation' involves some degree of 'communication', but that communication may well occur without consultation following upon it. Finally there may be an agreement to go further than the

---

[1] See, for example, Heather J. Harvey, *Consultation and Co-operation in the Commonwealth*; and *Report of the Imperial Committee on Economic Consultation and Co-operation, 1933*, Cmd. 4335.

exchange of information and consultation about it; it may be agreed that the parties may take action in common, either by negotiating together with some foreign country, or by administering some activity together. It is always implied in this that the parties have voluntarily agreed to administer or negotiate together and that they are free at any time to withdraw and that they are not bound by the outcome of their co-operative action any further than they have agreed in advance to be bound.

Co-operation may then be used to cover a wide range of action taken together by the parties concerned. Communication and consultation are examples of co-operation; they are not different from it. And in this chapter 'co-operation' is thought to cover all examples of working together by Members of the Commonwealth, including especially communication and consultation.

When the Members of the Commonwealth in 1926 chose free co-operation as their instrument, they were rejecting two methods of achieving co-ordination or common action which were conceivable. One had already been used and was available —action through the parliament and government of the United Kingdom. Members could have decided that they would meet together and decide upon a common line of action and that this line would be carried through by the government or parliament of the United Kingdom. On the other hand was the alternative of a federal government, in which each Member would have been represented, and through whose executive and legislature decisions would have been carried out. Neither alternative was acceptable, for it conflicted with the decision and determination of each Member to be independent and sovereign and to carry out its decisions through its own government and parliament.

2

How far, then, are Members of the Commonwealth obliged to co-operate?[2] Are there any rules or understandings about this

---

[2] The exposition which follows is based upon resolutions of Imperial Conferences, Prime Ministers' meetings, and other Commonwealth conferences. Strictly speaking the conventions bind only those Members which were represented at the conferences and agreed to them. At those held before 1947, India,

subject? We may start with communication or the exchange of information. Here, it was already laid down in 1926 that Members of the Commonwealth would exchange information with each other on any matter of common concern. And, secondly, it was agreed that Members would consult each other on matters of common concern, and that each Member had a right to be consulted. Specific reference was made to certain spheres in which communication or consultation would be necessary. Thus, so far as legislation was concerned, it was laid down in the Report of 1926 that 'the appropriate procedure with regard to projected legislation in one of the self-governing parts of the Empire which may affect the interests of other self-govern-ing parts is previous consultation between His Majesty's Minis-ters in the several parts concerned'.[3] And again in 1930 the Imperial Conference discussed the need for uniformity in regard to such matters as merchant shipping or nationality among Members of the Commonwealth and resolved that no change should be made in the law relating to these subjects without previous consultation between Members. In discussing nation-ality, for example, the conference resolved 'that steps should be taken as soon as possible by consultation among the various governments to arrive at a settlement of the problems involved on the basis of these principles'.[4] 'With regard to such subjects as fugitive offenders', they added, 'foreign enlistment and extra-dition in certain of its aspects, we recommend that before any alteration is made in the existing law there should be prior con-sultation and, so far as possible, agreement.'

In the field of foreign affairs, similarly, the obligation to com-municate and consult was accepted.

It was agreed in 1923 [said the Report of 1926[5]] that any of the Governments of the Empire contemplating the negotiation of a

Pakistan, Ceylon, Ghana, and Malaya were not present, or not present as full Members. Ceylon, upon becoming a Member in 1948, formally declared its readiness to adopt and follow the resolutions of past Imperial Conferences (Cmd. 7257; see W. I. Jennings, *The Constitution of Ceylon* (3rd ed.), pp. 252 ff. for a full exposition of what was involved). Other Members of the Commonwealth are tacitly assumed to have taken on the obligations of mem-bership, but there is inevitably some doubt about how far they regard them-selves as bound by resolutions passed before they were Members.

[3] Cmd. 2768, pp. 17–18.
[4] Cmd. 3479, paras. 74 ff., adopted in Cmd. 3717.
[5] Cmd. 2768, p. 22 and Cmd. 3717 (1930), p. 28.

treaty should give due consideration to its possible effect upon other Governments and should take steps to inform Governments likely to be interested of its intention. This rule should be understood as applying to any negotiations which any Government intends to conduct, so as to leave it to the other Governments to say whether they are likely to be interested.

There is throughout great stress upon the need for full information and prior information if consultation is to be a reality. These rules were based at first upon experience which the Dominions had had of inadequate opportunities for consultation on the part of the United Kingdom, but they came to be applicable to the actions of other Members of the Commonwealth, when they began to exercise their powers and rights as independent states.

In one matter the Members of the Commonwealth positively resolved that no alteration should be made in the law without the assent of the parliaments of all the other Members. This was in connexion with the law touching the succession to the Throne and the Royal Style and Titles concerning which it was declared in the Preamble to the Statute of Westminster, after approval by the Imperial Conference of 1930 and by the parliaments of all the Dominions concerned, that 'any alteration in the law touching the succession to the Throne or the Royal Style and Titles shall hereafter require the assent as well of the parliaments of all the Dominions as of the parliament of the United Kingdom'.[6] It is to be noted that this declaration is a convention; it is not law. It does not prevent a Member of the Commonwealth from altering the law on these matters and any such alteration would not fail to be of full legal effect because the assent of other parliaments had not been obtained. This, however, is just one illustration of the basis upon which the obligation to co-operate in the Commonwealth exists—it is voluntary; it is not legally required or enforceable; it is a convention to co-operate to the extent and by the methods which each Member has voluntarily accepted for itself.

Another example of arrangements by which consultation is achieved is that of the admission of the stocks of Commonwealth Members to the list of trustee securities in the United Kingdom.[7]

[6] See Chap. VII for a further discussion of this passage.
[7] See Chap. II above.

The interesting point of this arrangement is that it is secured by joint legislation in the Members concerned. The United Kingdom has agreed that it will admit the stocks of a Commonwealth Member to the trustee list if the Member has undertaken in an act of its parliament to consult the United Kingdom before submitting for the royal assent any legislation by the Member which appears to the United Kingdom to alter any of the provisions affecting the stock to the injury of the stock holders or to involve a departure from the original contract, and to make any such amendments in the legislation as may be requested by the United Kingdom.[8]

Now this arrangement leaves the Member concerned free to enact what legislation it pleases about its stocks. All that has been agreed is that if it wishes its stocks to be on the trustee list of the United Kingdom, then it must consult the United Kingdom about the changes it proposes to make and it must conform to the wishes of the United Kingdom about the terms of the legislation. If it does not do this, then the United Kingdom is not obliged to place these stocks on the trustee list. Failure to consult involves a sanction; a procedure is prescribed through which consultation can take place. But there is nothing in law to prevent the Member taking what action it pleases. And it is open to a Member, if it chooses, to impose similar conditions upon legislation about securities by other Members of the Commonwealth.

3

Has the obligation of Members of the Commonwealth to co-operate gone beyond the stages of communication and consultation? Have they agreed to undertake co-operative decision or co-operative administration in any sphere? The answer to this question is that the Members have in fact established certain institutions for co-operative administration, but that the institutions which they administer co-operatively in fact do no more than provide opportunities for communication and consultation. The existence of these institutions illustrates the fact that, so far, the Members of the Commonwealth have refused to undertake an obligation to co-operate beyond the stage of

[8] Colonial Stock Act, 1934, 24 & 25 Geo. V, c. 47, s. 1.

consultation. They may in particular cases administer together; in war and in peace they have decided and executed policies co-operatively, and with a co-ordination and unity as great as or greater than that shown by federations of comparable size. But these are *ad hoc* arrangements. No standing convention of co-operative decision and administration has been adopted.

The co-operatively administered institutions are almost all in the United Kingdom. They are normally financed by a contribution from each Member on an agreed basis, and they are administered by a governing body upon which each Member is represented. There is, for example, the Executive Council of the Commonwealth Agricultural Bureaux which administers the Commonwealth Institute of Entomology, the Commonwealth Mycological Institute, the Commonwealth Institute of Biological Control (which is in Ottawa), the Commonwealth Bureau of Animal Breeding and Genetics, the Commonwealth Bureau of Animal Health, the Commonwealth Bureau of Animal Nutrition, the Commonwealth Bureau of Dairy Science and Technology, the Commonwealth Forestry Bureau, the Commonwealth Bureau of Helminthology, the Commonwealth Bureau of Horticulture and Plantation Crops, the Commonwealth Bureau of Pastures and Field Crops, the Commonwealth Bureau of Plant Breeding and Genetics, and the Commonwealth Bureau of Soils. All these bureaux exist to collect and spread information in their respective fields, and they act as a clearing house and a centre of communication in these matters for Members. The Executive Council makes an annual report to each of the Members.

So also the Commonwealth Economic Committee, the Commonwealth Shipping Committee, and the Commonwealth Telecommunications Board are examples of institutions set up by the Members of the Commonwealth and administered by them through governing bodies upon which they are represented, whose functions are those of providing information and advice and acting as a medium for consultation. The Commonwealth Economic Committee provides economic and statistical services on subjects affecting Commonwealth production and trade, and issues, for example, monthly intelligence bulletins about particular commodities. The Commonwealth Shipping Committee has the functions of inquiring into complaints from persons or bodies interested with regard to ocean projects, facilities, and conditions in Commonwealth trade, and of surveying the facilities for maritime transport on such routes as appear to them to be necessary for trade within the Commonwealth and of making recommendations to the proper authority for the co-ordination and improvement of such facilities with regard to the type, size, and speed of ships, depth of water in docks and channels, construction of harbour works and similar matters; and in doing so to take into account facilities for air transport on the routes in question.

The Commonwealth Telecommunications Board is established by an act of the parliament of the United Kingdom,[9] but it is the result of an agreement among the Members of the Commonwealth to have such a board and the act of parliament does no more than incorporate the board and give it a legal status. The functions of the board are largely advisory and its advice is given to the 'Partner governments' (as they are called in the constitution of the board) who are represented on the board by one member each who jointly appoint the chairman. In addition to advice, the board is permitted to conduct research and to acquire patent rights which might be useful in connexion with the functions of the board or with the business of any of the public corporations engaged in telecommunications of a Partner government. Here, again, however, Members of the Commonwealth take part in this co-operative institution voluntarily, and they may withdraw from the agreement if they wish. While they remain under the agreement, too, it is clear that their obligations consist almost entirely in receiving advice from the board which they may take or disregard as they please.

It is interesting to notice, also, how the operation of the Colombo Plan was arranged. There is a Consultative Committee, which was set up when the plan was adopted in January 1950, and the task of this committee is confined to surveying the needs and assessing the resources available and required to carry out economic development in the countries in South and South-East Asia. Each year an economic survey of the region is prepared and published by the committee. But when it comes to providing capital aid and technical assistance to the countries in the region, decisions are in the hands of the countries

[9] Commonwealth Telegraphs Act, 1949, 12 & 13 Geo. VI, c. 39.

involved. It is arranged independently between the giving and receiving countries. It should be added, perhaps, that the Consultative Committee is not confined to Commonwealth countries, for the Colombo Plan extends to countries in South and South-East Asia irrespective of whether they are in the Commonwealth or not, and what is more the United States is a member of the committee. It is perhaps natural, therefore, that administrative powers are not given to an international committee of this kind. None the less it is usual to find that Members of the Commonwealth, even when engaged in matters in which foreign countries are not concerned, tend to preserve their independence and freedom of action much as they do when engaged in other international discussions.

There is indeed only one example of co-operative administration through a permanent institution in the Commonwealth where the institution is not engaged almost exclusively in the exchange of information or in consultation and that is the Imperial War Graves Commission. This body, which owes its legal existence to a royal charter, is financed by Members of the Commonwealth and its function is to establish and maintain cemeteries and to compile records of civilian war dead. The exception goes far to prove the rule. It is only in a matter where policy can be agreed upon and politics can be ruled out that an institution with administrative functions can be set up by Commonwealth Members. War graves could be a contentious subject; the establishment and working of the commission was not always plain sailing. In fact, however, co-operative administration has proved possible and successful in its work.

4

When we consider co-operation in the Commonwealth, therefore, we start from the position that there is an obligation to communicate and consult, but there is no obligation beyond that. What is more there is no obligation to agree, or to refrain from action if others disagree; there is no veto. The development of institutions of co-operation within the Commonwealth has therefore been determined by these principles, that communication and consultation must be made full and effective, but that no obligation to go beyond this point could be undertaken. Wherever it seemed likely, in particular, that a Member government could be committed to any policy by the action of another Member, action was taken to make sure that no such consequences could occur.

On this basis the machinery for co-operation works. It falls under half a dozen heads. First there is communication and consultation between governments in the Commonwealth, carried out through the departments of external affairs in each of the overseas Members, while the government of the United Kingdom has a department of Commonwealth relations under a Secretary of State.[10] It is interesting to notice that none of the other Members of the Commonwealth has set up a separate department to deal with Commonwealth relations. They deal with Commonwealth relations either as part of the work of their department of external affairs or as part of their Prime Minister's department. In most cases, however, there would be a distinct subdivision of the larger department which specialized in questions of Commonwealth relations. No hard and fast rule can be laid down about the proper form of organization. The United Kingdom has contact with all the other Members of the Commonwealth and there may be a case for saying that it needs the attention of a separate minister. It means that there is one voice at least in the United Kingdom cabinet which can be raised on behalf of consultation and communication with the other Members of the Commonwealth. If Commonwealth relations were contained within the sphere of the Foreign Office, they might become submerged or confused in wider or more complicated matters and not receive the care and attention in the cabinet which they should have. So far as overseas Members of the Commonwealth are concerned their relations with each other may not be sufficiently extensive to justify the setting up of a separate department, or it may be that the external relations of these Members are not yet so extensive that relations with other Commonwealth countries are likely to be submerged.

A second method of communication and consultation is through the High Commissioners, the representatives in each Commonwealth Member of the other Commonwealth Members. This system of representation is now accepted as normal,

[10] A full account of the organization of the department is found in the *Third Report of the Select Committee on Estimates*, H.C. 252 of 1958-9.

though not all Members are represented in each other's capitals. Though High Commissioners are given the same status as ambassadors, they have retained their distinctive title to mark the fact that they are not the same as representatives of foreign countries. In earlier times it was objected that the representative of one of the Queen's realms could not enjoy diplomatic status in another of the Queen's realms because the Queen could not accredit an ambassador to herself. These legalistic objections, whatever their force, should not be allowed to stand in the way of the Members of the Commonwealth obtaining that form of representation in each other's capitals which seems to them in accordance with equality of status. In fact the objection could no longer be sustained so far as India or Pakistan or Malaya are concerned, since they have ceased to be Her Majesty's realms. The Presidents of India or Pakistan, and the King of Malaya, could properly accredit an ambassador to the Queen whether in the United Kingdom or in Canada, Australia, New Zealand, or any of her other realms. In practice High Commissioners are still appointed, though in the case of India and Malaya the High Commissioner presents Letters of Commission from the President of the Republic of India or the King of Malaya[11] to the Queen, while the United Kingdom High Commissioner in Delhi or Kuala Lumpur similarly presents Letters of Commission from the Queen to the President or the King. The use of a distinctive name for the representatives of the Members of the Commonwealth stresses their special relationship with each other and perhaps frees them from certain restrictions of procedure in carrying out their duties which might attach to them if they were ordinary members of the diplomatic corps.

The advantage of representation by High Commissioners instead of by ambassadors has been stated officially on behalf of the government of the United Kingdom in these words:

. . . Whereas the Ambassador must do all his business through the Department of External Affairs, the High Commissioner is entitled to deal direct with other departments of government. The result is that the High Commissioner and his staff at appropriate levels have contacts of an informal sort throughout the machinery

[11] I use 'King' as an equivalent of Yang di-Pertuan Agong.

of government. A point of particular note is that the U.K. High
Commissioner has closer and more frequent contact with the Prime
Minister of the Commonwealth country in which he is serving than
is the case with foreign heads of mission. Practice on this point
naturally varies, but in Australia, for instance, on all important
matters and whenever a formal approach is called for, the High
Commissioner deals direct with the Prime Minister.[12]

If, however, Members should come to feel that they would
prefer their representatives to be diplomats, like the representatives of foreign states, then the rules would need to be altered
to make this possible. In a matter of this kind, however, it is
worth emphasizing that the views of foreign states would have
to be taken into account, for it involves matters of diplomatic
practice and of international law and relations, and not merely
of Commonwealth relations. Thus when arrangements were
made for High Commissioners to be accorded the same status
as ambassadors, consultation had to be undertaken with foreign
states and their agreement obtained.

An interesting footnote to the matter is that the representative of the Republic of Ireland in the United Kingdom (as in
other Members of the Commonwealth) is an ambassador, which
is not surprising, for Ireland is not within the Commonwealth.
On the other hand, Ireland is not regarded as a foreign country.
Her ambiguous position is recognized by the fact that the Irish
ambassador conducts his relations with the United Kingdom
through the Commonwealth Relations Office, not the Foreign
Office, and that when he presents his letters of credence to the
Queen, he is accompanied by a representative of the Commonwealth Relations Office. In this way is symbolized Ireland's
position in relation to the Commonwealth since 1949 of 'exclude
me in' in place of 'include me out'.

Through these Commonwealth representatives and their
officers and staffs in each other's capitals, communication and
consultation can be carried out. In addition to this, however,
there has grown up in London, and in many of the other capitals,
an arrangement by which there are regular meetings between
the Secretary of State for Commonwealth Relations or the

[12] H.C. 252 of 1958–9, p. 56 (referred to above). The nature of a U.K. High
Commissioner's duties and the organization of his office is described on
pp. 56 ff.

Minister for External Affairs or some other appropriate minister in a given capital with the Commonwealth representatives in that capital. These meetings are sometimes regular and frequent, sometimes irregular. They provide, however, in each Member an opportunity for representatives to discuss and inform each other about matters of common concern as they are viewed in relation to the situation from the point of view of a particular Member.

Meetings between Commonwealth representatives are not confined, however, to Commonwealth countries. It is the custom in many foreign capitals, and at the headquarters of the United Nations in New York, for example, for regular meetings of Commonwealth representatives to occur, in addition to the informal and frequent consultation of each other which is carried out in the ordinary course of their work. Each Commonwealth Member is provided in this way with information and advice from foreign capitals of far greater breadth and significance than if it relied solely upon its own representative.

In addition to communication and consultation through these permanent institutions, there is the contact between ministers, including Prime Ministers, when they visit other Commonwealth Members. These are frequently held and discussions range from one or two specific topics to a wide variety of general problems. The meetings of Prime Ministers, which have replaced what was called the Imperial Conference, occur at irregular intervals—there were meetings, for example, in 1957, 1956, 1955, 1953, 1951, 1949, 1948, 1946, and 1944. In addition there have been finance ministers meetings (in 1949 and 1959 in London and in 1954 in Sydney) and there have been foreign ministers meetings, of which that in Colombo in 1950 was the first. Specialized conferences, whether of ministers or of officials or non-official representatives, occur frequently. Economic questions were discussed, for example, at conferences in Montreal in 1958 and in London in 1952. There were conferences on nationality and citizenship in 1947, on the Japanese peace settlement in Canberra in 1947, on defence in 1951, on supply and production also in 1951, and on science in 1952 in Canberra and Melbourne. Added to this, ministers, especially foreign ministers, meet each other at regular meetings of international organizations such as the United Nations, the North Atlantic

Treaty Organization, or the South-East Asia Treaty Organization.

5

It is unnecessary to describe in detail the methods by which consultation occurs. They are indeed not markedly different from those through which the relations of independent states are conducted outside the Commonwealth. What difference there is, apart from the difference of name applied to High Commissioners, will come from the quality of the co-operation, the extent to which it is in some special way friendly, intimate, full, and frank. It is not very easy to discover how effective this machinery is. To start with, what test should be applied? At times people speak as if the test they apply is whether Members of the Commonwealth agree about a common policy. Yet that surely is not a proper test. Communication and consultation may assist other Members to know what you are proposing to do and to understand why you are doing it, but there is no reason why it should convert them to your point of view. The test that should be applied is rather whether consultation is full, and above all, whether it is carried out in time for the opinion of other Members to be obtained. And whether this is so or not only those inside the governments themselves really know, and they will not always say. There are, however, examples from time to time where it is clear that some Members of the Commonwealth at least have doubted the efficiency of the system of communication and consultation and have suggested improvements.

Thus Mr. John Curtin, the Prime Minister of Australia, advocated in 1943 that some standing machinery of consultation should be established.

I believe [he said] some form of Imperial consultation must emerge as a result of the experiences of the world. . . . I believe some Imperial authority must be evolved so that the British Commonwealth of Nations will have, if not an executive body, at least a standing consultative body. . . . I visualise a council with a structure similar to the present Pacific War Council, on which representatives of the Dominions could consult regularly with representatives of the British Government. Dominion representatives could be the respective High Commissioners, and they could be replaced at appropriate intervals by a special representative who would be a

Minister. The Empire Council could be a permanent body and its meetings held regularly. Because of everything that is inherent in Dominion status, I consider that meetings should, on occasions, be held in Ottawa, Canberra, Pretoria and Wellington as well as London. . . . The Empire Council should have a permanent secretariat of men as expert in the problems of peace as those who are expert in war advising the councils of the Empire and the United Nations today.

Mr. Curtin's suggestion of a secretariat aroused a good deal of discussion. Meetings of High Commissioners and ministers could certainly be held and were held, without for one moment suggesting that the sovereign independence of each Member was abridged. But a permanent secretariat looked like the beginnings of a government.

Mr. Curtin described what he had in mind. He spoke of it as 'the Secretariat of the Imperial Conference'.

This would normally be located in London, but it would be an ambulatory body and function for conferences at the place of meeting. All Dominions would be represented on the Secretariat. It would be responsible for seeing to the preparation and presentation of information on subjects to be considered by the Conference from time to time. It would have regard to the completion of action or resubmissions to the Conference. It would provide the Conference with an agency for continuity in its detailed work which is important in view of changes which occur in governments and Prime Ministers. The Secretariat would not supersede the present established direct channels of communication between governments though its members would be directly responsible to their respective Prime Ministers.[13]

Proposals of this kind—and they are put forward from time to time—must not be misunderstood. Their object is not to modify the sovereign independence of a Member but to make it more effective. 'I do not believe,' said Mr. Curtin, 'that Britain can manage the Empire on the basis purely of a government sitting in London.' The Australian Prime Minister thought, on the basis of experience in the conduct of the war, that his country was being left out of things, that it was not being fully and

[13] These quotations are taken from statements by Mr. Curtin on 14 Aug., 6 Sept., and 14 Dec. 1943, and are reprinted in Mansergh, op. cit., vol. i, pp. 562–5.

effectively informed and consulted. And there were many occasions in the conduct of the Pacific War in which this happened, though neglect to consult by the United States was much more frequent than neglect by the United Kingdom. None the less, the proposals for a Commonwealth secretariat were critically received. In the view of the Prime Ministers of the Commonwealth, then and since, there are plenty of institutions in existence through which consultation can occur. The question is: are they used as much as they should be? In practice, however, the organization of any Commonwealth conference usually means the bringing together at some stage in advance of an *ad hoc* Commonwealth secretariat which prepares the agenda, organizes the conference itself, and tidies up afterwards. Speaking generally Members have felt that standing Commonwealth secretariats of councils or conferences are in fact not likely to have enough to do. They are bound to prove less effective than organizations and meetings called together at a particular time to deal with a particular problem or set of problems.

It is proper, however, to express some doubt about the extent to which Members of the Commonwealth carry out their obligation to communicate and consult with each other on matters of common concern. Reference is made from time to time to the 'shoals of telegrams'[14] that go out every day from Commonwealth capitals to each other. Is there much that is important in them? Does anyone of importance read them? And if they are important, has enough time been allowed for the governments of the various Members to make comments and to give advice? How much is communication and how much consultation? And does consultation take place when a Member proposes to do something of which other Members will strongly disapprove? These questions cannot be answered in detail. Suffice it to mention one or two notorious cases where consultation either never occurred or if it did occur, was ineffective because of insufficient time; when it was in fact communication and not consultation.

When the United Kingdom decided upon and executed the landings at Suez in 1956, it did so without effective consultation

---

[14] Lord Salisbury's phrase in the House of Lords when he was speaking as Secretary of State for Dominion Affairs, 2 Nov. 1943. 129 *H.L. Deb.* 5 s., col. 512.

with the other Members of the Commonwealth. Sir Anthony Eden said in the House of Commons on 30 October 1956: 'We have also kept in close consultation with the Commonwealth governments, but the responsibility for the decision was that of the French and British Governments owing to the information reaching us of the situation in the neighbourhood of the Canal.'[15] Mr. Selwyn Lloyd, the Foreign Secretary, said on 31 October 1956: 'This specific course of conduct was not put to the other governments. It could not have been. It was decided upon only shortly before the Prime Minister came down and informed the House.'[16]

Who can doubt also, that in many matters of defence, and particularly with the development of nuclear weapons, Members of the Commonwealth feel unable to give each other full information about what they are doing or propose to do. Nor could it be supposed that communication and consultation between India and Pakistan or between India and South Africa, is as full as it is between Australia and New Zealand or New Zealand and the United Kingdom.

These are political factors. They do not fall for full discussion in an essay on the constitutional as distinct from the political structure of the Commonwealth. They are mentioned as examples of what must be borne in mind in assessing the value of the Commonwealth machinery for co-operation. They assist us in deciding also how far the convention to co-operate, and in particular to communicate and consult, a convention which is part of the constitutional structure of the Commonwealth, is modified by practice. For practice and custom can modify and even nullify a convention, just as it can modify or nullify a rule of strict law. It would not be far wide of the mark to say that the Members of the Commonwealth, in carrying out consultation and communication, are bound to be governed to an important extent by their conception of their own interests and by their reluctance on many occasions to disclose information even to other Members of the Commonwealth, which these other Members would in fact be very glad to have. In a Commonwealth of sovereign states, this is to be expected. Each Member is the judge of what is in its own interests and it acts accordingly.

[15] 558 *H.C. Deb.* 5 s., col. 1291.   [16] Ibid., col. 1568.

6

There is one matter upon which co-operation has been attempted and which deserves mention, and that is the subject of nationality. For a long time it was possible to say that one of the things which was common in the Commonwealth was the common nationality, that all the peoples of the Members of the Commonwealth were British subjects. With the assertion of a sovereign independence by the Commonwealth countries it was to be expected that each Member would wish to obtain control over so important a matter as the law relating to its own nationals. In such a matter, however, consultation was an obvious necessity—and accordingly a conference of Commonwealth countries was held in London in 1947.[17] The conference recommended that each Commonwealth Member should have its own citizenship law, defining whom its citizens are, and how citizenship is lost and acquired; and that, at the same time, each Commonwealth Member would recognize as British subjects or as Commonwealth citizens, if that term were preferred, its own citizens and the citizens of other Commonwealth Members. It was recommended also that naturalization of aliens and of British protected persons according to the law of any Commonwealth Member, would automatically confer the status of British subjects or Commonwealth citizens and should be recognized throughout the Commonwealth. And it was proposed also that citizenship in a Commonwealth Member would be more easily obtainable by a citizen of another Commonwealth Member than by an alien.

When the Members of the Commonwealth came to deal with these questions, however, common action was not taken. The Irish Free State had already passed legislation in 1936 defining Irish citizenship and declaring that Irish citizens were not also British subjects. They rejected the idea of the double status of citizen of a Member and citizen also of the Commonwealth. In the eyes of the law of the United Kingdom Irish citizens were still British subjects and the matter rested in this ambiguous position for some years. After the Conference of 1947, however, other Members of the Commonwealth preferred to follow the Irish example, so that while the United Kingdom, Canada,

[17] Cmd. 7326.

Australia, New Zealand, Pakistan, and Ghana have passed acts defining citizenship for their own peoples and conferring upon them at the same time the status of British subjects or Commonwealth citizens, South Africa, India, Ceylon, and Malaya have all adopted a single status for their people, and have not granted them also the status of Commonwealth citizens. Thus while co-operation on citizenship went so far as consultation and a conference, when it came later to decision and execution, a common policy was not carried out.[18]

In place of common citizenship there has been developed, however, the idea of reciprocal citizenship. This arose through the action of the Irish Free State or Eire, for when in April 1949 Eire left the Commonwealth, it was necessary to take some action about citizenship, particularly for those thousands of people living in Britain who were, under the law of Eire, Irish citizens. If the Republic of Ireland left the Commonwealth, surely it became a foreign country and its citizens were foreigners. To avoid this situation it was agreed between Ireland and the United Kingdom and later with other Members of the Commonwealth that, though Ireland was no longer in the Commonwealth, it was not to be regarded as a foreign country, nor were Irish citizens to be regarded as aliens. They were to be accorded reciprocal citizenship rights in the United Kingdom, while citizens of the United Kingdom and colonies would be accorded the rights of citizens in Ireland. And this arrangement was extended gradually throughout Commonwealth Members.

The Irish device of reciprocal citizenship has been applied also by those other Members of the Commonwealth—India, Pakistan, and Malaya—which did not provide for a status of Commonwealth citizen in their law. They treat citizens of other Commonwealth Members and of Ireland on a favourable basis, as compared with aliens. In the outcome, therefore, while in some Commonwealth Members—the United Kingdom, Canada, Australia, New Zealand, and Ceylon—citizens of all other Members are regarded as Commonwealth citizens, in others, like India, Pakistan, and Malaya—and paradoxically Ireland—citizens of Commonwealth Members are accorded some degree of rights of reciprocal citizenship. It should be added, however,

[18] See J. M. Jones, *British Nationality Law* (revised ed. 1956).

that Commonwealth citizenship or reciprocal citizenship carries with it—except in the United Kingdom—in most Commonwealth Members only a limited number of rights. In particular it is into the United Kingdom alone that a person by virtue of his Commonwealth citizenship may immigrate.

7

It is easy to overestimate or to underestimate the efficiency of the arrangements for co-operation between the Members of the Commonwealth. It is extremely hard to assess truly how far the conventions of co-operation which are reaffirmed in successive meetings of Commonwealth Prime Ministers are obeyed in practice. Two observations may be hazarded. The first is that with the extension of the membership of the Commonwealth to Asian and African nations, so that the Commonwealth is no longer British in any real sense but predominantly an Afro-Asian Commonwealth, it is almost unavoidable that for a period at least co-operation could not be as close and smooth-running as it was in the Commonwealth of the years before 1945. It is wrong, of course, to believe that relations between Commonwealth Members before 1945 were always smooth and effective, but the scale of operations and the predominantly European outlook of the Members may have made co-operation easier. Whether this is so or not, it is clear that in a world-wide Commonwealth with Members whose vital interests are affected by different forces in different parts of the world and whose policies consequently are extremely difficult to harmonize, co-operation must be expected to be difficult and to get more difficult before it gets easier.

In the second place, Members of the Commonwealth have close relations with many countries outside the Commonwealth and co-operate with them. This has always been true of the United Kingdom and Canada, and it has become true of other Members of the Commonwealth. In the result it is not surprising if some Members regard their relations with other Members as just a part of their international relations and find themselves more and more inclined not to give them a special status or to adopt a special procedure or set of institutions for them. Commonwealth co-operation to them is a part of international co-operation.

In these circumstances it is not surprising to find that Members of the Commonwealth commit themselves to the closest co-operation with each other when they are associated also, first, with independent countries outside the Commonwealth, and secondly in arrangements that apply to a region of the world with which they conceive their interests to be most closely concerned. The best example of this is the North Atlantic Treaty Organization. Here Canada and the United Kingdom have undertaken obligations towards each other which go far beyond anything that could have been contemplated in the years before 1939 when Canada's membership of the Commonwealth was founded upon the understanding that it would not bind itself in advance to the United Kingdom in regard to any commitment in Europe. But these new and far-reaching obligations undertaken in NATO are not obligations between Canada and the United Kingdom alone; they are shared also with the United States, France, Belgium, Holland, Luxembourg, Norway, Denmark, Portugal, Iceland, Turkey, Greece, and the Federal Republic of Germany.

Under the terms of the North Atlantic Treaty, signed in Washington in April 1949, the Parties undertake 'to consult together whenever, in the opinion of any of them, the territorial integrity, political independence or security of any of the parties is threatened'.[19] This goes no further than the convention of consultation which applies among Members of the Commonwealth. But the parties to the treaty went further. They agreed

that an armed attack against one or more of them in Europe or North America shall be considered an attack against them all, and consequently they agree that if such an armed attack occurs, each of them, in exercise of the right of individual or collective self-defence recognised by Article 51 of the Charter of the United Nations, will assist the Party or Parties so attacked by taking forthwith, individually and in concert with the other Parties, such action as it deems necessary including the use of armed force, to restore and maintain the security of the North Atlantic area.[20]

To make sure that these obligations might be carried out effectively, the parties established a council, on which each of them

<hr/>

[19] Article 4.   [20] Article 5.

is represented, to consider matters concerning the implementation of the treaty.[21] As a result of this treaty a whole defence force was set up, under a single supreme commander (General Eisenhower was the first holder of the post), and a degree of co-operative administration of armed forces was established which went far beyond anything which Members of the Commonwealth had or would have contemplated among themselves. Whatever criticism there may be about the effectiveness of these arrangements, what is clear is that two Members of the Commonwealth, Canada and the United Kingdom, have entered into co-operative arrangements in defence which extend in practice beyond communication and consultation.

The obligations undertaken by the parties to the South-East Asia Collective Defence Treaty, which was signed at Manila in 1954, do not go so far as that of the North Atlantic Treaty. Each party recognizes that armed attack against any of the parties would endanger its own peace and safety and agrees that it will in that event act to meet the common danger in accordance with its constitutional processes.[22] Provision for common consultation is included in the treaty and there is a council as in the North Atlantic Treaty. To this South-East Asia Treaty Organization four Members of the Commonwealth adhered—Australia, New Zealand, Pakistan, and the United Kingdom—and they were associated with the United States, Thailand, France, and the Philippines. But although the obligations undertaken in SEATO were less than those in NATO, they went farther than the Members of the Commonwealth had gone among themselves.

So also, while all the Members of the Commonwealth are members of the United Nations Organization, they undertake obligations of mutual consultation and assistance there which they do not undertake with each other exclusively. And it will be noted that in regional arrangements not all the Members of the Commonwealth in the region concerned are invited or are willing to join with the others in accepting obligations. India and Ceylon do not belong to SEATO, while Pakistan, Australia, and New Zealand do. Again when Australia and New Zealand joined with the United States in making the ANZUS Pact the United Kingdom was not invited to join it.

[21] Article 9.   [22] Article 4.

It is apparent, then, that no co-operative arrangements exist for Members of the Commonwealth exclusively which commit them to the extent which Members are prepared to be committed either in the United Nations Organization or in regional arrangements such as NATO or SEATO. Differences in political attitudes make this position inevitable. It may well be also that it corresponds with the strategic realities of the situation.

VII · SYMBOLS

I

IT is common for the members of a group, whether it be a club or a school or a state or the United Nations, to adopt some symbol of their association. It may be a flag or a badge or a motto; it may be animal, vegetable, or mineral; it may be a person. There is, be it noted, no logical necessity for a symbol; an association is not less an association because it lacks a symbol of its members' unity. In practice, however, it is commonly found that unity is maintained and promoted by the possession of a symbol. At the same time it is to be remembered that where members differ about what form a symbol should take, unity in the association may be preserved only by deciding to go without a symbol.

In the Commonwealth, as it is organized at present, the Members have decided that there shall be a symbol of their association, and that that symbol should be what they describe either as 'the Crown' or 'the Queen'. In the preamble to the Statute of Westminster, 1931, for example, we find it declared that 'the Crown is the symbol of the free association of the Members of the British Commonwealth of Nations'—at that time the United Kingdom, Canada, Australia, New Zealand, South Africa, Newfoundland, and the Irish Free State.

And in the communiqué issued on 27 April 1949 by the Commonwealth Prime Ministers the following paragraphs appear:

The Governments of the United Kingdom, Canada, Australia, New Zealand, South Africa, India, Pakistan and Ceylon, whose countries are united as Members of the British Commonwealth of Nations and owe a common allegiance to the Crown, which is also the symbol of their free association, have considered the impending constitutional changes in India.

The Government of India have informed the other Governments of the Commonwealth of the intention of the Indian people that under the new constitution which is about to be adopted India shall become a sovereign, independent republic. The Government of

India have however declared and affirmed India's desire to continue her full membership of the Commonwealth of Nations and her acceptance of The King as the symbol of the free association of its independent member nations and as such the Head of the Commonwealth.

The Governments of the other countries of the Commonwealth, the basis of whose membership of the Commonwealth is not hereby changed, accept and recognise India's continuing membership in accordance with the terms of this declaration.

Accordingly the United Kingdom, Canada, Australia, New Zealand, South Africa, India, Pakistan and Ceylon hereby declare that they remain united as free and equal members of the Commonwealth of Nations, freely co-operating in the pursuit of peace, liberty and progress.

When, in 1955, Pakistan decided to establish a republican form of government, a similar declaration was adopted at a meeting of Commonwealth Prime Ministers. The position of the Queen as the symbol of the Commonwealth's association was explicitly recognized by the proclamation at the time of her Coronation in 1953 of new royal styles and titles in which she was described as 'Head of the Commonwealth'.

In the outcome, therefore, all the Members of the Commonwealth recognize the Queen as the symbol of their association, and, as such, the Head of the Commonwealth. Some Members go further, however, and recognize the Queen as the head of their own national government. For the United Kingdom, Canada, Australia, New Zealand, South Africa, Ceylon, and Ghana, the Queen is not only the Head of the Commonwealth but also the head of their state. For India and Pakistan, however, and for South Africa, Ceylon, and Ghana, when they carry out their declared intentions of becoming republics, the head of the state is a president, as a result of their adopting a republican constitution. But this situation is not confined to the republican Members of the Commonwealth. Malaya is not a republic; the head of the state is a King (Yang di-Pertuan Agong) elected for a period by the rulers of the states of the federation. The Queen is not therefore the head of the state in Malaya, although Malaya is a kingdom. In relation to India, Pakistan, and Malaya, therefore (and to South Africa, Ceylon, and Ghana in due course), the Queen is no more than the symbol of their association with each other and other Members of the Commonwealth. As Head

of the Commonwealth she has no position within the govern-
mental system of any individual Member, nor has she any
powers in the Commonwealth as a whole.

It might be argued that for India, Pakistan, and Malaya, the
symbol of the Commonwealth association is the Queen, whereas
for the other Members it is the Crown. After all, is not that
what was said in the Declaration of 1949? It is true that this was
said in 1949, but it is also true that the Members of the Commonwealth which acknowledged a common allegiance to the Crown
in 1949 and spoke of the Crown as the symbol of their association, all declared, in 1953, in proclaiming a new title for Elizabeth the Second, that she was Head of the Commonwealth. If
this proclamation is to have any meaning it must surely mark
the acceptance by these Members of the Queen as the symbol
of their association. It remains a fact that they owe a common
allegiance to the Crown, an allegiance which they do not share
with the republican Members or with Malaya, but they can be
regarded as having chosen to speak of the Queen rather than of
the Crown as the symbol of their association.

2

The present rule of the Commonwealth association is, then,
that the association does have a symbol and that the Queen is
the symbol. As long as this rule stands, a country which wishes
to be a Member of the Commonwealth must accept the Queen
as the symbol. If it wishes to leave the Commonwealth it will
mark its departure by declaring that it no longer recognizes the
Queen as the symbol. And if it wishes to stay in the Commonwealth, but does not accept the Queen as a symbol, then it will
be deemed to have left the Commonwealth. Of course if a situation of this kind arose, it might well happen that Members of
the Commonwealth would consider whether another or an
alternative symbol of association should be devised which could
allow Members who wished to continue in the Commonwealth
but could not accept the Queen as a symbol, to remain as Members. As things stand at present, however, a test of membership
of the Commonwealth is acceptance of the Queen as the symbol
of association and, as such, Head of the Commonwealth.

The position is well illustrated by what happened, in 1948,

when Eire decided that it could no longer recognize the King in connexion with the external relations of the country. The Irish Free State (as it was called until 1937) had by legislation passed in 1936 upon the abdication of Edward VIII, reduced the functions of the King in relation to the government of the country. A somewhat involved and ambiguous section of the Executive Authority (External Relations) Act[1] read as follows:

It is hereby declared and enacted that, so long as Saorstat Eireann is associated with the following nations,[2] that is to say, Australia, Canada, Great Britain,[3] New Zealand and South Africa, and so long as the King recognised by those nations as the symbol of their co-operation continues to act on behalf of those nations (on the advice of the several Governments thereof) for the purposes of the appointment of diplomatic and consular representatives and the conclusion of international agreements, the King so recognised may, and is hereby authorised to, act on behalf of Saorstat Eireann for the like purposes as and when advised by the Executive Council so to do.

This interesting section was remarkable for what it did not say. It did not explicitly say that the Irish Free State recognized the King as the symbol of its association and co-operation with the other countries named in the section. It did not say that the King would act in external affairs on behalf of the Irish Free State, but only that he 'may'. Whatever the section did or did not say, however, there was no doubt that in some undefined and incomprehensible way, the King still retained some position in relation to the Irish Free State. When in 1937 a new constitution of Eire was adopted, with a President as head of the state, the situation in relation to the King was unchanged. Moreover, the new state was not described as a republic, but as 'a sovereign, independent, democratic State'.[4]

In 1948, however, the Prime Minister of Eire, Mr. Costello, announced that legislation would be introduced to abolish entirely any connexion between Eire and the Monarchy. The

---

[1] No. 58 of 1936.

[2] It will be noted that the countries are arranged in alphabetical order, not in the more usual order of seniority as self-governing countries as in s. 1 of the Statute of Westminster.

[3] The term 'United Kingdom' is not used, for the Irish Free State did not recognize the union of Northern Ireland with Great Britain.

[4] Constitution of Eire, Article 5.

resulting Republic of Ireland Act, 1948,[5] repealed the Executive Authority (External Relations) Act of 1936, declared that the description of the state should be the Republic of Ireland, and provided that 'the President, on the authority and on the advice of the government, may exercise the executive power or any executive function of the state in or in connexion with its external relations'. It was accepted at once by the United Kingdom and all other Members of the Commonwealth that when the Republic of Ireland Act came into force—as it did on 18 April 1949—the Republic would no longer be a Member of the Commonwealth because it had abolished all links with the King. It was assumed that when the Irish parliament passed the act it meant at one and the same time to make a republic and to secede from the Commonwealth.

It is worth while to recall that these steps were taken and completed before, but only shortly before, India had placed before the meeting of Commonwealth Prime Ministers its intention to become a republic combined with its desire to remain in the Commonwealth, and had been permitted to do so in the declaration issued on 27 April 1949. How could Ireland automatically cease to be a Member of the Commonwealth because it had become a republic on 18 April 1949, and India be welcomed on 27 April 1949 as a continuing Member of the Commonwealth although it proposed to become a republic? The explanation lay in the fact that Ireland, by the repeal of the External Relations (Executive Authority) Act had abolished all relations with the King, including recognition of the King as the symbol of co-operation, whereas India had expressed its willingness to accept the King as the symbol of association, and as such the Head of the Commonwealth. There was no inconsistency between the two declarations.

What is more difficult to assess is whether, had the King not been the symbol of association, or had there been no symbol or a different symbol, the Republic of Ireland would have been willing to continue as a Member of the Commonwealth. It was clear that Ireland wished to continue its close relations with Britain, and other Members of the Commonwealth, and this wish was reciprocated. No sooner had the Republic come into existence than legislation was passed by the Members of the

[5] No. 22 of 1948.

Commonwealth establishing reciprocal citizenship with Ireland and asserting that Ireland, though no longer a Member of the Commonwealth, was not a foreign country.[6] It was difficult to resist the conclusion that Ireland was still a Member of the Commonwealth in all but name. It seemed to be not the association so much as the nature of the symbol to which it objected.

There is a good deal of evidence to support this view. When Mr. Costello announced his intention of abolishing links with the monarchy, he spoke of the long history of aggression and persecution by an alien government.

During all that period [he said] the Crown was a symbol of a political and religious ascendancy and became anathema to the vast majority of the Irish people. The harp without the Crown symbolised the ideal of Irish independence and nationhood. The harp beneath the Crown was the symbol of conquest. The bitter facts of history have inevitably prevented our people from having that outlook which the people of the great self-governing Members of the British Commonwealth of Nations may have for the Crown as their traditional link.[7] . . . the question had become *not* whether our association with the Commonwealth and the constitutional provisions in which it was expressed represented a limitation of our freedom or sovereignty, but whether our constitutional arrangements relating to these matters were in a *form* which the people as a whole could accept as being compatible with our national sentiment and historical tradition.[8] . . . Irish national instincts, deep-rooted in history, recoiled from the forms which were to them, not the embodiment of their national pride in the social structure, but the symbol of centuries of civil and religious persecution and confiscation.[9]

How much weight should be attached to these sentiments it is difficult to decide. Irish neutrality might well have had its expression in a desire to withdraw from association with the Commonwealth, whatever the symbol of the association might be. It may be that a desire to leave the Commonwealth was as strong a motive for the passing of the Republic of Ireland Act

[6] See, for example, the Ireland Act, 1949 (12 & 13 Geo. VI, c. 41), of the parliament of the United Kingdom.

[7] In a speech to the Canadian Bar Association in Montreal, 1 Sept. 1948, printed in Mansergh, *Documents and Speeches on British Commonwealth Affairs*, vol. ii, p. 799.   [8] Ibid., p. 800.

[9] Ibid., p. 798.

as was the objection to the symbol. Whatever the answer may be, it is remarkable that Mr. Costello should find intolerable a situation which Mr. De Valera, no less a patriot than he, had invented in 1936 and had been content to accept thereafter while he was in office. It is interesting, too, that India, for whom the Crown and the King represented an alien monarchy at least as much as they did for Ireland, and for whom the establishment of a republic represented the goal of national independence, just as much as it did for Ireland, should have been willing to accept the King as the symbol of association and the Head of the Commonwealth, while Ireland found such an arrangement totally unacceptable. It is tempting but profitless to speculate what Ireland's attitude would have been had the arrangements made for the Republic of India in April 1949 been in existence and in operation before these issues had come to the fore in Ireland.

3

As the Members of the Commonwealth have agreed that there is to be a symbol of association, and that this symbol is to be the Queen, it follows that they all have a common concern in deciding who the Head of the Commonwealth is to be and what titles, if any, shall be attached to the Head. This was expressed in the preamble to the Statute of Westminster by the declaration that 'it would be in accord with the established constitutional position of all the Members of the Commonwealth in relation to one another that any alteration in the law touching the succession to the throne or the royal style and titles shall hereafter require the assent as well of the parliaments of all the Dominions as of the Parliament of the United Kingdom'. That declaration embodied a constitutional convention; it was not enacted in the Statute itself. The reason for its adoption was partly to recognize the equality of the Dominions with Great Britain in this matter of common concern, but also to provide for the situation which arose upon the passing of the Statute of Westminster when, for the first time, some of the Dominions at least—South Africa for example—would themselves be able to alter the law relating to the succession to the throne and the royal style and titles—a subject which theretofore had lain within the exclusive competence of the parliament of the United

Kingdom. As this matter was a matter of common concern to all Members of the Commonwealth it was necessary for the United Kingdom to say that if it proposed to alter the law it would obtain the consent of all the other Members, and for the other Members to say that if they proposed to alter the law they would obtain the consent of the United Kingdom and of each other.

Although there have been changes in the membership of the Commonwealth since 1931—the Irish Free State has left,[10] Newfoundland has become a province of Canada, and India, Pakistan, Ceylon, Malaya, and Ghana have assumed the status of membership—the principles enunciated in the preamble to the Statute of Westminster remain substantially operative today. To understand their operation, however, it is necessary to consider the position of Members of the Commonwealth in some detail, for in this matter of their relation to the monarchy they exhibit individual differences of some importance. And since 1931 there have been several opportunities of observing these differences. With the abdication of Edward VIII in 1936, it was thought necessary to make provision concerning the succession to the throne; with the passing of the Indian Independence Act in 1947 it was necessary to abolish the King's title of Emperor of India; and with the accession of Elizabeth II in 1952, action was taken to alter the royal style and titles.

The basic rule, as has been said, is that no such alteration may be made save with the assent of the parliaments of all Members of the Commonwealth. This assent may be given in any way which the parliament deems appropriate: by resolution, by an address to the monarch, or by act of parliament. In practice acts of parliament have generally been employed.[11] It must be emphasized that the withholding of assent does not invalidate in

[10] S. 3 (3) of the Ireland Act, 1949, provides that the assent of the parliament of the Republic of Ireland shall not be required for any alteration in the law touching the succession to the throne or the royal style and titles.

[11] The exceptions were Australia and New Zealand which assented by resolutions of both houses of their parliaments to the alteration in the law concerning the succession to the throne made by the Abdication Act of the parliament of the United Kingdom in 1936 (see *Australian Commonwealth Parliamentary Debates*, vol. 152, and *New Zealand Parliamentary Debates*, vol. 248). The explanation probably was that at that time, as neither Australia nor New Zealand had adopted the Statute of Westminster, their parliaments were not competent to pass laws concerning the succession to the throne, and an act of assent might be thought void for repugnancy.

law the alteration made by another Member of the Commonwealth, though it might in practice destroy the symbolic unity
of the Commonwealth. Although it would seem desirable that
prior assent should be obtained before any parliament makes an
alteration in the law, this has not always occurred in practice.
Prior consultation and an assurance from a government that
assent will be sought has been considered sufficient. When
Edward VIII expressed his intention to abdicate in 1936, the
government of the United Kingdom decided that it would be
necessary to pass an act which might be held to alter the law
touching the succession to the throne for it was to contain a
section excluding from the succession any children which Edward VIII might have after his abdication. It wished to proceed
speedily and, as the parliaments of some Members of the Commonwealth were not sitting, their assent could not be obtained
in time. Thus, while the parliament of the Commonwealth of
Australia signified its assent to the alteration on 11 December
1936, the very day upon which the Abdication Act was assented
to in the United Kingdom, the assents of the parliaments of
Canada, New Zealand, South Africa, and the Irish Free State
were not given until after the United Kingdom act had been
passed.[12]

Giving assent to alterations is one thing; making the alterations is another. Both may be linked together, but there are
possible differences in procedure which deserve attention. Consider, for example, the Republic of India. So far as India is
concerned the position of the Queen as symbol of the Commonwealth association is not a matter of law at all. It rests upon
a basis of constitutional convention—the Declaration of the
Commonwealth Prime Ministers in 1949. India proclaimed no
title for the Queen as did the other Members of the Commonwealth in 1953, although upon the Queen's accession in 1952
the Prime Minister of India addressed a message to her welcoming her as 'the new Head of the Commonwealth'. The view in
India would seem to be that since the Queen is Head of the
Commonwealth, but is not Head of the State and therefore
forms no part of the government of India and performs no
functions within India, it is not necessary for the Queen's

---

[12] The New Zealand resolution of assent was not passed until the parliament
resumed in Sept. 1937.

accession to be proclaimed in India nor for her title to be part of the law of India. If, therefore, any change should be proposed either in the succession to the Headship of the Commonwealth or to the titles of the Head of the Commonwealth, the change could be carried out so far as India was concerned without any alteration in the law of India. At the same time it is difficult to see that this could properly be done without the assent of the parliament of India, though this assent could of course be given by resolution, and would not need to be expressed in the form of an act. Whether this view is accepted in India is not clear. When the royal style and titles were altered in 1953, at the time of the Coronation of the Queen, India not only abstained from proclaiming a title for the Queen but apparently the parliament of India was not called upon to give its assent to the changes of title which all the other Members of the Commonwealth were making. It may be that India considered that changes in the title of the Queen concerned only those Members of the Common-wealth in which the Queen was the Head of the State, yet it would seem of great importance that the title of the Head of the Commonwealth should not be altered save with the assent of the parliaments of all the Members.

Although Pakistan joined in the proclamation of a new title for the Queen in 1953, while it was still a 'Dominion' under the Indian Independence Act, 1947, and a kingdom, curiously enough the assent of the parliament of Pakistan (at that time the Constituent Assembly) was not sought. The new title was simply proclaimed by the Governor-General. It may be ex-pected that Pakistan in future will adopt the view that the position of the Queen in relation to Pakistan, as to India, rests no longer upon law but convention, in this case upon the Declaration of the Prime Ministers' meeting in 1955. Pakistan may therefore feel that changes in succession and in title may be made without the enactment of a law, although the assent of the parliament of Pakistan would surely be required.[13] It seems apparent, too, that Malaya is in the same position, though the question has not yet arisen.

[13] So long as Pakistan has no parliament, it must be presumed that assent could be given by the person or body recognized as competent to legislate. It is interesting to ask: What is a parliament in the convention under discus-sion? Is it the supreme law-making body or is it a representative legislative assembly? No authoritative answer has been given to this question.

When we come to consider those Members of the Commonwealth for which the Queen is not only the symbol of association but also the Head of the State, it is apparent that changes
in the law of succession and of title almost certainly require
legal action to be effective. The position of the Queen within
the system of government is regulated by law and can only be
altered by law. It will usually be necessary for the parliaments
of those Members not only to express their assent to the changes
being made by other Members, in accordance with the constitutional convention declared in the preamble to the Statute of
Westminster, but also to pass an act making or authorizing the
change for themselves.

Two possible lines of action are open to some Members of the
Commonwealth at least in this matter. One is to enact the change
themselves; the other is to ask the parliament of the United
Kingdom to enact the change on their behalf. It may be that
some Members might feel that, although they could enact the
change themselves, they could express their unity with each
other and the United Kingdom by arranging for the change to
be made in one single act of the parliament at Westminster. It
is perhaps unlikely that this line will be followed in the future
for feelings of independence and self-sufficiency are strong in
the Members of the Commonwealth. The legal possibility exists,
however, for some Members, and it is perhaps worth while to
indicate how it could be done.

If Canada wished to enact a change in the succession or the
titles, and if it were deemed that the parliament of Canada had
power to enact such a law (for the matter has been disputed), it
would be open to the Canadian parliament to pass such a law
itself. On the other hand, Canada could ask the parliament at
Westminster to enact the change for it under the provisions of
section 4 of the Statute of Westminster. To be effective such an
enactment must contain a declaration that it had been passed at
the request and with the consent of Canada, and it would then
extend to Canada as part of the law of Canada. This, in fact, is
what was done on the abdication of Edward VIII in 1936. The
government of Canada asked for the Abdication Act of the parliament at Westminster[14] to be extended to Canada. In the
preamble to the act there appear the words: 'Whereas . . . the

_____

[14] 1 Edw. VIII and 1 Geo. VI, c. 3.

Dominion of Canada, pursuant to the provisions of section four of the Statute of Westminster, 1931, has requested and consented to the enactment of this Act.' By virtue of this declaration of request and consent, the Abdication Act extended to Canada under the provisions of section 4 of the Statute of Westminster. The request and consent was made by the government of Canada and this was in accordance with the law.[15] As, however, the act requested and consented to was an act altering the succession, there arose the further requirement that the 'assent' of the parliament of Canada must be obtained in accordance with the preamble to the Statute of Westminster. So in the case of Canada in 1936—and in any future case where this course is chosen—it was essential that the assent of the parliament of Canada should be obtained to the making of the change. In 1936, in fact, the request and consent of the government of Canada was made and declared in the Abdication Act which came into effect on 11 December 1936, but the assent of the parliament of Canada to the change was not obtained—because the parliament was not in session—until later.[16]

New Zealand is in the position of being able either to make a change in the succession or the titles by an enactment of the parliament of New Zealand, or to request and consent to a change being made by the parliament of the United Kingdom so as to extend to New Zealand under the provisions of section 4 of the Statute of Westminster. The request and consent would have to be recited in the United Kingdom act, if the act was to be construed as applying to New Zealand, and it would be necessary for the parliament of New Zealand to signify request and consent.[17] In addition the assent of the parliament of New Zealand to the change would be required in accordance with the constitutional convention recited in the preamble to the Statute of Westminster.

In fact in 1947 and 1953 New Zealand proceded by means of an act of its own parliament, assenting to the deletion of the

---

[15] Unlike Australia, where the request and consent must be made by the government and parliament of the Member, and New Zealand where the parliament must request and consent.

[16] By the Succession to the Throne Act, 1937, 1 Geo. VI, c. 16, which assented to the Abdication Act of the United Kingdom.

[17] By the terms of the Statute of Westminster Adoption Act of New Zealand, No. 38 of 1947, s. 3 (1).

words 'Emperor of India' from the King's title by the Royal
Titles Act, No. 11 of 1947, and assenting to a new title for
the Queen in 1953 in respect of New Zealand and for other
Commonwealth Members by the Royal Titles Act, No. 2 of
1953.

Before New Zealand adopted the Statute of Westminster in
1947, its parliament, though competent to assent to a change in
the succession and the titles, was not competent to make that
change itself. To do so, it would have had to pass a law repugnant to an act of the parliament of the United Kingdom and
such a law would have been void by virtue of the Colonial Laws
Validity Act. When Edward VIII abdicated in 1936, therefore,
it was necessary for the required changes in the law so far as
New Zealand was concerned to be made by the parliament of
the United Kingdom. The Abdication Act of the United Kingdom extended to New Zealand, but it contained no declaration
of request and consent, because New Zealand had not yet
adopted section 4 of the Statute of Westminster. Its application
to New Zealand followed from the terms of the Colonial Laws
Validity Act. The parliament of New Zealand assented to the
change,[18] but the change itself was made for New Zealand by
the parliament of the United Kingdom.

Australia was in a similar position before it adopted the Statute
of Westminster in 1942. The Abdication Act of the parliament
of the United Kingdom extended to Australia by virtue of the
Colonial Laws Validity Act: there was no declaration of Australia's request and consent because it had not adopted section 4
of the Statute. The parliament of the Commonwealth assented
to the change[19] but it was not competent to make it itself.

What is the position since the adoption of the Statute in 1942?
If we assume that under the Australian constitution the parliament of the Commonwealth is empowered to make laws on the
succession and the titles (and it is not undisputed), then it is open
to Australia to proceed either by the method of the parliament
of the Commonwealth enacting the change[20] or by the method

[18] By resolution passed on 9 Sept. 1937 (*New Zealand Parliamentary
Debates*, vol. 248).
[19] By resolution passed on 11 Dec. 1936 (*Australian Commonwealth Parliamentary Debates*, vol. 152).
[20] As in Royal Style and Titles Acts, No. 70 of 1947 and No. 32 of 1953.

of the parliament and government[21] of the Commonwealth requesting and consenting to the making of the change for Australia by the parliament of the United Kingdom.

South Africa has the power to make these changes by an enactment of the Union Parliament and has in fact done so in 1937 (following the abdication of Edward VIII)[22] and in 1948 and 1953,[23] and these enactments constitute also the requisite assent of the parliament of the Union to the changes by other Members. It is true also that the Union could, if it wished, invite the parliament of the United Kingdom to enact a change by virtue of section 4 of the Statute of Westminster, expressing its request and consent to such an enactment, but this United Kingdom act would not extend to the Union unless, by section 2 of the Status Act of 1934, it was expressly extended thereto by the parliament of the Union. If such a procedure were followed— and it is difficult to see why it should be—the act of the parliament of the Union extending the United Kingdom act to the Union would no doubt constitute a declaration of the 'assent' to the change by the parliament of the Union.

Ceylon, under the provisions of the Ceylon Independence Act, 1947, is in the same position as New Zealand. It may either enact a change itself,[24] or it may request and consent to the enactment of a change by the parliament of the United Kingdom under the provision of section 1 (1) of the Ceylon Independence Act, which embodies the terms of section 4 of the Statute of Westminster. Ghana, under the terms of the Gold Coast Independence Act of 1957, is in the same position as Ceylon and New Zealand.

It will be seen, then, that the Members of the Commonwealth differ in the procedures open to them when a question arises of altering the succession to or the titles of the Headship of the

---

[21] Both parliament and government must request and consent by Statute of Westminster, s. 9 (3).

[22] H.M. King Edward VIII's Abdication Act, No. 2 of 1937. This act was made to apply from 10 Dec. 1936—one day before the passing of the Abdication Act in the United Kingdom, so that George VI was King in South Africa (retrospectively) while Edward VIII was still King in the rest of the Commonwealth. To add to the confusion, the Irish Free State brought Edward VIII's abdication into effect on 12 Dec. 1936, so that Edward VIII was King in Ireland after George VI was King in the rest of the Commonwealth.

[23] Royal Style and Titles Act, No. 17 of 1947 and No. 6 of 1953.

[24] As was done by the Royal Titles Act, No. 22 of 1953.

Commonwealth and the symbol of their association. What is common to them all is that, for any change, the assent of the parliaments of all the Members is required, by constitutional convention, though not by law.[25] All have power to make a change by act of their own parliaments if they choose to do so.[26] India, Pakistan, and Malaya, it is submitted, may if they choose make a change without resorting to a legal enactment: Canada, South Africa, Australia, New Zealand, Ceylon, and Ghana, on the other hand, would have to enact any change in the law, but they have open to them a choice between passing the act themselves or inviting the parliament of the United Kingdom to make the change on their behalf through the appropriate procedure laid down in the relevant acts.

5

The differences in attitude of the individual Members of the Commonwealth towards the Queen as Head of the Commonwealth or as Head of the State may be illustrated by looking at the titles proclaimed for the Queen by certain of the Members at her Coronation in 1953. Until that date it had been considered proper that the Queen should have one title only throughout the whole Commonwealth, and that if any alteration were to be made, it should apply uniformly to all Members. The action taken in 1953, however, illustrated a new departure. While it was still necessary for changes to obtain the assent of the parliaments of all the Members, it was not thought necessary that the same title should be adopted by all Members. Each Member, indeed, was to be free to choose that title which suited it best. There was one element in common—all Members embodied in the title they chose the phrase 'Head of the Commonwealth'.

When Elizabeth II came to the throne in 1952 her title was: 'Elizabeth II, by the grace of God, of Great Britain, Ireland, and the British Dominions beyond the seas, Queen, Defender of the Faith'. This title was based upon proclamations made under the Royal Titles Act, 1927. In particular, a proclamation in 1948 which received the assent of the parliaments of all the

[25] Pakistan and India have not followed this convention, as has been seen above.

[26] Subject to doubts expressed by some authorities concerning Canada and Australia.

Members of the Commonwealth,[27] as was requisite, had removed the words 'Emperor of India' from the title of George VI in recognition of the independence granted to India and Pakistan in 1947. But the secession of the Republic of Ireland from the Commonwealth in 1949, the adoption of the republican form of government by India, and the explicit recognition of the King as Head of the Commonwealth at the Prime Ministers' Conference in 1949, made it clear that further changes would be needed.

The accession of Queen Elizabeth II on 6 February 1952 brought the opportunity to consider the position. Already some Members, in proclaiming the Queen's accession, showed that they were ready for changes, but the variety in the forms which they adopted in their proclamations showed the diversity of the Commonwealth once more. In London the government of the United Kingdom described the Queen as 'Elizabeth the Second, by the Grace of God, Queen of this Realm and of all Her other Realms and Territories, Head of the Commonwealth, Defender of the Faith'. The phrase 'Head of the Commonwealth' was used also in the proclamations issued in Australia, New Zealand, Pakistan, and Ceylon. India issued no proclamation but the Prime Minister addressed a message to the Queen welcoming her as 'the new Head of the Commonwealth'. In South Africa and Canada, the phrase 'Head of the Commonwealth' was not used. Instead she was proclaimed 'Elizabeth the Second, by the Grace of God, of Great Britain, Ireland and the British Dominions beyond the Seas, Queen Defender of the Faith', and in addition there were added, in the case of Canada, the words 'Supreme Liege Lady in and over Canada' and in the case of South Africa, 'Sovereign in and over the Union of South Africa'. It is interesting to observe that Canada and South Africa, both always in the forefront in asserting independence, should have adopted the old-fashioned formula while the United Kingdom and the other Members should have broken new ground. Strictly speaking, Canada and South Africa were acting correctly. They recited the Queen's title as it was established by law.

The divergence in the form of the proclamations made it

---

[27] See acts referred to above. The assent of the parliament of the United Kingdom was given in the Indian Independence Act, 1947, s. 7 (2).

clear, however, that it was time to discuss the question of the title and the matter was accordingly taken up at a Commonwealth Conference in December 1952, and a declaration was issued. It was agreed, in the words of the communiqué:

that the present Title is not in accord with current constitutional relations within the Commonwealth, and that there is need for a new form of title which will, in particular, reflect the special position of the Sovereign as Head of the Commonwealth. [The governments] concluded, after full consideration, that in the present stage of development of the Commonwealth relationship, it would be in accord with the established constitutional position that each member country should use for its own purposes a form of title which suits its own particular circumstances but retains a substantial element which is common to all. They agreed that the various forms of the Title should, in addition to an appropriate territorial designation, have as their common element the description of the Sovereign as Queen of Her other Realms and Territories and Head of the Commonwealth.[28]

As a result of this declaration the parliaments of the Members of the Commonwealth except India and Pakistan passed legislation[29] to authorize a form of title for the Queen in respect of each of them and in due course proclamations were issued on 29 May 1953, in the capitals of the Members of the Commonwealth bringing the new titles into effect simultaneously in respect of the different Members. It is worth while to set them out in order so that the resemblances and the differences may stand out.

United Kingdom. Elizabeth the Second, by the Grace of God, of the United Kingdom of Great Britain and Northern Ireland, and of Her other Realms and Territories, Queen, Head of the Commonwealth, Defender of the Faith.

Canada. Elizabeth the Second, by the Grace of God, of the United

[28] Cmd. 8748.
[29] See acts referred to above. The acts differ in content, from the Australian act which both authorizes a new title in respect of Australia and assents to the proclaiming of new titles in respect of other Members of the Commonwealth, to the South African act which authorizes a new title in respect of South Africa but makes no reference to assent to changes by other Members. It is submitted that the Australian procedure is constitutionally entirely correct. The Australian act, both in preambles and in operative sections, is a model of how the conventions of the Commonwealth should be carried out in this matter.

Kingdom, Canada, and Her other Realms and Territories, Queen, Head of the Commonwealth, Defender of the Faith.

Australia. Elizabeth the Second, by the Grace of God, of the United Kingdom, Australia and Her other Realms and Territories, Queen, Head of the Commonwealth, Defender of the Faith.

New Zealand. Elizabeth the Second, by the Grace of God, of the United Kingdom, New Zealand, and Her other Realms and Territories, Queen, Head of the Commonwealth, Defender of the Faith.

South Africa. Elizabeth the Second, Queen of South Africa and of Her other Realms and Territories, Head of the Commonwealth.

Pakistan. Elizabeth the Second, Queen of the United Kingdom and of Her other Realms and Territories, Head of the Commonwealth.[30]

Ceylon. Elizabeth the Second, Queen of Ceylon and of Her other Realms and Territories, Head of the Commonwealth.

It is interesting to speculate upon the differences of principle and of sentiment that lie behind these differing titles. To start with, the Queen's title in respect of the United Kingdom has been amended to take account of the partition of Ireland, and there is a specific reference to Northern Ireland. It will be noticed that Canada, Australia, and New Zealand all wished to lay some stress upon the fact that their own Queen was also the Queen of the United Kingdom and they made specific reference to this fact in the titles they chose. In this way we may think they chose to stress their association in a *British* Commonwealth, which is, perhaps, of particular significance in the case of Canada, for a large proportion of its population is not of British stock, but of French stock. The Prime Minister of Canada said in the debate on the Canadian bill authorizing the title:

Her Majesty is now Queen of Canada but she is the Queen of Canada because she is Queen of the United Kingdom and because the people of Canada are happy to recognise as their sovereign the person who is the sovereign of the United Kingdom. It is not a separate office . . . it is the sovereign who is recognised as the sovereign of the United Kingdom who is our sovereign. . . .[31]

The same three Members chose also to recite the Queen's title

[30] This title was proclaimed by the Governor-General, not enacted by the parliament.

[31] *Canadian House of Commons Debates,* 3 Feb. 1953, p. 1566. See note by W. P. M. Kennedy, 10 *University of Toronto Law Journal,* p. 83.

as 'Defender of the Faith', following the United Kingdom in this matter. In South Africa—no less staunch in the Christian faith than these other Members—it was decided none the less to drop the title 'Defender of the Faith'. Nor does South Africa follow the United Kingdom, Canada, Australia, or New Zealand in using the phrase 'by the Grace of God', preferring perhaps to think that the Queen holds her position by act of parliament. It was not surprising, of course, that in Moslem Pakistan and Buddhist Ceylon the title Defender of the Faith should be omitted as inapplicable, and there too no use was made of the phrase 'by the Grace of God'.

It was significant, also, that in South Africa and Ceylon no reference was made explicitly to the United Kingdom in the titles adopted, though that country is included in the reference to 'Her other Realms and Territories'. The majority of South Africans are not of British stock, and the government of the Union had laid great stress upon the fact that the Queen was Queen of South Africa in a distinct and separate capacity. Ceylon naturally followed the same plan. Pakistan's choice of title was significant not only for what it omitted, but also for what it contained. It was at first sight very surprising that in the Pakistan title there was an explicit reference to the United Kingdom, but no explicit reference to Pakistan itself. The explanation, it may be suggested, is that Pakistan was engaged upon drawing up her new constitution and it was still to be decided whether it would adopt a republican form of government or continue to be a monarchy. In these circumstances it was no doubt wise to make no explicit reference to Pakistan but to describe the Queen truthfully enough as 'Queen of the United Kingdom and of Her other Realms and Territories', one of which, if you chose to be explicit, was Pakistan. If Pakistan should become a republic, the title would still be correct, though Pakistan would no longer be one of 'Her Realms and Territories'.[32]

[32] One footnote may be added, which may interest those who have followed the controversy in the United Kingdom as to whether the Queen should be described in Scotland as Elizabeth I or Elizabeth II. Apparently Australia, South Africa, New Zealand, Ceylon, and Pakistan, for whom the Queen was certainly the first Elizabeth to reign over them as distinct kingdoms, were content to describe her as the second Elizabeth. Yet the case for describing the Queen as Elizabeth I of South Africa is surely as strong as the case for

6

It is apparent, then, that on the present organization of the Commonwealth, the Members are agreed that a symbol of their association is needed and that this symbol is the Queen, who, in her symbolic capacity, is the Head of the Commonwealth. The acceptance of the Queen as the symbol is, at present, a condition of becoming a Member of the Commonwealth. It may not always be so; it may be that the Members may find it essential, if they are to preserve or extend the association, that they should adopt a different symbol or no symbol at all. These are matters of speculation. For the present, although we may no longer say, in the words of the Declaration of 1926, that the Members of the Commonwealth are 'united by a common allegiance to the Crown', we may assert that they are 'united by a common recognition of the Queen as the symbol of their free association and, as such, the Head of the Commonwealth'.

calling her Elizabeth I of Scotland. The argument does not appear to have been invoked by the Scottish Nationalists.

APPENDIX I

THE COLONIAL LAWS VALIDITY ACT, 1865
(28 & 29 Vict., c. 63)

An Act to remove Doubts as to the Validity of Colonial Laws
(29 June 1865)

WHEREAS Doubts have been entertained respecting the Validity of divers Laws enacted or purporting to have been enacted by the Legislatures of certain of Her Majesty's Colonies, and respecting the Powers of such Legislatures, and it is expedient that such Doubts should be removed:

Be it hereby enacted by the Queen's most Excellent Majesty, by and with the Advice and Consent of the Lords Spiritual and Temporal, and Commons, in this present Parliament assembled, and by the Authority of the same, as follows:

1. The Term 'Colony' shall in this Act include all of Her Majesty's Possessions abroad in which there shall exist a Legislature, as herein-after defined, except the Channel Islands, the *Isle of Man*, and such Territories as may for the Time being be vested in Her Majesty under or by virtue of any Act of Parliament for the Government of *India*:

The Terms 'Legislature' and 'Colonial Legislature' shall severally signify the Authority, other than the Imperial Parliament or Her Majesty in Council, competent to make Laws for any Colony:

The Term 'Representative Legislature' shall signify any Colonial Legislature which shall comprise a Legislative Body of which One Half are elected by Inhabitants of the Colony:

The Term 'Colonial Law' shall include Laws made for any Colony either by such Legislature as aforesaid or by Her Majesty in Council:

An Act of Parliament, or any Provision thereof, shall, in construing this Act, be said to extend to any Colony when it is made applicable to such Colony by the express Words or necessary Intendment of any Act of Parliament:

The Term 'Governor' shall mean the Officer lawfully administering the Government of any Colony:

The Term 'Letters Patent' shall mean Letters Patent under the Great Seal of the United Kingdom of *Great Britain* and *Ireland*.

2. Any Colonial Law which is or shall be in any respect repugnant to the Provisions of any Act of Parliament extending to the Colony to which such Law may relate, or repugnant to any Order or Regulation made under Authority of such Act of Parliament, or having in the Colony the Force and Effect of such Act, shall be read subject to such Act, Order or Regulation, and shall, to the Extent of such Repugnancy, but not otherwise, be and remain absolutely void and inoperative.

3. No Colonial Law shall be or be deemed to have been void or inoperative on the Ground of Repugnancy to the Law of *England*, unless the same shall be repugnant to the Provisions of some such Act of Parliament, Order or Regulation as aforesaid.

4. No Colonial Law, passed with the Concurrence of or assented to by the Governor of any Colony, or to be hereafter so passed or assented to, shall be or be deemed to have been void or inoperative by reason only of any Instructions with reference to such Law or the Subject thereof which may have been given to such Governor by or on behalf of Her Majesty, by any Instrument other than the Letters Patent or Instrument authorising such Governor to concur in passing or to assent to Laws for the Peace, Order, and good Government of such Colony, even though such Instructions may be referred to in such Letters Patent or last-mentioned Instrument.

5. Every Colonial Legislature shall have, and be deemed at all Times to have had, full Power within its Jurisdiction to establish Courts of Judicature, and to abolish and reconstitute the same, and to alter the Constitution thereof, and to make Provision for the Administration of Justice therein; and every Representative Legislature shall, in respect to the Colony under its Jurisdiction, have, and be deemed at all Times to have had, full Power to make Laws respecting the Constitution, Powers, and Procedure of such Legislature; provided that such Laws shall have been passed in such Manner and Form as may from Time to Time be required by any Act of Parliament, Letters Patent, Order in Council, or Colonial Law for the Time being in force in the said Colony.

6. The Certificate of the Clerk or other proper Officer of a Legislative Body in any Colony to the Effect that the Document to which it is attached is a true Copy of any Colonial Law assented to by the Governor of such Colony, or of any Bill reserved for the Signification of Her Majesty's Pleasure by the said Governor, shall be *prima facie* Evidence that the Document so certified is a true Copy of such Law or Bill, and, as the Case may be, that such Law has been duly and properly passed and assented to, or that such Bill has been duly and properly passed and presented to the Governor; and any Proclamation purporting to be published by Authority of

the Governor in any Newspaper in the Colony to which such Law or Bill shall relate, and signifying Her Majesty's Disallowance of any such Colonial Law, or Her Majesty's Assent to any such reserved Bill as aforesaid, shall be *prima facie* Evidence of such Disallowance or Assent.

And whereas Doubts are entertained respecting the Validity of certain Acts enacted or reputed to be enacted by the Legislature of *South Australia*: Be it further enacted as follows:

7. All Laws or reputed Laws enacted or purporting to have been enacted by the said Legislature, or by Persons or Bodies of Persons for the Time being acting as such Legislature, which have received the Assent of Her Majesty in Council, or which have received the Assent of the Governor of the said Colony in the Name and on behalf of Her Majesty, shall be and be deemed to have been valid and effectual from the Date of such Assent for all Purposes whatever; provided that nothing herein contained shall be deemed to give Effect to any Law or reputed Law which has been disallowed by Her Majesty, or has expired, or has been lawfully repealed, or to prevent the lawful Disallowance or Repeal of any Law.

(*Note*: It may be worth mentioning that in 1937, s. 1 of this act was amended by the substitution of the words 'British India and British Burma' for 'and such territories . . . India'. The object of this amendment was to bring the act into line with the provisions of the Government of India Act, 1935, which *inter alia* separated Burma from India. The amendment was made by statutory order issued under the authority of the Government of India Act, 1935, s. 311 (5). See Government of India (Adaptation of Acts of Parliament) Order, 1937. S.R. and O. No. 230 of 1937, art. 2, Sched., Part II, p. 966.)

APPENDIX II

THE STATUTE OF WESTMINSTER, 1931
(22 Geo. V, c. 4)

An Act to give effect to certain resolutions passed by Imperial Conferences held in the years 1926 and 1930

(11 December 1931)

WHEREAS the delegates of His Majesty's Governments in the United Kingdom, the Dominion of Canada, the Commonwealth of Australia, the Dominion of New Zealand, the Union of South Africa, the Irish Free State and Newfoundland, at Imperial Conferences holden at Westminster in the years of our Lord nineteen hundred and twenty-six and nineteen hundred and thirty did concur in making the declarations and resolutions set forth in the Reports of the said Conferences:

And whereas it is meet and proper to set out by way of preamble to this Act that, inasmuch as the Crown is the symbol of the free association of the members of the British Commonwealth of Nations, and as they are united by a common allegiance to the Crown, it would be in accord with the established constitutional position of all the members of the Commonwealth in relation to one another that any alteration in the law touching the Succession to the throne or the Royal Style and Titles shall hereafter require the assent as well of the Parliaments of all the Dominions as of the Parliament of the United Kingdom:

And whereas it is in accord with the established constitutional position that no law hereafter made by the Parliament of the United Kingdom shall extend to any of the said Dominions as part of the law of that Dominion otherwise than at the request and with the consent of that Dominion:

And whereas it is necessary for the ratifying, confirming and establishing of certain of the said declarations and resolutions of the said Conferences that a law be made and enacted in due form by authority of the Parliament of the United Kingdom:

And whereas the Dominion of Canada, the Commonwealth of Australia, the Dominion of New Zealand, the Union of South Africa, the Irish Free State and Newfoundland have severally requested and consented to the submission of a measure to the

Parliament of the United Kingdom for making such provision with regard to the matters aforesaid as is hereafter in this Act contained:

Now, therefore, be it enacted by the King's most Excellent Majesty by and with the advice and consent of the Lords Spiritual and Temporal, and Commons, in this present Parliament assembled, and by the authority of the same, as follows:—

1. In this Act the expression 'Dominion' means any of the following Dominions, that is to say, the Dominion of Canada, the Commonwealth of Australia, the Dominion of New Zealand, the Union of South Africa, the Irish Free State and Newfoundland.

2. (1) The Colonial Laws Validity Act, 1865, shall not apply to any law made after the commencement of this Act by the Parliament of a Dominion.

(2) No law and no provision of any law made after the commencement of this Act by the Parliament of a Dominion shall be void or inoperative on the ground that it is repugnant to the law of England, or to the provisions of any existing or future Act of Parliament of the United Kingdom, or to any order, rule or regulation made under any such Act, and the powers of the Parliament of a Dominion shall include the power to repeal or amend any such Act, order, rule or regulation in so far as the same is part of the law of the Dominion.

3. It is hereby declared and enacted that the Parliament of a Dominion has full power to make laws having extra-territorial operation.

4. No Act of Parliament of the United Kingdom passed after the commencement of this Act shall extend, or be deemed to extend, to a Dominion as part of the law of that Dominion, unless it is expressly declared in that Act that that Dominion has requested, and consented to, the enactment thereof.

5. Without prejudice to the generality of the foregoing provisions of this Act, sections seven hundred and thirty-five and seven hundred and thirty-six of the Merchant Shipping Act, 1894, shall be construed as though reference therein to the Legislature of a British possession did not include reference to the Parliament of a Dominion.

6. Without prejudice to the generality of the foregoing provisions of this Act, section four of the Colonial Courts of Admiralty Act, 1890 (which requires certain laws to be reserved for the signification of His Majesty's pleasure or to contain a suspending clause), and so much of section seven of that Act as requires the approval of His Majesty in Council to any rules of Court for regulating the practice and procedure of a Colonial Court of Admiralty, shall cease to have effect in any Dominion as from the commencement of this Act.

7. (1). Nothing in this Act shall be deemed to apply to the repeal, amendment or alteration of the British North America Acts, 1867 to 1930, or any order, rule or regulation made thereunder.

(2) The provisions of section two of this Act shall extend to laws made by any of the Provinces of Canada and to the powers of the legislatures of such Provinces.

(3) The powers conferred by this Act upon the Parliament of Canada or upon the legislatures of the Provinces shall be restricted to the enactment of laws in relation to matters within the competence of the Parliament of Canada or of any of the legislatures of the Provinces respectively.

8. Nothing in this Act shall be deemed to confer any power to repeal or alter the Constitution or the Constitutional Act of the Commonwealth of Australia or the Constitution Act of the Dominion of New Zealand otherwise than in accordance with the law existing before the commencement of this Act.

9. (1) Nothing in this Act shall be deemed to authorize the Parliament of the Commonwealth of Australia to make laws on any matter within the authority of the States of Australia, not being a matter within the authority of the Parliament or Government of the Commonwealth of Australia.

(2) Nothing in this Act shall be deemed to require the concurrence of the Parliament or Government of the Commonwealth of Australia in any law made by the Parliament of the United Kingdom with respect to any matter within the authority of the States of Australia, not being a matter within the authority of the Parliament or Government of the Commonwealth of Australia, in any case where it would have been in accordance with the constitutional practice existing before the commencement of this Act that the Parliament of the United Kingdom should make that law without such concurrence.

(3) In the application of this Act to the Commonwealth of Australia the request and consent referred to in section four shall mean the request and consent of the Parliament and Government of the Commonwealth.

10. (1) None of the following sections of this Act, that is to say, sections two, three, four, five and six, shall extend to a Dominion to which this section applies as part of the law of that Dominion unless that section is adopted by the Parliament of the Dominion, and any Act of that Parliament adopting any section of this Act may provide that the adoption shall have effect either from the commencement of this Act or from such later date as is specified in the adopting Act.

(2) The Parliament of any such Dominion as aforesaid may at any

time revoke the adoption of any section referred to in subsection (1) of this section.

(3) The Dominions to which this section applies are the Commonwealth of Australia, the Dominion of New Zealand and Newfoundland.

11. Notwithstanding anything in the Interpretation Act, 1889, the expression 'Colony' shall not, in any Act of the Parliament of the United Kingdom passed after the commencement of this Act, include a Dominion or any Province or State forming part of a Dominion.

12. This Act may be cited as the Statute of Westminster, 1931.

APPENDIX III

THE INDIAN INDEPENDENCE ACT, 1947

(10 & 11 Geo. VI, c. 30)

An Act to make provision for the setting up in India of two independent Dominions, to substitute other provisions for certain provisions of the Government of India Act, 1935, which apply outside those Dominions, and to provide for other matters consequential on or connected with the setting up of those Dominions

(18 July 1947)

BE it enacted by the King's most Excellent Majesty, by and with the advice and consent of the Lords Spiritual and Temporal, and Commons, in this present Parliament assembled, and by the authority of the same, as follows:

1. (1) As from the fifteenth day of August, nineteen hundred and forty-seven, two independent Dominions shall be set up in India, to be known respectively as India and Pakistan.

(2) The said Dominions are hereafter in this Act referred to as 'the new Dominions', and the said fifteenth day of August is hereafter in this Act referred to as 'the appointed day'. . . .

[Sections 2–4 omitted.]

5. For each of the new Dominions, there shall be a Governor-General who shall be appointed by His Majesty and shall represent His Majesty for the purposes of the government of the Dominion:

Provided that, unless and until provision to the contrary is made by a law of the Legislature of either of the new Dominions, the same person may be Governor-General of both the new Dominions.

6. (1) The Legislature of each of the new Dominions shall have full power to make laws for that Dominion, including laws having extra-territorial operation.

(2) No law and no provision of any law made by the Legislature of either of the new Dominions shall be void or inoperative on the ground that it is repugnant to the law of England, or to the provisions of this or any existing or future Act of Parliament of the United Kingdom, or to any order, rule or regulation made under any such Act, and the powers of the Legislature of each Dominion include the power to repeal or amend any such Act, order, rule or regulation in so far as it is part of the law of the Dominion.

(3) The Governor-General of each of the new Dominions shall have full power to assent in His Majesty's name to any law of the Legislature of that Dominion and so much of any Act as relates to the disallowance of laws by His Majesty or the reservation of laws for the signification of His Majesty's pleasure thereon or the suspension of the operation of laws until the signification of His Majesty's pleasure thereon shall not apply to laws of the Legislature of either of the new Dominions.

(4) No Act of Parliament of the United Kingdom passed on or after the appointed day shall extend, or be deemed to extend, to either of the new Dominions as part of the law of that Dominion unless it is extended thereto by a law of the Legislature of the Dominion.

(5) No Order in Council made on or after the appointed day under any Act passed before the appointed day, and no order, rule or other instrument made on or after the appointed day under any such Act by any United Kingdom Minister or other authority, shall extend, or be deemed to extend, to either of the new Dominions as part of the law of that Dominion.

(6) The power referred to in subsection (1) of this section extends to the making of laws limiting for the future the powers of the Legislature of the Dominion.

7. (1) As from the appointed day—

(a) His Majesty's Government in the United Kingdom have no responsibility as respects the government of any of the territories which, immediately before that day, were included in British India;

(b) the suzerainty of His Majesty over the Indian States lapses, and with it, all treaties and agreements in force at the date of the passing of this Act between His Majesty and the rulers of Indian States, all functions exercisable by His Majesty at that date with respect to Indian States, all obligations of His Majesty existing at that date towards Indian States or the rulers thereof, and all powers, rights, authority or jurisdiction exercisable by His Majesty at that date in or in relation to Indian States by treaty, grant, usage, sufferance or otherwise; and

(c) there lapse also any treaties or agreements in force at the date of the passing of this Act between His Majesty and any persons having authority in the tribal areas, any obligations of His Majesty existing at that date to any such persons or with respect to the tribal areas, and all powers, rights, authority or jurisdiction exercisable at that date by His Majesty in or in relation to the tribal areas by treaty, grant, usage, sufferance or otherwise:

Provided that, notwithstanding anything in paragraph (*b*) or paragraph (*c*) of this sub-section, effect shall, as nearly as may be, continue to be given to the provisions of any such agreement as is therein referred to which relate to customs, transit and communications, posts and telegraphs, or other like matters, until the provisions in question are denounced by the Ruler of the Indian State or person having authority in the tribal areas on the one hand, or by the Dominion or Province or other part thereof concerned on the other hand, or are superseded by subsequent agreements.

(2) The assent of the Parliament of the United Kingdom is hereby given to the omission from the Royal Style and Titles of the words 'Indiae Imperator' and the words 'Emperor of India' and to the issue by His Majesty for that purpose of His Royal Proclamation under the Great Seal of the Realm.

8. (1) In the case of each of the new Dominions, the powers of the Legislature of the Dominion shall, for the purpose of making provision as to the constitution of the Dominion, be exercisable in the first instance by the Constituent Assembly of that Dominion, and references in this Act to the Legislature of the Dominion shall be construed accordingly.

(2) Except in so far as other provision is made by or in accordance with a law made by the Constituent Assembly of the Dominion under subsection (1) of this section, each of the new Dominions and all Provinces and other parts thereof shall be governed as nearly as may be in accordance with the Government of India Act, 1935; and the provisions of that Act, and of the Orders in Council, rules and other instruments made thereunder, shall, so far as applicable, and subject to any express provisions of this Act, and with such omissions, additions, adaptations and modifications as may be specified in orders of the Governor-General under the next succeeding section, have effect accordingly:

Provided that—

(*a*) the said provisions shall apply separately in relation to each of the new Dominions and nothing in this subsection shall be construed as continuing on or after the appointed day any Central Government or Legislature common to both the new Dominions;

(*b*) nothing in this subsection shall be construed as continuing in force on or after the appointed day any form of control by His Majesty's Government in the United Kingdom over the affairs of the new Dominions or of any Province or other part thereof;

(*c*) so much of the said provisions as requires the Governor-General or any Governor to act in his discretion or exercise his individual judgment as respects any matter shall cease to have effect as from the appointed day;

(*d*) as from the appointed day, no Provincial Bill shall be reserved under the Government of India Act, 1935, for the signification of His Majesty's pleasure, and no Provincial Act shall be disallowed by His Majesty thereunder; and

(*e*) the powers of the Federal Legislature or Indian Legislature under that Act, as in force in relation to each Dominion, shall, in the first instance, be exercisable by the Constituent Assembly of the Dominion in addition to the powers exercisable by that Assembly under subsection (1) of this section.

(3) Any provision of the Government of India Act, 1935, which, as applied to either of the new Dominions by subsection (2) of this section and the orders therein referred to, operates to limit the power of the legislature of that Dominion shall, unless and until other provision is made by or in accordance with a law made by the Constituent Assembly of the Dominion in accordance with the provisions of subsection (1) of this section, have the like effect as a law of the Legislature of the Dominion limiting for the future the powers of that Legislature. . . .

[Sections 9–20 and the three schedules omitted.]

APPENDIX IV

THE CEYLON INDEPENDENCE ACT, 1947
(11 Geo. VI, c. 7)

An Act to make provision for, and in connexion with, the attainment by Ceylon of fully responsible status within the British Commonwealth of Nations

(10 December 1947)

BE it enacted by the King's most Excellent Majesty, by and with the advice and consent of the Lords Spiritual and Temporal, and Commons, in this present Parliament assembled, and by the authority of the same, as follows—

1. (1) No Act of the Parliament of the United Kingdom passed on or after the appointed day shall extend, or be deemed to extend, to Ceylon as part of the law of Ceylon, unless it is expressly declared in that Act that Ceylon has requested, and consented to, the enactment thereof.

(2) As from the appointed day His Majesty's Government in the United Kingdom shall have no responsibility for the government of Ceylon.

(3) As from the appointed day the provisions of the First Schedule to this Act shall have effect with respect to the legislative powers of Ceylon.

2. As from the appointed day Ceylon shall be included in the definition of 'Dominion' in paragraph (23) of section one hundred and ninety of the Army Act and of the Air Force Act (which section, in each Act, relates generally to the interpretation of the Act), and accordingly in the said paragraph (23), in each Act, for the words 'and Newfoundland' there shall be substituted the words 'Newfoundland and Ceylon'. . . .

[Sections 3–5 omitted.]

First Schedule

Legislative Powers of Ceylon

1. (1) The Colonial Laws Validity Act, 1865, shall not apply to any law made after the appointed day by the Parliament of Ceylon.

(2) No law and no provision of any law made after the appointed

day by the Parliament of Ceylon shall be void or inoperative on the ground that it is repugnant to the law of England, or to the provisions of any existing or future Act of Parliament of the United Kingdom, or to any order, rule or regulation made under any such Act, and the powers of the Parliament of Ceylon shall include the power to repeal or amend any such Act, order, rule or regulation in so far as the same is part of the law of Ceylon.

2. The Parliament of Ceylon shall have full power to make laws having extra-territorial operation.

3. Without prejudice to the generality of the foregoing provisions of this Schedule, sections seven hundred and thirty-five and seven hundred and thirty-six of the Merchant Shipping Act, 1894, shall be construed as though reference therein to the legislature of a British possession did not include reference to the Parliament of Ceylon.

4. Without prejudice to the generality of the foregoing provisions of this Schedule, section four of the Colonial Courts of Admiralty Act, 1890 (which requires certain laws to be reserved for the signification of His Majesty's pleasure or to contain a suspending clause), and so much of section seven of that Act as requires the approval of His Majesty in Council to any rules of Court for regulating the practice and procedure of a Colonial Court of Admiralty, shall cease to have effect in Ceylon.

[Second Schedule omitted.]

APPENDIX V

THE GHANA INDEPENDENCE ACT, 1957
(5 & 6 Eliz. II, c. 6)

An Act to make provision for, and in connection with, the attainment by the Gold Coast of fully responsible status within the British Commonwealth of Nations

(7 February 1957)

BE it enacted by the Queen's most Excellent Majesty, by and with the advice and consent of the Lords Spiritual and Temporal, and Commons, in this present Parliament assembled, and by the authority of the same, as follows—

1. The territories included immediately before the appointed day in the Gold Coast as defined in and for the purposes of the Gold Coast (Constitution) Order in Council, 1954, shall as from that day together form part of Her Majesty's dominions under the name of Ghana, and—

   (a) no Act of the Parliament of the United Kingdom passed on or after the appointed day shall extend, or be deemed to extend, to Ghana as part of the law of Ghana, unless it is expressly declared in that Act that the Parliament of Ghana has requested, and consented to, the enactment thereof;

   (b) as from the appointed day, Her Majesty's Government in the United Kingdom shall have no responsibility for the government of Ghana or any part thereof;

   (c) as from the appointed day, the provisions of the First Schedule to this Act shall have effect with respect to the legislative powers of Ghana;

   Provided that nothing in this section other than paragraphs (a) to (c) thereof shall affect the operation in any of the territories aforesaid of any enactment, or any other instrument having the effect of law, passed or made with respect thereto before the appointed day.

2. As from the appointed day, the British Nationality Act, 1948, shall have effect—

   (a) with the substitution in subsection (3) of section one thereof (which provides for persons to be British subjects or Commonwealth citizens by virtue of citizenship of certain countries) for the words 'and Ceylon' of the words 'Ceylon and Ghana';

(*b*) as if in the British Protectorates, Protected States and Protected Persons Order in Council, 1949, the words 'Northern Territories of the Gold Coast' in the First Schedule thereto and the words 'Togoland under United Kingdom Trusteeship' in the Third Schedule thereto were omitted:

Provided that a person who, immediately before the appointed day, was for the purposes of the said Act and Order in Council a British protected person by virtue of his connection with either of the territories mentioned in paragraph (*b*) of this section shall not cease to be such a British protected person for any of those purposes by reason of anything contained in the foregoing provisions of this Act, but shall so cease upon his becoming a citizen of Ghana under any law of the Parliament of Ghana making provision for such citizenship.

3. (1) No scheme shall be made on or after the appointed day under the Colonial Development and Welfare Acts, 1940 to 1955, wholly or partly for the benefit of Ghana.

(2) Any scheme in force under the said Acts immediately before the appointed day which was made solely for the benefit of Ghana or any part thereof shall cease to have effect on that day without prejudice to the making of payments in pursuance of that scheme on or after that day in respect of any period falling before that day; and, so far as practicable, no part of any sums paid out of moneys provided by Parliament for the purposes of any other scheme made under those Acts before that day shall be employed in respect of any period falling on or after that day for the benefit of Ghana.

(3) Nothing in the two foregoing subsections shall restrict the making of, or the employment of sums paid out of moneys provided by Parliament for the purposes of, any scheme under the said Acts with respect to a body established for the joint benefit of Ghana and one or more of the following territories, that is to say, the Federation or any Region of Nigeria, Sierra Leone and the Gambia, in a case where Ghana has undertaken to bear a reasonable share of the cost of the scheme.

(4) Without prejudice to the continuance of any operations commenced by the Colonial Development Corporation in any part of Ghana before the appointed day, as from that day the expression 'colonial territories' in the Overseas Resources Development Acts, 1948 to 1956, shall not include Ghana or any part thereof.

4. (1) Notwithstanding anything in the Interpretation Act, 1889, the expression 'colony' in any Act of the Parliament of the United Kingdom passed on or after the appointed day shall not include Ghana or any part thereof.

(2) As from the appointed day, the expression 'colony' in the

Army Act, 1955, and the Air Force Act, 1955, shall not include Ghana or any part thereof, and in the definitions of 'Commonwealth force' in subsection (1) of section two hundred and twenty-five and subsection (1) of section two hundred and twenty-three respectively of those Acts and in section eighty-six of the Naval Discipline Act as amended by the Revision of the Army and Air Force Acts (Transitional Provisions) Act, 1955, for the words 'or Ceylon' there shall be substituted the words 'Ceylon or Ghana'.

(3) Any Order in Council made on or after the appointed day under the Army Act, 1955, or the Air Force Act, 1955, providing for that Act to continue in force beyond the date on which it would otherwise expire shall not operate to continue that Act in force beyond that date as part of the law of Ghana.

(4) As from the appointed day, the provisions specified in the Second Schedule to this Act shall have effect subject to the amendments respectively specified in that Schedule, and Her Majesty may by Order in Council, which shall be subject to annulment in pursuance of a resolution of either House of Parliament, make such further adaptations in any Act of the Parliament of the United Kingdom passed before this Act, or in any instrument having effect under any such Act, as appear to her necessary in consequence of section one of this Act; and any Order in Council made under this subsection may be varied or revoked by a subsequent Order in Council so made and, though made after the appointed day, may be made so as to have effect from that day:

Provided that this subsection shall not extend to Ghana as part of the law thereof.

5. (1) This Act may be cited as the Ghana Independence Act, 1957.

(2) In this Act, the expression 'the appointed day' means the sixth day of March, nineteen hundred and fifty-seven, unless before that date Her Majesty has by Order in Council appointed some other day to be the appointed day for the purposes of this Act.

First Schedule

Legislative Powers of Ghana

1. The Colonial Laws Validity Act, 1865, shall not apply to any law made on or after the appointed day by the Parliament of Ghana.

2. No law and no provision of any law made on or after the appointed day by the Parliament of Ghana shall be void or inoperative on the ground that it is repugnant to the law of England, or to the provisions of any existing or future Act of the Parliament of the

United Kingdom, or to any order, rule or regulation made under any such Act, and the powers of the Parliament of Ghana shall include the power to repeal or amend any such Act, order, rule or regulation in so far as it is part of the law of Ghana.

3. The Parliament of Ghana shall have full power to make laws having extra-territorial operation.

4. Without prejudice to the generality of the foregoing provisions of this Schedule, sections seven hundred and thirty-five and seven hundred and thirty-six of the Merchant Shipping Act, 1894, shall be construed as though reference therein to the legislature of a British possession did not include reference to the Parliament of Ghana.

5. Without prejudice to the generality of the foregoing provisions of this Schedule, section four of the Colonial Courts of Admiralty Act, 1890 (which requires certain laws to be reserved for the signification of Her Majesty's pleasure or to contain a suspending clause) and so much of section seven of that Act as requires the approval of Her Majesty in Council to any rules of court for regulating the practice and procedure of a Colonial Court of Admiralty shall cease to have effect in Ghana.

6. Notwithstanding anything in the foregoing provisions of this Schedule, the constitutional provisions shall not be repealed, amended or modified otherwise than in such manner as may be specified in those provisions.

In this paragraph, the expression 'the constitutional provisions' means the provisions for the time being in force on or at any time after the appointed day of the Gold Coast (Constitution) Orders in Council, 1954 to 1956, and of any other Order in Council made before that day, or any law, or instrument made under a law, of the Parliament of Ghana made on or after that day, which amends, modifies, re-enacts with or without amendment or modification, or makes different provisions in lieu of, any of the provisions of any such Order in Council or of any such law or instrument previously made.

[Second Schedule omitted.]

APPENDIX VI

THE FEDERATION OF MALAYA INDEPENDENCE ACT, 1957

An Act to make provision for and in connection with the establishment of the Federation of Malaya as an independent sovereign country within the Commonwealth

(31 July 1957)

BE it enacted by the Queen's most Excellent Majesty, by and with the advice and consent of the Lords Spiritual and Temporal, and Commons, in this present Parliament assembled, and by the authority of the same, as follows—

1. (1) Subject to the provisions of this section, the approval of Parliament is hereby given to the conclusion between Her Majesty and the Rulers of the Malay States of such agreement as appears to Her Majesty to be expedient for the establishment of the Federation of Malaya as an independent sovereign country within the Commonwealth.

(2) Any such agreement as aforesaid may make provision—

(a) for the formation of the Malay States and of the Settlements of Penang and Malacca into a new independent Federation of States under a Federal Constitution specified in the agreement, and for the application to those Settlements, as States of the new Federation, of State Constitutions so specified;

(b) for the termination of Her Majesty's sovereignty and jurisdiction in respect of the said Settlements, and of all other Her power and jurisdiction in and in respect of the Malay States or the Federation as a whole, and the revocation or modification of all or any of the provisions of the Federation of Malaya Agreement, 1948, and of any other agreements in force between Her Majesty and the Rulers of the Malay States.

(3) Any such agreement shall be conditional upon the approval of the new Federal Constitution by enactments of the existing Federal Legislature and of each of the Malay States; and upon such approval being given Her Majesty by Order in Council may direct that the said Federal and State Constitutions shall have the force of law within the said Settlements, and, so far as She has jurisdiction in that behalf, elsewhere within the Federation, and may make such

other provision as appears to Her to be necessary for giving effect to the agreement.

(4) Any Order in Council under this section shall be laid before Parliament after being made.

(5) In this Act 'the appointed day' means such day as may be specified by Order in Council under this section as the day from which the said Federal Constitution has the force of law as aforesaid.

2. (1) On and after the appointed day, all existing law to which this section applies shall, until otherwise provided by the authority having power to amend or repeal that law, continue to apply in relation to the Federation or any part thereof, and to persons and things in any way belonging thereto or connected therewith, in all respects as if no such agreement as is referred to in subsection (1) of section one of this Act had been concluded;

Provided that—

(a) the enactments referred to in the First Schedule to this Act shall have effect as from the appointed day subject to the amendments made by that Schedule (being amendments for applying in relation to the Federation certain statutory provisions applicable to Commonwealth countries having fully responsible status within Her Majesty's dominions);

(b) Her Majesty may by Order in Council make such further adaptations in any Act of the Parliament of the United Kingdom passed before the appointed day, or in any instrument having effect under any such Act, as appear to Her necessary or expedient in consequence of the agreement referred to in subsection (1) of section one of this Act;

(c) in relation to the Colonial Development and Welfare Acts, 1940 to 1955, this subsection shall have effect only so far as may be necessary for the making of payments on or after the appointed day in pursuance of schemes in force immediately before that day and in respect of periods falling before that day;

(d) nothing in this section shall be construed as continuing in force any enactment or rule of law limiting or restricting the legislative powers of the Federation or any part thereof.

(2) An Order in Council made under this section shall be subject to annulment in pursuance of a resolution of either House of Parliament.

(3) An Order in Council made under this section may be varied or revoked by a subsequent Order in Council so made and may, though made after the appointed day, be made so as to have effect from that day.

(4) In this section 'existing law' means any Act of Parliament or other enactment or instrument whatsoever, and any rule of law, which is in force on the appointed day or, having been passed or made before the appointed day, comes into force after that day; and the existing law to which this section applies is law which operates as law of, or of any part of, the United Kingdom, Southern Rhodesia, or any colony, protectorate or United Kingdom trust territory except that this section—

(a) does not apply to any law passed by the Federal Legislature of Rhodesia and Nyasaland;

(b) applies to other law of, or of any part of, Southern Rhodesia so far only as concerns law which can be amended neither by a law passed by the Legislature thereof nor by a law passed by the said Federal Legislature; and

(c) applies to other law of, or of any part of, Northern Rhodesia or Nyasaland so far only as concerns law which cannot be amended by a law passed by the said Federal Legislature.

(5) References in subsection (4) of this section to a colony, a protectorate and a United Kingdom trust territory shall be construed as if they were references contained in the British Nationality Act, 1948.

3. (1) Her Majesty may by Order in Council confer on the Judicial Committee of the Privy Council such jurisdiction in respect of appeals from the Supreme Court of the Federation as appears to Her to be appropriate for giving effect to any arrangements made after the appointed day between Her Majesty and the Head of the Federation for the reference of such appeals to that Committee.

(2) An Order in Council under this section may determine the classes of cases in which, and the conditions as to leave and otherwise subject to which, any such appeal may be entertained by the said Committee, and the practice and procedure to be followed on any such appeal, and may in particular make such provision with respect to the form of the report or recommendation to be made by the Committee in respect of any such appeal, and the transmission to the Head of the Federation of such reports or recommendations, as appears to Her Majesty to be appropriate having regard to the said arrangements.

(3) Except so far as otherwise provided by Order in Council under this section, and subject to such modifications as may be so provided, the Judicial Committee Act, 1833, shall apply in relation to appeals under this section as it applies in relation to appeals to Her Majesty in Council.

(4) Arrangements made in pursuance of this section may apply to any appeal to Her Majesty in Council, or any application for

leave to bring such an appeal, which is pending on the appointed day; but except as aforesaid nothing in this Act shall be construed as continuing in force any right of appeal to Her Majesty in Council from any court in the Federation.

(5) An Order in Council made under this section may be varied or revoked by a subsequent Order in Council so made.

4. (1) References in this Act to any other enactment are references thereto as amended or extended by any subsequent enactment.

(2) The enactments described in the Second Schedule to this Act are hereby repealed, as from the appointed day, to the extent specified in the third column of that Schedule.

(3) This Act may be cited as the Federation of Malaya Independence Act, 1957.

[Schedules One and Two omitted.]

APPENDIX VII

THE NIGERIA INDEPENDENCE ACT, 1960

An Act to make provision for, and in connexion with, the attainment by Nigeria of fully responsible status within the Commonwealth

BE it enacted by the Queen's most Excellent Majesty, by and with the advice and consent of the Lords Spiritual and Temporal, and Commons, in this present Parliament assembled, and by the authority of the same, as follows:

1. (1) On the first day of October, nineteen hundred and sixty (in this Act referred to as 'the appointed day'), the Colony and the Protectorate as respectively defined by the Nigeria (Constitution) Orders in Council, 1954 to 1960, shall together constitute part of Her Majesty's dominions under the name of Nigeria.

(2) No Act of the Parliament of the United Kingdom passed on or after the appointed day shall extend, or be deemed to extend, to Nigeria or any part thereof as part of the law thereof, and as from that day—

(a) Her Majesty's Government in the United Kingdom shall have no responsibility for the government of Nigeria or any part thereof; and

(b) the provisions of the First Schedule to this Act shall have effect with respect to legislative powers in Nigeria.

(3) Without prejudice to subsection (2) of this section, nothing in subsection (1) thereof shall effect the operation in Nigeria or any part thereof on and after the appointed day of any enactment, or any other instrument having the effect of law, passed or made with respect thereto before that day.

2. (1) As from the appointed day, the British Nationality Acts, 1948 and 1958, shall have effect as if—

(a) in subsection (3) of section one of the said Act of 1948 (which provides for persons to be British subjects or Commonwealth citizens by virtue of citizenship of certain countries) the word 'and' in the last place where it occurs were omitted, and at the end there were added the words 'and Nigeria';

(b) in the First Schedule to the British Protectorates, Protected States and Protected Persons Order in Council, 1949, the words 'Nigeria Protectorate' were omitted:

Provided that a person who immediately before the appointed day is for the purposes of the said Acts and Order in Council a British protected person by virtue of his connexion with the Nigeria Protectorate shall not cease to be such a British protected person for any of those purposes by reason of anything contained in the foregoing provisions of this Act, but shall so cease upon his becoming a citizen of Nigeria under the law thereof.

(2) Subject to the subsequent provisions of this section, any person who immediately before the appointed day is a citizen of the United Kingdom and Colonies shall on that day cease to be such a citizen if—

(a) under the law of Nigeria he becomes on that day a citizen of Nigeria; and

(b) he, his father or his father's father was born in any of the territories comprised in Nigeria.

(3) Subject to subsection (8) of this section, a person shall not cease to be a citizen of the United Kingdom and Colonies under the last foregoing subsection if he, his father or his father's father—

(a) was born in the United Kingdom or in a colony; or

(b) is or was a person naturalized in the United Kingdom and Colonies; or

(c) was registered as a citizen of the United Kingdom and Colonies; or

(d) became a British subject by reason of the annexation of any territory included in a colony.

(4) A person shall not cease to be a citizen of the United Kingdom and Colonies under subsection (2) of this section if he was born in a protectorate, protected state or United Kingdom trust territory, or if his father or his father's father was so born and is or at any time was a British subject.

(5) A woman who is the wife of a citizen of the United Kingdom and Colonies shall not cease to be such a citizen under subsection (2) of this section unless her husband does so.

(6) Subsection (2) of section six of the British Nationality Act, 1948 (which provides for the registration as a citizen of the United Kingdom and Colonies of a woman who has been married to such a citizen) shall not apply to a woman by virtue of her marriage to a person who ceases to be such a citizen under subsection (2) of this section, or who would have done so if living on the appointed day.

(7) Subject to the next following subsection, the reference in paragraph (b) of subsection (3) of this section to a person naturalized in the United Kingdom and Colonies shall include a person who would, if living immediately before the commencement of the British Nationality Act, 1948, have become a person naturalised in

the United Kingdom and Colonies by virtue of subsection (6) of section thirty-two of that Act (which relates to persons given local naturalisation before that commencement in a colony or protectorate).

(8) Any reference in subsection (3) or (4) of this section to a territory of any of the following descriptions, that is to say, a colony, protectorate, protected state or United Kingdom trust territory, shall, subject to the next following subsection, be construed as a reference to a territory which is of that description on the appointed day; and the said subsection (3) shall not apply to a person by virtue of any certificate of naturalisation granted or registration effected by the governor or government of a territory outside the United Kingdom which is not on that day of one of those descriptions.

(9) The protectorates of Northern Rhodesia and Nyasaland shall be excepted from the operation of any reference in subsection (4) or (8) of this section to a protectorate.

(10) Part III of the British Nationality Act, 1948 (which contains supplemental provisions) shall have effect for the purposes of subsections (2) to (9) of this section as if those subsections were included in that Act.

3. (1) Notwithstanding anything in the Interpretation Act, 1889, the expression 'colony' in any Act of the Parliament of the United Kingdom passed on or after the appointed day shall not include Nigeria or any part thereof.

(2) As from the appointed day—

(*a*) the expression 'colony' in the Army Act, 1955, the Air Force Act, 1955, and the Naval Discipline Act, 1957, shall not include Nigeria or any part thereof; and

(*b*) in the definitions of 'Commonwealth force' in subsection (1) of section two hundred and twenty-five and subsection (1) of section two hundred and twenty-three respectively of the said Acts of 1955, and in the definition of 'Commonwealth country' in subsection (1) of section one hundred and thirty-five of the said Act of 1957—

(i) the word 'or' (being, in the said Acts of 1955, that word in the last place where it occurs in those definitions) shall be omitted; and

(ii) at the end there shall be added the words 'or Nigeria'.

(3) Any Order in Council made on or after the appointed day under either of the said Acts of 1955 providing for that Act to continue in force beyond the date on which it would otherwise expire shall not operate to continue that Act in force beyond that date as part of the law of Nigeria or any part thereof.

(4) As from the appointed day, the provisions specified in the Second Schedule to this Act shall have effect subject to the amendments respectively specified in that Schedule, and Her Majesty may by Order in Council, which shall be subject to annulment in pursuance of a resolution of either House of Parliament, make such further adaptations in any Act of the Parliament of the United Kingdom passed before this Act, or in any instrument having effect under any such Act, as appear to Her necessary in consequence of section one of this Act; and any Order in Council made under this subsection may be varied or revoked by a subsequent Order in Council so made and, though made after the appointed day, may be made so as to have effect from that day:

Provided that this subsection shall not extend to Nigeria or any part thereof as part of the law thereof.

4. (1) In relation to any person who at the date of the passing of this Act is serving in the naval forces of the Federation of Nigeria established by section three of the Nigeria (Constitution) Order in Council, 1954, the Overseas Service Act, 1958 (which authorises the Secretary of State to appoint officers to be available for civilian employment in the public service of an overseas territory in accordance with arrangements made by the Secretary of State with the government of that territory and to make provision as to superannuation in respect of officers so appointed) shall have effect as if service in those forces and service on or after the appointed day in the naval forces of Nigeria were civilian employment in the public service of that Federation or, as the case may be, of Nigeria.

(2) In relation to any person who, having served in the naval forces of the said Federation in accordance with arrangements made by the Secretary of State with the government of that Federation, has by reason of death or retirement ceased so to serve before the date of the passing of this Act, subsection (2) of section four of the said Act of 1958 (which authorises the Secretary of State to pay pensions to or in respect of persons who have served as officers to whom that Act applies) shall have effect as if that person were a person who has served as such an officer and as if those arrangements were such arrangements as are mentioned in subsection (1) of section one of that Act.

5. (1) This Act may be cited as the Nigeria Independence Act, 1960.

(2) References in this Act to any enactment are references to that enactment as amended or extended by or under any other enactment.

SCHEDULES

First Schedule

Legislative Powers in Nigeria

1. The Colonial Laws Validity Act, 1865, shall not apply to any law made on or after the appointed day by any legislature established for Nigeria or any part thereof.

2. No law and no provision of any law made on or after the appointed day by any such legislature as aforesaid shall be void or inoperative on the ground that it is repugnant to the law of England, or to the provisions of any Act of the Parliament of the United Kingdom, including this Act, or to any order, rule or regulation made under any such Act, and, subject to paragraph 6 of this Schedule, the powers of any such legislature shall include the power to repeal or amend any such Act, order, rule or regulation in so far as it is part of the law of Nigeria or any part thereof and in so far as it relates to matters within the legislative powers of that legislature.

3. Any such legislature as aforesaid shall have full power to make laws having extra-territorial operation, so far as those laws relate to matters within the legislative powers of that legislature.

4. Without prejudice to the generality of the foregoing provisions of this Schedule, sections seven hundred and thirty-five and seven hundred and thirty-six of the Merchant Shipping Act, 1894, shall be construed as though reference therein to the legislature of a British possession did not include reference to any such legislature as aforesaid.

5. Without prejudice to the generality of the foregoing provisions of this Schedule, section four of the Colonial Courts of Admiralty Act, 1890 (which requires certain laws to be reserved for the signification of Her Majesty's pleasure or to contain a suspending clause) and so much of section seven of that Act as requires the approval of Her Majesty in Council to any rules of court for regulating the practice and procedure of a Colonial Court of Admiralty shall cease to have effect in Nigeria.

6. Nothing in this Act shall confer on any such legislature as aforesaid any power to repeal, amend or modify the constitutional provisions otherwise than in such manner as may be provided for in those provisions.

In this paragraph, the expression 'the constitutional provisions' means this Act, any Order in Council made before the appointed day which revokes the Nigeria (Constitution) Orders in Council,

1954 to 1960, and any law, or instrument made under a law, of any such legislature as aforesaid made on or after that day which amends, modifies, re-enacts with or without amendment or modification, or makes different provision in lieu of, any of the provisions of this Act, that Order in Council or any such law or instrument previously made.

Second Schedule

Amendments not affecting Law of Nigeria

Diplomatic immunities

1. In section four hundred and sixty-one of the Income Tax Act, 1952 (which relates to exemption from income tax in the case of certain Commonwealth representatives and their staffs)—
   (a) in subsection (2), the word 'or' (in the last place where it occurs before the words 'for any state') shall be omitted, and immediately before the words 'for any state' there shall be inserted the words 'or Nigeria';
   (b) in subsection (3), immediately before the words 'and "Agent-General"' there shall be inserted the words 'or for Nigeria'.

2. In subsection (6) of section one of the Diplomatic Immunities (Commonwealth Countries and Republic of Ireland) Act, 1952, immediately before the word 'and' in the last place where it occurs there shall be inserted the word 'Nigeria'.

Financial

3. In section two of the Import Duties Act, 1958, in subsection (4), after the words 'New Zealand' there shall be inserted the word 'Nigeria'.

4. In the Colonial Stock Act, 1934 (which extends the stocks which may be treated as trustee securities), the expression 'Dominion' shall include Nigeria; and, during any period falling on or after the appointed day during which there is in force as part of the law of Nigeria any instrument passed or made before that day which makes provision corresponding to the undertaking required to be given by the Government of a Dominion under paragraph (a) of subsection (1) of section one of that Act, paragraphs (a) and (b) of the said subsection (1) shall be deemed to have been complied with in the case of Nigeria.

Visiting forces

5. In the Visiting Forces (British Commonwealth) Act, 1933, section four (which deals with attachment and mutual powers of command) and the definition of 'visiting force' for the purposes of

that Act which is contained in section eight thereof shall apply in relation to forces raised in Nigeria as they apply in relation to forces raised in Dominions within the meaning of the Statute of Westminster, 1931.

6. In the Visiting Forces Act, 1952—

   (a) in paragraph (a) of subsection (1) of section one (which specifies the countries to which that Act applies) the word 'or' in the first place where it occurs shall be omitted, and at the end there shall be added the words 'Nigeria or';

   (b) in paragraph (a) of subsection (1) of section ten the expression 'colony' shall not include Nigeria or any part thereof;

and, until express provision with respect to Nigeria is made by an Order in Council under section eight of that Act (which relates to the application to visiting forces of law relating to home forces), any such Order for the time being in force shall be deemed to apply to visiting forces of Nigeria.

Ships and aircraft

7. In subsection (2) of section four hundred and twenty-seven of the Merchant Shipping Act, 1894, as substituted by section two of the Merchant Shipping (Safety Convention) Act, 1949, the word 'or' (in the last place where it occurs before the words 'or in any') shall be omitted, and immediately before the words 'or in any' there shall be inserted the words 'or Nigeria'.

8. In the proviso to subsection (2) of section six of the Merchant Shipping Act, 1948, the word 'or' in the last place where it occurs shall be omitted and at the end there shall be added the words 'or Nigeria'.

9. In the definition of 'excepted ship or aircraft' in paragraph 3 of the Third Schedule to the Emergency Laws (Repeal) Act, 1959, the word 'or' (in the last place where it occurs before the words 'or in any') shall be omitted, and immediately before the words 'or in any' there shall be inserted the words 'or Nigeria'.

10. The Ships and Aircraft (Transfer Restriction) Act, 1939, shall not apply to any ship by reason only of its being registered in, or licensed under the law of, Nigeria or any part thereof; and the penal provisions of that Act shall not apply to persons in Nigeria (but without prejudice to the operation with respect to any ship to which that Act does apply of the provisions thereof relating to the forfeiture of ships).

11. In the Whaling Industry (Regulation) Act, 1934, the expression 'British ship to which this Act applies' shall not include a British ship registered in Nigeria.

Copyright

12. The references in section thirty-one of the Copyright Act, 1956, to a colony shall not include Nigeria or any part thereof.

13. If the Copyright Act, 1911, so far as in force in the law of Nigeria or any part thereof is repealed or amended by that law at a time when sub-paragraph (2) of paragraph 39 of the Seventh Schedule to the Copyright Act, 1956 (which applies certain provisions of that Act in relation to countries to which the said Act of 1911 extended) is in force in relation to Nigeria or that part thereof, the said sub-paragraph (2) shall thereupon cease to have effect in relation thereto.

Divorce jurisdiction

14. In subsection (2) of section two of the Indian and Colonial Divorce Jurisdiction Act, 1926 (which enables section one of that Act to be extended to certain countries, but not to any of the countries named in the said subsection (2)), the word 'and' shall be omitted in all places where it occurs except the first such place and except in the expression 'Rhodesia and Nyasaland', and at the end there shall be added the words 'and Nigeria'.

Commonwealth Institute

15. In subsection (2) of section eight of the Imperial Institute Act, 1925, as amended by the Commonwealth Institute Act, 1958 (which relates to the power to vary the provisions of the said Act of 1925 if an agreement for the purpose is made with the governments of certain territories which for the time being are contributing towards the expenses of the Commonwealth Institute) the word 'and' shall be omitted and at the end there shall be added the words 'and Nigeria'.

INDEX

Allegiance to the Crown, and membership of Commonwealth, 114-15, 116-17.

Attlee, Mr. C. R., 1-2.

Australia, Commonwealth of: legislative powers of parliament of, 25-28, 32-36; and disallowance, 36-37; and reservation, 40-41; and appeals to Privy Council, 50-52; member of Commonwealth, 1; authority of constitution of, 59-63, 65-68, 70, 108-9.

Banerjee, A. C., *The Making of the Indian Constitution*, 97.

British Commonwealth, use of term, 1-2; *and see* Commonwealth.

British Commonwealth and Empire, use of term, 5-6.

British Empire, use of term, 1-6.

Bryce, Lord, *Studies in History and Jurisprudence*, 108-9.

Burma, independence of, 20.

Callard, K., *Pakistan: A Political Study*, 101.

Canada: called a 'Dominion', 6, 9, 10, 13; disuse of term, 13-14; as member of Commonwealth, 1-2; and disallowance, 36-37; and reservation, 40-41; legislative powers of parliament of, 25-28, 32-36; and appeal to Privy Council, 47-49; authority of constitution of, 59-63, 65, 68-72, 108-9, 110-11.

Ceylon: not called a Dominion, 15-16; and disallowance, 38-40; and reservation, 41-42; as member of Commonwealth, 1-2, 6, 122-3; legislative powers of parliament of, 25-28, 32-36; and appeals to Privy Council, 50, 52; authority of constitution of, 72, 83-84.

Churchill, Mr. Winston, 5, 122.

Colombo Plan, 134-5.

Colonial Conference of 1907, 6-10.

Colony: use of term, 7-10; disuse, 12.

Commonwealth: use of term, 1-6; adopted by Lionel Curtis, 2-4; Lord Rosebery's use, 2; constitutional structure of, meaning of, 17-19; members of, 1; membership of, Chapter V.

Commonwealth Agricultural Bureaux, list of, 133.

Commonwealth and Empire, use of term, 5-6.

Commonwealth Economic Committee, 133.

Commonwealth Prime Ministers Conferences, 139; of 1948, 122-3; of 1949, 2, 122, 150-1, 154; of 1955, 122, 151; of 1957, 124.

Commonwealth Relations Office, 16, 136.

Commonwealth Shipping Committee, 133-4.

Commonwealth Telecommunications Board, 134.

Conferences, Commonwealth, 139-40; *and see* Imperial Conferences.

Costello, Mr., 117, 153, 155, 156.

Coupland, Sir R., *The Cripps Mission*, 125.

Cowen, D. V., 81, 82, 108, 110; *Parliamentary Sovereignty and the Entrenched Sections of the South Africa Act*, 78.

Crewe, Marquess of, *Lord Rosebery*, 2.

Cripps, Sir Stafford, 124-5.

Curtin, Mr. J., on Commonwealth consultation, 140-2.

Curtis, Lionel, views on Commonwealth, 2-6; *The Problem of the Commonwealth*, 2, 4, 5; *The Commonwealth of Nations*, 2, 3.

Danesfort, Lord, 73.

Deakin, Alfred, on use of term 'Dominion', 8-9.

Delany, V. T. H., 90.

De Valera, E., 94, 156.

Dewey, A. C., *The Dominions and Diplomacy*, 55.

Disallowance, 23-24; and Australia, 36-37; and Canada, 36-37; and Ceylon, 38-40; and Ghana, 38, 40; and India, 38; and Irish Free State, 36-37; and Malaya, 38, 40; and New Zealand, 36-37; and Pakistan, 38; and South Africa, 36-39; and Rhodesia and Nyasaland, 40; and West Indies, 40.

Dixon, Sir Owen, 66-67, 88.

PRINTED IN GREAT BRITAIN
AT THE UNIVERSITY PRESS, OXFORD
BY VIVIAN RIDLER
PRINTER TO THE UNIVERSITY